The Private Letters of Sir James Brooke, K.C.B., Rajah of Sarawak, Narrating the Events of His Life, from 1838 to the Present Time, Volume 3

James Brooke

PRIVATE LETTE[

OF

SIR JAMES BROOK[

~~Ind 9046.10~~ Ind 9046.10 (3)

1873, June 10.
Minot Fund.

PRIVATE LETTERS

OF

SIR JAMES BROOKE,

house, that plenty of defenders have started up. Every *day now*, will bring answers to the statements which have been set forth through the original agency of *one man*, *i. e.* Mr. Wise, my former agent, and now the managing Director of the Eastern Archipelago Company. This gentleman offered to make me a " second Arkwright," and " one of the richest commoners in England," if I would place implicit confidence in him. His plan was, that I should sell Sarawak to a company, remaining its governor, and this was to be a vast company. This I indignantly refused, and would not *accept* any money from such schemes. Mr. Wise, finding me likely to become a very unpleasant clog to his golden prospects, determined to get such a hold over me, as to prevent my acting against his project, but in doing this, he committed some acts, which opened my eyes wide. I broke through his thongs like cobwebs, and referred him to my legal adviser, begging him candidly, to produce all his accounts, and to offer the fullest explanations; adding, at the same time, if the explanation was satisfactory, he would stand higher in my opinion than ever. He would not do this—he would not produce the accounts, or explain; but whilst he threatened to prosecute, he was wise enough to know that a persecution would be safer. Fortunately copies of my letters are in my possession since 1845. They tell a tale, and are

that the strength of our opponents is weakness, and their wisdom folly; and I am getting comfortably hardened to this steady flow of abuse which, coming from men whom I never respected, ought not to depress my mind.

Mr. Hume's reference to my correspondence was very weak: the way would be, to challenge him to publish it at length; and I have given Templer full power to act, in regard to the correspondence in his possession, as he may think fit. Placed in circumstances of unprecedented novelty and great difficulty, I did not embrace my position *at once*—and, indeed, the position itself altered very rapidly. I am free to confess, too, before the world, that my views of duty and responsibility were not so high at first as they have since been. Year after year expending my fortune, to support those views, I was harassed with the notion of my means coming to an end, before the government was stable, and I should then willingly have embraced assistance from such a company, as I proposed in 1843. As time proceeded, and I became firmer, I began to fear involving the good done, by risking it. I thought Sarawak would stand alone; it was the temptation offered by Mr. Wise, the " golden prize," the "vast fortune," which first staggered me, and caused me to reflect. The idea of participating in such schemes, shocked my independence. I deserve little merit, for

No. 130.

JOHN C. TEMPLER, ESQ.

Singapore, October 6, 1850.

MY DEAR JACK,

I DO not attempt to thank you, for I am unable to do so, and have done so before; but I feel that I like to be obliged to you, and would do as much for you, as you have done for me, provided you are unlucky enough to give me the chance.

Nothing can be kinder than Mr. Drummond, nothing better than his speeches; nothing weaker than Hume's case, and nothing more decisive than the majority. Mr. Drummond was very right to attack Mr. Wise; the motive cannot be too strongly brought to light, and Mr. Wise should not be allowed secretly to work the strings of his puppets. I quite approve likewise, if you do, of your publishing the letters or anything else. I send you some others; you will see, that they are to my mother, and she treasured them, and I found them when she left the world. What pain would all this have given her! for she was sensitive in the extreme.

There should be a preface by you, and a running commentary. I leave it and everything in your hands, and you need only refer to me, when you think it necessary.

~~Ind 9046.10~~ Ind 9046.10 (3)

✓

1873, June 10.

Minot Fund.

English colours employed between Sarawak and this place, and the trade of the entire coast has vastly increased. Borneo government is still the great impediment to a more rapid and even better state of affairs.

There has been a fight, between the Dutch and the Chinese Kunsi, a Company in Sambas. This is the Iron Trade Company, which, pushed on its own ground, made a sally against a place called Pawowkat, inhahabited by other Chinese, and took it: the people, some four thousand, have all fled to Sarawak in great distress; but they will be a useful population, though I want no large body of Chinese for fear of the natives Farewell, my dear Jack; I have no time for anything about Greenwich or Bridport or the dear folks there. My kindest regards to the dear wife and children and all the rest; and ever believe me,

Your affectionate and obliged friend,

J. BROOKE.

———

October 7, 1850.

I enclose a small literary curiosity, a letter from the Prince Chow-Fa-Mungkuk, or, literally, the Crown Prince or Lord of Heaven. How I rejoiced to hear such good accounts of your dear folks, and how much I should have liked to have made that excursion with

PRIVATE LETTE[R]

OF

SIR JAMES BROOK[E]

To

His Excellency Sir James Brooke
K. C. B. Her Britanic Majesty's Ambassador extraordinary and pleni
potentiary to Siam &c &c &c

The Prince Thunksum
momfah Yui Chow-Fa-
Mongkuk has most rejoiced
for highest honour of acknowledging the rejoyful receipt
of the graceful gift or present
of Great Valued Astronomi
cal telescope to-gether
its implements & standing
round table & with three
notes from His Most cele
brated Excellency Sir
James Brooke. K. C. B.
Her Britanic Majesty's
Ambassador extraordinary
plenipotentiary to Siam
through the care or receipt of
his dear genuant cousin
His Honour " Rhun Phranai
waiwosnarth " & his intimate friend James Hayes Esqre
on 27th September 1850.
9–o'clock P. M. of Astronomi

house, that plenty of defenders have started up. Every *day now*, will bring answers to the statements which have been set forth through the original agency of *one man*, *i. e.* Mr. Wise, my former agent, and now the managing Director of the Eastern Archipelago Company. This gentleman offered to make me a " second Arkwright," and " one of the richest commoners in England," if I would place implicit confidence in him. His plan was, that I should sell Sarawak to a company, remaining its governor, and this was to be a vast company. This I indignantly refused, and would not *accept* any money from such schemes. Mr. Wise, finding me likely to become a very unpleasant clog to his golden prospects, determined to get such a hold over me, as to prevent my acting against his project, but in doing this, he committed some acts, which opened my eyes wide. I broke through his thongs like cobwebs, and referred him to my legal adviser, begging him candidly, to produce all his accounts, and to offer the fullest explanations ; adding, at the same time, if the explanation was satisfactory, he would stand higher in my opinion than ever. He would not do this—he would not produce the accounts, or explain ; but whilst he threatened to prosecute, he was wise enough to know that a persecution would be safer. Fortunately copies of my letters are in my possession since 1845. They tell a tale, and are

No. 131.

JOHN C. TEMPLER, ESQ.

Singapore, October 11, 1850.

MY DEAR JACK,

In my hurried letter by the last mail, I told you that I was, in 1843, anxious to find support from any quarter, excepting from a foreign nation; and my correspondence, if published at full length, instead of being garbled, would prove, not only this, but a great deal more; and would show that the light expressions quoted, refer to real objects, worthy of attention, and not to any personal views. Thus "the orators dinging it into the long ears of the public," refers, I am certain, either to the sufferings of the Dyaks, or to the slavery carried on by the pirates, and, in like manner, "philanthropy being in fashion," refers to the same crimes meeting with sympathy in Africa, and not in Borneo. You may safely challenge the production of the correspondence.

In proposing a company, in 1843, when ruin stared me in the face—when I saw the probability of ruin coming once more upon the people of Sarawak, unless I could find support—when I was disbursing large sums from my private fortune, to establish security and government, was it much to ask to be governor under

and my popularity, a large sum might have been shared between us.

  *   *   *   *   *

Let me now turn to what is called my trading affairs.

1st. It is fairly to be admitted, that I did trade before I entered the government service; but it is false to say, that I used my position to advance that trade, for, on the contrary, I declared all trade free, with the exception of antimony, reserved as revenue, and opium, which was held for the same purpose.

How did I trade, however? I who do not know how to keep an ordinary ledger account—who boggle over the multiplication table—to whom is denied the faculty of figures—I who never kept an account of private expenditure, and would rather face a row of soldiers than a row of figures—how did I trade? Why, by letting a gentleman do everything for me, and supplying the money when it was wanted!

Thus all my trade—all my revenue—all my means in Sarawak, did not pay the current expenses, and year by year I drew on my private fortune to support the country. This lasted till about 1845, and may be shown any day.

In 1846, the antimony and opium were leased, and the revenue of Sarawak amounted to 2500*l.* from these sources, and about 500*l.* (or less) from other sources. All the expenses of the establishment, and all the

I have thus touched upon points more or less known to you before, and I could write a small folio, were I to detail the rise and progress of Sarawak. Sarawak is now a large town, containing at least twelve thousand inhabitants. The Dyaks amount to twelve thousand or fifteen thousand more, the Chinese to six thousand, and the other population of Malays at Lundu, and along the coast, to some three thousand or four thousand. And yet the country is quiet—our crimes are not numerous, and the general spirit of the population is good, and highly in favour of the government. If any man would compare the state of things in Sarawak, with that in any other river, he would not doubt of the good done—of the great advancement of commerce, if the measures applied at Sarawak were applied to the other localities—and of the blessings of government and security. Samarahan is so close to Sarawak, that it is moderately prosperous—Sadong is in a wretched state, from the imbecility and rapacity of its native rulers (Datus). I cannot interfere, though Malay and Dyak population are imploring me to do so; and the Bruné government cannot interfere, or if it did interfere, it would make matters worse. I say cannot, because their oppression, added to what is now inflicted, would drive the people desperate. Thus a noble river, quite as fine as Sarawak, is without government and without security, and as it is with

No. 132.

REV. RICHARD COXE.

Singapore, October 16, 1850.

MY DEAR DICK,

I HAVE not heard from you for some time, and being in Siam, I have been unable to write. My mission was a dead failure, as the Siamese are as hostile, and as opposed to Europeans, as any people can well be. I had a very trying time of it, and altogether got out of an unpleasant and critical position, without loss of national or individual credit; although I was sore tempted, and my temper sorely tried. You may fancy how bad it was, when I mention, that I secluded myself, and never took or breathed the fresh air of heaven, during a long month of my stay. This was a defensive measure, to avoid all chance of insult, and that inevitable lowering in public estimation, which these arrogant and semi-barbarous people, always attempt with Europeans. In short, I am convinced that there is no earnestness in our eastern policy—it is nothing but a slipshod expediency, which we shall some day rue; for it will force us into strong measures, when the cup of insult and humiliation has been drained to the dregs. I would be just, but commanding. I would use the power we undoubtedly possess, to amend native governments, whose existence is a prolonged

~~Ind 9046.10~~ Ind 9046.10 (3)

1873, June 10.

Minot Fund.

himself, some to Keppel, and some to others. Templer will now publish all these, and it will be evident what my motives have been, and whether I have ever sought any selfish advantage, in what I have undertaken; in fact, being 10,000*l.* minus in raising this country to its present happy condition—often with pecuniary ruin staring me in the face, and always in pecuniary difficulties, from the expenditure I could not avoid—I am told that I have been speculating selfishly. However, it is no use writing what you will see in a book; but I beg you to remark how the enemy have been beaten from pillar to post, shifting their ground, as fresh facts have been brought forward, and now, they are fighting a defensive battle.

I should have believed it impossible, when younger, that I could have borne, to be held up as a mark for public defamation and obloquy; but there is a stern self-reliance in innocence, which shields us from the storm, and, in my case, my compassion for the authors of all these falsehoods, is tinged with a touch of unchristian contempt. My character is no longer to be lost or lowered in public; but how it may fare with my purse, is another matter.

I have nothing more to add, as there is never any news in this dull place, and if there was, you would not be interested in it. I am thinking of coming home in the early part of 1852. I need a freezing, to set

PRIVATE LETTE

OF

SIR JAMES BROOKI

.

after these matters, unless I am reminded of them.   It will please me much at all times to hear of your well-being, and that rest and quiet have improved your health.   I hope too to see you again in a year or two, when I propose coming home.

> Believe me,
>> My dear Martha,
>>> Your sincerely and obliged,
>>>> J. BROOKE.

No. 134.

JOHN C. TEMPLER, ESQ.

Sarawak, October 26, 1850.

MY DEAR JACK,

I ARRIVED yesterday, rejoiced to be once again in my own country.   Without all is quiet, within highly prosperous.   M'Dougall's church is a great feature in the scene.   The Chinese population is greatly increased, and the trade this year will exceed ten thousand tons.   The jungle is fast receding. We have now our Arabs to take a canter on, and in another year I hope to have a road, between my farm and the town, a distance of seven or eight miles.

I go up the river in a few days, to settle matters with the Chinese.

house, that plenty of defenders have started up. Every *day now*, will bring answers to the statements which have been set forth through the original agency of *one man*, *i. e.* Mr. Wise, my former agent, and now the managing Director of the Eastern Archipelago Company. This gentleman offered to make me a " second Arkwright," and " one of the richest commoners in England," if I would place implicit confidence in him. His plan was, that I should sell Sarawak to a company, remaining its governor, and this was to be a vast company. This I indignantly refused, and would not *accept* any money from such schemes. Mr. Wise, finding me likely to become a very unpleasant clog to his golden prospects, determined to get such a hold over me, as to prevent my acting against his project, but in doing this, he committed some acts, which opened my eyes wide. I broke through his thongs like cobwebs, and referred him to my legal adviser, begging him candidly, to produce all his accounts, and to offer the fullest explanations ; adding, at the same time, if the explanation was satisfactory, he would stand higher in my opinion than ever. He would not do this—he would not produce the accounts, or explain ; but whilst he threatened to prosecute, he was wise enough to know that a persecution would be safer. Fortunately copies of my letters are in my possession since 1845. They tell a tale, and are

morrow I go up the main river, to the Chinese settlement, in order to arrange the future management with
the gold-working Company, and to bring down as
many of the new comers as I can, to locate them here
and at Sundu.

By forming two or three nuclei in proper situations,
the Chinese will increase, and yet continue under control. The difficulty at Sambas is, their having been
allowed to congregate and rule, in a place difficult of
access. At the close of the year, I will send you our
export and import account. The tonnage will be at
least ten thousand tons, mostly under the English flag.
We, yesterday, had five vessels in the river, viz., a
barque, a brig, two schooners, and a tope.

I am not anxiou sto revert to Mr. Wise; but I may
mention what I have recently done, and you can judge
whether it will be of any use bringing it forward,
though probably not.

In the Singapore " Straits Times," and directly afterwards in the " Daily News," appeared some scandalous
and positive statements respecting my expedition up
the Kaluka river, in March or April, 1849.* I had,
it was said, allowed a captive woman to be led away
into slavery, permitted the murder of a boat's crew,
after they were made prisoners, murdered a *toothless*

* See the correspondence with the Singapore authorities on this
subject, *post*, Nos. 148 and 149.

old man, who was unarmed, and invaded the peaceful haunts of native commerce. All these *positive* statements were afterwards dropped, but I kept my attention fixed on them, because they could only have been derived, from within a small circle of persons, or else must have been invented by the enemy. Having some grounds for the proceeding, I brought Mr. Miller,* the surgeon of the " Nemesis," to a Court of Inquiry, upon which trial, he and every gun-room officer of the " Nemesis " disclaimed any knowledge whatever of these statements. Subsequently, Captain Wallage pledged me his honour, in writing, for himself and the engineers of the steamer, that they were not the authors, nor acquainted with them ; and lastly, every white person in Sarawak made affidavit of the same. Therefore there is now proof, that these statements were not originated by any person present up the Kaluka river, unless he was a common seaman, and further, that they did not originate with any European (unless a common seaman) within three hundred miles of the scene of action. From whence then did the " Straits Times " obtain this information ? That a native should furnish it, is a preposterous supposition ; *ergo,* it must have been obtained, from a man before the mast, or have been invented. These are the original

* See Parliamentary Papers, entitled Dr. Miller, 11th May 1852, where all the details of this case are given.

slanders which heralded the rest. I have no doubt, however, that there are honest men enough, who have been misled, to bring the truth ultimately to light, of the steps taken to cause the outcry.

Adieu, my dear Jack. With kind regards to your wife.

Believe me, ever,

Your affectionate friend,

J. BROOKE.

The documents above referred to are all in my hands.

———————

No. 136.

JOHN C. TEMPLER, ESQ.

Sarawak, December 7, 1850.

MY DEAR JACK,

I HAVE had a fresh accession of fever, from which I have partially rallied, but the great prostration of strength, warns me of the consequences of longer delaying to seek relief from a total change of climate. I obey the dictates of prudence the more readily, as here I am useless, and unable to do what I am obliged to attempt.

In February, therefore, I have resolved to leave Singapore for Malta, and thence, travelling viâ Naples, Rome, Florence, and Milan, to Geneva. At Geneva I

shall halt; and have written to the Johnsons to join me
there. If nothing occurs to accelerate my motions, I
shall be in England in July or August, and thus be
able to see much of you. I have resolved to live at
Greenwich. I want a home of my own; I hate
London, and your society decides me in favour of the
old place. I could not, however, live comfortably any-
where but at Rose Cottage, if it is to be had; and I
know old Mrs. Crofts will take care of me. I will
take the cottage for a year, from the 1st August to
1st September or 1st June; and I shall desire my
servant Channon to lodge my traps, which he will
carry home direct, a pledge to Mrs. Crofts for my
appearance. I fully authorize you, therefore, to take
Rose Cottage. If that is not to be had, I will wait till
can choose another. Dear Jack, we will have many
yarn yet, in spite of our enemies; and I can tell you
en thousand things by word of mouth which it is im-
ossible to explain in writing; only pray don't expect
e to do lion again, the work is too hard, and does
ot pay at the price. My love to Mrs. Templer, and
l your party, and believe me ever,

Your affectionate friend,

J. Brooke.

No. 137.

JOHN C. TEMPLER, ESQ.

Labuan, December 21, 1850.

MY DEAR JACK,

A MERRY Christmas, and a happy new year to you. I arrived at this place three days ago, weak and sickly after a rough passage; but on the whole I am better, or at any rate, not worse. I feel, however, that the mental exertion of business destroys me, and I must fly from it, as soon as I can. It is, indeed, miserable to be the witness of human suffering, such as the poor Muruts of Bruné are now exposed to; to feel the power of being able to relieve this misery, and to know that forms and shadows prevent one doing so.

This is only, however, to say that I trust to your advice, and Cameron's, to hurry me, if there be any advantage to be gained. I wish you to exert this privilege, without consideration for my comfort or health. I feel that a cool climate will set me up quickly, and, at any rate, no personal consideration shall prevent my obeying your summons.

*   *   *   *   *

The objects of the Eastern Archipelago Company I approve. The company as constituted, or rather the bubble called a compány, is an imposition on Government and the public. Mr. Burns has been at his tricks in the Barram River. I write this, on the mere chance of catching the January mail; how I wish it was February! I am an overworked horse.

Ever, dear Jack,

Your affectionate friend,

J. BROOKE.

Let Mr. Cameron know about me, as I have not written to my own family, and they will be glad to hear.

No. 138.

REV. F. M'DOUGALL.

Singapore, January 28, 1851.

MY DEAR M'DOUGALL,

I HAVE before expressed to you my wish, that he labourers employed in the mission should be inreased, so as to embrace the more distant rivers, where iere is a large Dyak population. I cannot, however, ave this part of the world, without letting you know y strong opinion, as to the necessity of caution in all ur proceedings. In the prosecution of the best course, iere are dangers to be avoided; and great and pro-ising, as I consider the field of missionary labour in

Kanowit and Sakarran, and amongst the Dyaks generally, yet I do not hesitate to say that great prudence
with forbearance will be required to cultivate this field
with success, and to crown the exertions of the church,
with a substantial success in due time.   There is a
proper season to speak; and I must say that any
measures, that tend to satisfy the craving at home for
spurious and speedy results, by showing a list of con-
verts monthly and yearly, should be discouraged and
suppressed.   It is building the superstructure on a
foundation of sand; it would be permanently injurious
to the ultimate object of the mission, and it would be
dangerous to the public peace.   The Dyak population
must be moved in the mass; and, as a rule, the jealousy
of the Mahomedan population must not be roused.
We have now toleration, charity, and peace, and these
blessings must not be risked, by the indiscreet zeal of
Christian men, strong to introduce their faith amongst
others.

You are aware of this danger from experience.   You
know that I speak only the words of sober reason,
when I say that, let the bigotry of Islam be once
aroused, the mission will *not succeed*, and wars and
bloodshed may attend our attempt to introduce Chris-
tianity.   Zeal begets controversy; controversy begets
heat and strife; and thus every evil passion accrues
from an indiscreet attempt to convert our brother men,

and by rashly interfering with opinions (however wrong in themselves) sacred and dear to their professors.

History; the state of religious opinion in England; and above all, our local happiness and experience, warn us to guard against danger, and to establish some authority to prevent its arising.

The Government, of course, is the ultimate judge of what concerns the safety of the country, or is likely to disturb the public peace; but there ought to be some power in the church itself, to give unity of design and execution; and to prevent, and check the slightest tendency towards the evil I have mentioned. How is this to be done?

Have you any ecclesiastical authority to control and direct other clergymen? If you have not, and I do not perceive how you can have, what objection could there be, to making you the Bishop of Sarawak? There could be no objection on my part; and I consider, certainly, that some authority within the church itself necessary to control the clergy; and to offer to the Government a responsible person, with whom it could act, and in whom it could confide. The details I must leave with you; but I have thus freely, though somewhat hurriedly, expressed my own opinions, and you will consider them, and impress them, on all concerned. My apprehensions of divided councils, and controversial crusade, may be ill-founded, but it is well to guard against every danger, where the happiness of so many thousands is concerned, and where (in my opinion) a wrong step may impede the prospect of diffusing our religion.

Farewell: may peace and goodwill be with you in Sarawak; and if God so wills, I shall once more return.

Yours, my dear M'Dougall,

Very sincerely,

J. BROOKE.

No. 139.

JOHN C. TEMPLER, ESQ.

Point de Galle, February 15, 1851.

MY DEAR JACK,

I SEND through you a full and fair account of Mr. Napier's administration, the inquiry on him, and his dismissal. There could not have been a simpler or more straightforward public duty, or one more embarrassing or painful.*

Mr. Napier is likewise led and advised by Mr. Woods, a newspaper editor, who is the *calumniator*, not only of

---

* This refers to the Lieutenant-Governor of Labuan, who had been dismissed from the execution of his office by Sir James Brooke, and Earl Grey confirmed Sir James's decision.

myself, but of all the officers engaged. The exaltation of this man to a public situation, has drawn a remonstrance in no measured terms from me on *moral grounds.* I will send the papers if I have time to you by this mail.*

I am moved by a just indignation; and if Government does not support me, I shall act independently, for my blood being up, I shall not shrink, and I am not to be cowed by any earthly considerations, or ruled by a base expediency.

Yet, dear Jack, I am quite good-tempered about it, because I am right, or at any rate convinced that I am right, which is as much as a poor mortal man can say in this world. The —— business will end in smoke, or in disgrace to those who have concocted it. Send or take the letters to —— without delay.

God bless you, ever yours,

J. BROOKE.

* See these letters, Nos. 148, 149.

CHAPTER II.

FEBRUARY 22, 1851, TO APRIL 17, 1851.

No. 140.

JOHN C. TEMPLER, ESQ.

Steam Packet "Hindostan," three days from Aden,
February 22, 1851.

MY DEAR JACK,

I have already by this mail, forwarded to you three large packets, and the present one is to be for public, miscellaneous, and my private letter. There is always a last word to say on the points under discussion, so as to guard each, from every possible chance of misconstruction. In the first place, therefore, it may in Napier's case be urged that he was burdened by *many duties*, and therefore failed in some. Were it so, it would not affect the case; but it was not so, as the accounts sent home, will show how little there was to do in that way, and how it was done, and the enclosure No. 1 is the sum total of judicial cases for the year 1849 ; and besides this, the duty *was very light*.   Mr. Scott now does the same duties added to his *laborious office* of Surveyor-General, and is far from complaining.

The Siam mission may be brought up, and on this point it may be boldly affirmed, that the propositions made were just and moderate ; and that I strictly obeyed my instructions, in avoiding all ground of dispute ; that I was a favourite personally with the Siamese, though I was *unbending*, and that the English and American inhabitants fully approved of every step I took.   If the enemy accuse me of delay in proceeding on the mission, answer, that when I first received the appointment, it was *physically impossible* that I could undertake the duty, and had I been able to do so, 1 could not have procured a vessel of war, as Admiral Austen was expected, and the commanding officer would not have felt authorized to detach vessels, under the circumstances on a distant, and perhaps prolonged, mission.   When I returned from Penang (which I did before I ought to have done), I waited at Singapore, ready at any hour to embark, until the Admiral's arrangements were completed.   No blame is, however, to be implied, as the disposition of the squadron, rendered it impossible for the new commander-in-chief to arrange it otherwise.   You are aware likewise that

I have erected a fort at Sakarran, and that I have recently placed Mr. Brereton in charge of it. This step may be questioned in various ways. The answer is, that the fort is necessary to prevent the Sakarrans from issuing forth on piratical expeditions, and adviseable likewise, to check the feuds which have arisen in consequence of these piratical expeditions. It is a measure reported to H.M. Government, approved of by the better-disposed Malays and Dyaks of Sakarran, and of the Batong Lupar, pleasing likewise to the Sultan of Borneo and his government, which for the last fifty or seventy years have lost all power and control over the Batong Lupar and Sakarran—and this nucleus of a fort will create a trade in noble rivers, and gradually, by affording protection to those within and without, and curbing the system of retaliation, introduce peace, and advance commerce. If Brereton's appointment is called in question, urge that he is the fittest person for it, that I have no native who will go, on whom I can rely; that Brereton has small independent means, and the revenue he can derive from the river, will not more than cover (if it will do that) the expenses which must be met. I make nothing either by Sakarran, Serebas, or any river; and though the government of Borneo has long ceased to exercise the functions, or perform the duties of government, yet when these rivers are more developed, it will be time so to apportion the revenue, as to establish security, and a strong and just local rule, and the claims of the native state may then be fairly considered, with reference to the more important objects of general peace and the good of the people.   What is said of Sakarran, may with equal truth be said of Rejang.   There the proposal of a fort, and the establishment of a just government is not only pleasing to the Dyaks, but Kum Nipa, the Kayàn chief, has come from the interior, to help in building it; and has agreed that if I govern he will come down below the rapids of the Rejang, for the greater convenience of trade.   We have now established firm relations with the Kayans of the Barram, and have exchanged friendly letters with the Kinneah chiefs (a name unknown before), in the interior of that noble river.   Labuan is struggling through its difficulties, kept back by the dilatory operations of the company, yet possessing substantial elements of success.   The Dusans of the north are now guided by our councils;—the Lanoons controlled;— the city of Bruné from want of all internal government, and security of person and property, is gradually dissolving.   The results of good government are everywhere apparent, and known to all; and I may truly say that a course of policy mixed, as I have always mixed it, of mercy and severity, has prevented the effusion of blood; and the bloodshed has been the blood of the

guilty and not of the innocent. At this moment, when
I am broken down by sickness and exertion, the
measures I have pursued are eminently successful, and
their development in their infancy. The man, perse-
cuted in his own country, is respected and loved in
Borneo, and I may say throughout the Archipelago.
And what assistance have I had? A weak and
vacillating course has been pursued for thirty years
past, and will be pursued still. There are no systematic
measures taken, no power granted, no real confidence
manifested in myself, or any one else—no efficient support given. I feel, I know instinctively, that the war
of words will supersede all the benefits of action; that
supineness and indifference to distant spheres, render
England unfit to carry out a consistent course of policy
in the East. The age of noble confidence is gone, and
the bagman distrust of Manchester has taken its place
—yet, whilst I live, will I not turn my hand from the
plough; nor do I wish to complain. There is a moral
might developed in a man's soul, by persecution in a
right cause, which is superior to fortune's gifts, or
earthly treasure. There is a self-reliance, and a re-
liance on a good cause, which raises us above the
world's opinion and men's judgment. I trust I am
learning something of this, and I can sincerely say that
beyond a just indignation, I entertain no vindictive
feeling towards those who are pleased to be my enemies.

They may injure me in prospects and in peace; but they cannot deprive me of the consciousness of right, —the love of my friends—the attachment and respect of the native communities—or the gratification of duty done. They cannot reduce me to their own level of feeling, or of language. That I have faults enough, heaven knows. I have a fixedness of purpose, and a devotion in any cause I embrace, so unfortunately mixed up with a lightness of temper, and a scoffing playfulness, and an abhorrence of cant, that the solemn and silly will never comprehend my character, and the suspicious and worldly never will trust, and always will abuse me. So be it. The love of pleasing the multitude is a base token of a base nature. I must be content, my dear Jack, with my friends, and d——n the rest of the world—the chosen to me, I am content to live with, and wish not to live without. Poor, poor Jem! how often do I think of him, and your love of his memory is worthy of you and of him. He had many good and rare qualities, all of which would have been refined by age; but it would please you to listen, as I have listened lately, to his praises from Earl and others. I think I have now mentioned every point which it is necessary for you to know; and I do not lay down any course of action, for you know far better than I do myself, what is proper to be done. Remember, above all things, that I am ready to come home at any time to face my enemies, if it be necessary ; but I do not desire to mix myself up in these wordy contentions, unless it be advisable.　I often think what could have been the end, had I not had you to advocate my cause, and to arrange a defence against this unworthy and malignant persecution.　I should have been condemned unheard, —too proud to volunteer a defence, and too careless, and too ignorant, to seek the means necessary for rebutting false accusations.　*And this would have been justice !*　I often ask myself how can these men, Hume and Cobden, reconcile it before God, or to their own consciences, to denounce an absent man, to condemn a man unheard—and this is what they call fair play and manly English feeling; they preach of peace, whilst they banish charity from the earth.

I express what I feel, a warm gratitude to those who have defended me ; who have taken the trouble to inquire into the truth, and to expose the falsehood; amongst these prominently are Henry Drummond, and ——, and your friends —— and ————; but is it not strange that I have no Government defender, not one influential ministerial voice in the House of Commons to support my reputation,* and to avow the approbation of ministers.　Am I right, dear Jack, in feeling hurt at this ? in regarding it as less than my due, and beneath their dignity ?　In a position *more responsible,*

* This was before the Session of 1851.

perhaps, than any other under the Crown, as being solely dependent on my *own judgment*, and beyond the reach of ministerial assistance, or advice to guide or rule, am I to be left half disowned? or is it the support which Government finds from Cobden and his party that cools its zeal, and renders it unrighteously cautious?

All these things have struck me much, and as I shall stay at Malta till I receive an answer to this letter, pray (however shortly) tell me am I right or not? I feel quite independent. I never, from nature, can play a *truckling* or expedient game. I am, I trust, not selfish enough to turn Sarawak into a mere means of personal exaltation. *I have power and influence* not to be appreciated at a distance, and will never fritter it away by engaging in any paltry antagonism with a company, or rival governor, or any one else, whom Government may permit or encourage to oppose a course of policy, which depends on a systematic and dignified action and support. *My first duty* is to secure the happiness of Sarawak, and to place it in a situation of permanent security and independence. This done, the rest is but "leather or prunella." My horse, my gun, and books, are a stock of content and employment enough, and if there be some disappoiutment left, it is but the dregs of a cup which every mortal man must drink ere he die. However, these subjects are for our cool and serious deliberation, when we meet, and I shall not act hastily without your advice; though my natural temperament, my habits, my feelings, my appreciation of independence, all conspire to urge me to cast off the trammels of office, and all the expedient shifts which office now requires, but requires in vain from me. You will see with what vivacity and bitterness I have attacked the Court at Singapore. I would no more blink a public principle for private convenience than I would sell Sarawak to Mr. Wise's company to be made a mercantile bubble of.

I stay, as I before told you, for an answer to my letter, and an acknowledgment of my packets in Malta. After that, if you give me leave, I proceed to Naples, Rome, Leghorn, Genoa, by sea; then to Milan, over the Simplon, to Switzerland, where I wish to recruit. I have written to the Johnsons to come and join me. Is there any just impediment to Mrs. Templer and the children, led by yourself, coming to the Leman Lake? I only mention this, but otherwise I should like much to join you during a portion at least of your holidays. At Bridport or where? I shall call myself Smith, John Smith, at your service. Pray what news do you intend to send me about Rose Cottage? Am I to get it, and at a moderate rent? If I cannot get Rose Cottage, I shall take some other small house in your vicinity, and a thorough-bred steed, picked up at Tattersall's, will enable me to jog quietly to chambers, between Prior and yourself. Charlie Grant comes home with me, and Charlie Johnson I hope will be at home, and I have my servant Channon. If I remember right, Rose Cottage has three bedrooms, and as the two Charlies will not be often there together, we shall manage.

We are now getting on to Aden, and I shall close this last packet and write you a short note, to inform you of my arrival in Malta. It may be that your letters, or the Government may induce me to come on.

My kind love to all the party; I hope soon to be amongst you all, and to be living a quiet life, far from crowds, and public feasts, or public spouting. Farewell, my dear friend, and believe me

Your sincere and affectionate friend,

J. BROOKE.

I enclose my correspondence with the President of the United States and the American envoy. I sent the President's letter to Lord ———, who, thinking it a public matter, referred it to the Foreign Office, but I do not think it a question, in which the English Government have any concern.

Show whatever papers will interest, to Cameron and my uncle.

No. 141.

JOHN C. TEMPLER, ESQ.

Ripon, approaching Malta,
March 13, 1851.

MY DEAR JACK,

I HAVE wonderfully recovered during my passage, and feel quite a different man from what I did, when I left the East; my only ailment being, at present, a cold caught in the climate of Egypt, which is as treacherous, as a cold wind and scorching sun, can make it.

Our passage has been very agreeable and calm, till within the last 24 hours, and we are now struggling towards Malta, in half a gale of wind, right in our teeth.

I write this preliminary to our arrival, and I do not anticipate that you will order me home. The change of ministry will scarcely affect my position, either with my friends or my foes, but as far as I am *personally* concerned, I shall regret any change which removes Lord —— or Lord ——, for I have always met from them every public consideration and private kindness.

I have sent to you, directed to ——, four large packets, dropped from the saloon of the steamer into the mail bag, as we have gone along.

The first was a full and particular account of

the —— affair.   The second, relating to piracy. The third, the reports and decisions on ——'s case. The fourth, my correspondence with the President of the United States.

There are likewise some newspapers, all relating to these topics. I saw in the "Home News" paper, that a Parliamentary return was furnished by the India House, for military and naval expenses of Labuan, from 1848 to 1849. The military is correct from 1848, but Labuan has never had any separate naval establishment. The Company's vessels employed there, occasionally, have been part of the naval squadron employed at Labuan, or *any other* place, or in cruizing, according to pleasure, of the Commander-in-Chief. No settlement, therefore, can in fairness be charged for the naval expenses, which come under the general Admiralty administration; and the vessels employed, being available for the service of any or every settlement within the limits of the East India command. I think it as well to mention this, in case an effort is made to pervert the simple fact.

I have written you a long letter, and now only hope to hear from you soon; and if need be, shall write from Malta, should there be a letter from you. My love to all, my dear Jack, and believe me,

Your affectionate friend,

J. BROOKE.

No. 142.

COMMANDER HOSKEN, R.N.

Malta, March 27, 1851.

MY DEAR HOSKEN,

I HAVE learned, that Commander Daniel of the Indian Navy, in reply to a letter addressed to him by Mr. Hume, has said, that he neither saw nor heard of pirates whilst on the coast of Borneo.

As it is not the custom of pirates to visit ships of war, and as the " Semiramis" was not employed to search for pirates, it would have been remarkable if Captain Daniel had seen them, or seeing them, had known them to be pirates ; but it seems strange that he should never have heard of piracy whilst stationed at Labuan ; and I can account for this in no other way, than that he never troubled himself to make any inquiries on the subject, for, being ignorant of the native language, he could learn nothing from the ordinary topics of conversation carried on.

Will you tell me whether, in your opinion, Captain Daniel or any other man might not, at any time he took the trouble to inquire, have *heard* of the existence of pirates, and the atrocities they committed on the peaceable inhabitants of the coast?

I am sorry to give you this trouble, and believe me, my dear Hosken,

Very sincerely yours,
J. BROOKE.

———

(Answer.)

H. M. S. "Banshee," Malta,
March 27, 1851.

MY DEAR SIR JAMES,

I CANNOT understand how it happened that Captain Daniel never heard of pirates during the time he was stationed at the island of Labuan; he most certainly would have heard of several acts of piracy on the coast of Borneo, on both sides of the island, more particularly on the side towards Sarawak, if he had made inquiry.

The subject of the depredations, committed along the coast, was frequently talked of by the officers of the Government; and it was well known that six piratical vessels had stopped at the north end of Labuan, to obtain water, a few months before we came to the island, in June 1849.

Believe me, my dear Sir,
Yours very faithfully,
JAMES HOSKEN.

No. 143.

JOHN C. TEMPLER, ESQ.

Malta, March 24, 1851.

MY DEAR JACK,

I AM comfortably established at Dunsford's hotel, and am enjoying and benefiting by the charming weather, which has succeeded an inclement winter; the great folks are very kind and obliging, and amongst many agreeable persons I have found some old ac-acquaintances. Lord and Lady E——, Robert ——, formerly of the Colonial-office, and Graves, who has been for years employed in the survey of the Mediterranean, are the principal ones of the number. The latter is well known to your brother Harry, and remembers him too. I trust Harry is better of his awkward accident. He is getting too old for hunting, and must leave it for the boys, though your father used to hunt at a later time of day. Accidents, however, will happen in the best-regulated families, and your light weights, in my experience, are more liable to them than your fourteen stone men.

I am, all things considered, remarkably well, but I by no means like the cold, nor does it like me. I think there is a gouty tendency in my habit, which slumbers in the genial temperature of 85°, but which awakens in cold weather, and shows itself in a nasty cough, from that vulgar region, the stomach. You may remember how it annoyed me, when last in England, and it is always aggravated by good dinners, and strong drinks, and late hours. Now it is merely incipient, and bids me beware of turtle and claret. I am, however, wondrously moderate and feel young, and I ride daily for some hours, enjoying the balmy air and bright sunshine. During the course of next week I am going with Lord —— in his yacht, to visit Gergenti, in Sicily. It is an awkward place to get at in any other way, and though I hate sight-seeing, these temples are worth the trouble of a land-journey on donkeys, and I esteem myself very fortunate to have an opportunity of visiting them with so agreeable a party.

Charlie Johnson is here in the "Terrible," and I see as much of him as I can; but such are the thousand demands of naval duty, that it is not so much as I wish, for he is a great favourite of mine. Charlie Grant is fagging away at my long correspondence with Colonel Butterworth, which, when completed, shall be sent to you. There was, or rather is, in Singapore, the editor of a small newspaper. This man has habitually been abusing and vilifying all the officers, civil, naval, and military, employed on the coast of Borneo, not with an ordinary, but with an extraordinary abuse, accusing us of specific acts of murder. This newspaper editor has, from an almost unaccountable weakness, been chosen by Colonel Butterworth to fill two appointments in the Court of Singapore.

It appeared to me something monstrous, for a court of judicature to take into its pay, a newspaper editor who had made the most shameless and unsupported charges against officers in the performance of their duties. As the Court did not either accede to my views, or justify the appointment, but merely contented itself with presuming a man to be fit for office, whom they knew was not fit, I addressed them a letter which produced the correspondence I will send viâ Southampton, and a copy of which I have also forwarded to Lord ——, and he will probably let the India Board or the Court of Directors, or anybody else whom it may concern, judge the matter.

There are many things, my dear Jack, I wish to talk to you about, and Downe Hall shall be my abode, as you kindly propose in September, or sooner if possible.

1st. Will the Government place me in a position less anomalous than the one I at present hold? What can be a greater one than an independent prince, with, I may safely say, unlimited power over five hundred miles of coast, acting as Consul-general?

2nd. Will they back me (morally, not physically) in carrying the same government as previously in Sarawak to other places? The government of Bruné is dying in my hands. The people of numerous tribes desire good government. They have long *de facto* been independent in a great measure of Bruné, and will not allow the native rajahs to bully them as of yore.

I can advance good government, if I have a direct or even indirect authority, and by this means not only shall we benefit by *increase* of commerce, but the mass of the native population will benefit too; we shall come in contact with the native tribes of the interior, and the defunct rights of the Bruné government can be attended to, so as to pay it a just tribute from its possessions, from which it now gets nothing.

3rd. Will the Government act consistently and strictly against the pirates of the Archipelago? As I write, my dear Jack, I long to be with you; but in term time you are a man of business, and only accessible in the evening.

I am afraid I was hard upon ministers in my last letter; they have always been very kind and very considerate to me; but in the effort merely to hold their own in England, they allow the extremities of the empire to get cold. In the East, especially in the Hindu-Chinese nations and China, we ought to do everything or nothing; and the outcry on the score of humanity, roared forth by Cobden and Sturge, is humanity to vicious governments, but not to the mass of the people. The more experience I gain, the more I despise half-and-half measures. In private life it leads to the ruin of those who pursue this course, and it is no better in public affairs, though the result is not so quickly apparent. We can retrograde or we can advance, but we cannot stand still, any more than the globe—stillness, is the type of death—motion, of life—and whether in the moral or physical world, we can no more remain stationary than we can remain asleep all our lives. I am sorry to hear I cannot get Rose Cottage ; but Mrs. Templer, in her walks, may look out for some nice damp, dreary-looking abode, away from the haunts of men ; for I hate living in a row, and I like a little garden. Is there anything like a small house in the Park, or near the Park? or on Blackheath? However, there is time for all this. So farewell, my dear friend ; the Charlies send their love. I hope Mrs. Templer and the young ones are well. I was surprised to hear Master Jamie rode a pony. I send you some other non-business papers, with this very long letter. So adieu, with my kind regards to your dear wife, and believe me,

Your affectionate friend,

J. BROOKE.

No. 144.

JOHN C. TEMPLER, ESQ.

Malta, March 29, 1851.

MY DEAR JACK,

I SHOULD not have troubled you again so soon, but having learned a move* of the adversary, I thought it as well to counteract it, as you will see by the enclosed papers. This negative evidence cannot go far with reasonable men. I have been staying here for answers to my letters, and likewise on account of Charlie Johnson; but as the " Terrible " sails in a few days, I shall retire from Valetta to Bosquetto, in order to get out of the way of the dinner parties, which try my lately-amended health, and which I particularly dislike; for to be moderately agreeable, I am obliged to take more wine than is good for me; for it is wretched work to feel one cannot talk, or talk with pain. If the weather be fine, I believe Lord and Lady —— will cross over to Gergenti, in which case I shall accompany them. My future movements are not quite certain, but I shall keep you well informed in case of need.

The weather here is not so agreeable as I could

* The move referred to, was the address of some parties in Singapore to Mr. Hume, to the effect that they had never heard of the racies of the Serebas and Sakarrans.

wish; it is changeable, and the wind is often cold, besides which, there is a dryness in the atmosphere which is disagreeable, however healthy it may be.   If you are too busy, ask Mrs. Templer to write to me.   Farewell, and believe me,

Your affectionate friend,

J. BROOKE.

No. 145.

REV. FRANCIS M'DOUGALL.

Malta, March 30, 1851.

MY DEAR M'DOUGALL,

IT seems natural, that you should hear from me at Malta, and for this reason, and because I feel inclined, I write, rather than from any abundance of material.   Firstly, my health is greatly improved, and from the day I left Galle, I began to pick up, and to feel like another creature, which I attribute as much to relaxation and change, as to climate.   My only drawback now, is from the number of dinners which I cannot avoid going to, and when out, there is no alternative excepting being stupid without wine, or agreeable with it.   The first burst is passing away, and as Charlie Johnson will be off in the " Terrible " during the week, I propose returning to Boschetto, for greater quiet, and there awaiting my English letters, and the next India mail.   I shall afterwards go by sea to Naples, Civita Vecchia, Leghorn, and Genoa, visiting the principal towns from their respective seaports, and making my way to Switzerland about June, and to England in August. This is the present programme, but the Hume persecution may take me home sooner, should my friends deem it necessary. My mind is generally far away from my body, and lingers with you all, in Sarawak and Borneo. What are cities and temples, to jungles and Dyaks? and what are the knightly remains of Malta, compared to our little church? What is all the rubbish of the past, compared to the hopes of the future?—I am a man of one idea—Borneo; everything else in life, is a little snuff, which tickles my nostrils; or a little sound, or a little sight for amusement, but I am not in earnest, in anything else. I am not for ministerial crises, saving as they touch on Borneo prospects. I hope you are all happy, and have a little society and are gay, for I don't like solemn people, and I hope Mrs. M'Dougall continues strong and well. It would be very agreeable, if I escorted out Mrs. Bunyon, and Miss Bunyon, and Miss Bickersteth, but if any of them come, I will do my best, whether they journey by land or sea, to make their voyage agreeable; and if they leave before I do, I will, if you tell me, look out, that they have a better passage than yours was. The stick I entrusted to Sir —— (whom you knew as —— of the " Amazon") to deliver, according to the direction ; so by this time, I trust, Mrs. M'Dougall's mother is leaning on it for support. How does our school progress? that is my delight, and I often think of the " Good night, Sir," which greeted me in my evening drives.

Charlie Grant is writing to St. John. I am going to write to Brooke. What is Mr. Chambers doing? I hope you will send him to Sakarran—he will be a great support to Brereton. My best love to Mrs. M'Dougall, and all our dear folks. You will comfort poor ——, and I trust he bears his misfortunes in a proper spirit. Say all that is kind to the natives, tell them how often my thoughts are with them, and how I wish my person were too,

Ever your sincere friend,

J. BROOKE.

No. 146.

JOHN C. TEMPLER, ESQ.

Malta, March 31, 1851.

MY DEAR JACK,

I RE-OPENED my note of the 29th on the receipt of your welcome letters of the 22nd, 23rd and 24th ultimo.

All the arrangements you propose for Downe Hall will suit me admirably ; and our holidays passed, I can look out for a house, or cottage at Greenwich, for I could not then take up my abode with you, without subjecting Mrs. Templer to serious inconvenience, from the number of my visitors. Don't you know that I am a "*Lion ?*" I was delighted to hear that the papers I sent were so conclusive, and in good time; and as I agree with you, that in all probability the motion will be postponed till after Easter, I shall still continue to acquaint you with another branch of the subject, which Brereton writes me will come under discussion, this is what Mr. Hume calls the "Sakarran aggression." The case is very simple. The enclosed sketch will show you the river, and I may remark that Linga is not a piratical tribe, but, at feud with Serebas and Sakarran, and only restrained by my influence, from continuing the "*intertribal war*," but I allow no *intertribal wars.* You will observe the position of *my fort* at the junction of the Sakarran with the Batong Lupar. The Dyaks of Batong Lupar are very numerous, and not *piratical, therefore I have never attacked them, and we are excellent friends.*

This is preliminary. The place where my fort is built was inhabited by Sheriff Mullah, a brother of Sheriff Sahib, and it was taken by Captain Keppel in 1844, his attack having been justified by a decision in the Court of Admiralty.

Sheriff Mullah, and the piratical Malays having

D 3

been driven away, I became friends with some of these
people, both Malay and Dyak, and encouraged Abong
Kapi, a Sakarran Malay, to settle at the place, which
he did. This place, by way of distinction, is now
called "Sakarrana." Several of the Dyak chiefs
whose lands were nearest to Sakarrana, promised me
faithfully to renounce piracy, and to support Abong
Kapi. The three principal ones were Gasim, Lingi,
and Bulan. The two first were quite sincere, and I
have always trusted them since, even though opposed
to me afterwards. Evil councils were, however, too
strong with the Sakarran Dyaks; and two sheriffs, by
name Sheriff Baka and Sheriff Long, both now residing
in Sarawak, tempted them to make a piratical excursion, on which they were met by the Linga people.
The Dyaks most inclined to continue piracy, were
those located above the rapids; and these, moved by
evil advice, overbore the influence of Abong Kapi, of
Gasim, Lingi, and others, and went out with a large
fleet, attacking Linga, and doing other mischief.
Abong Kapi, Gasim, &c., afraid that I would retaliate
on them, left Sakarrana and its neighbourhood, and
retired above the rapids, where it was difficult to get
at them. I always had hopes of them, and as they did
not come out often, being kept in check by the Linga
people, I turned my attention to Serebas. The Dyaks
of the Batong Lupar were never meddled with, except-

ing once, by a blackguard named Bandar Cassim, and I paid him off for his bad act done, without my knowledge. The Sakarrans suffered severely in the fleet destroyed by Captain Farquhar, and Kapi, Gasim, &c., regained their influence, and promised once more to renounce piracy, and I once more believed them—but a town and fort at the mouth of the Sakarran was very desirable to prevent the good party from being overborne, as they were before; to protect Linga from Sakarran, and Sakarran from Linga, and to become a mart for commerce in a very noble country. Thus piracy would be *prevented*, and good government and security established.

I recommended the plan to our Government at home, before the defeat of the Serebas, but afterwards it became comparatively easy, and the only question was, who was I to get to govern the place? It will be proper to mention, that the rajahs of Borneo have not been acknowledged in this river for at least fifty years; but considering that the country was originally theirs, I mentioned my intention of establishing a government to the sultan and Mumein, and gained their willing assent to the measure. It was, I believe, last December, that I sent Crookshank with a few prahus from Sarawak, to build the fort, and I established Sheriff Hassim, a Pontiana man, in authority at Sakarrana. When Mr. Hume calls it an " aggression," pray ask

him who built the fort? Why, Sakarran Malays and
Dyaks. Who guard the fort? Sakarran Malays and
Dyaks. Who asked for the fort? Sakarran Malays
and Dyaks. I only provided the arms and ammuni-
tion, and other things necessary to start Sheriff Hassim;
but the Sakarran people chose him for their ruler, and
the Sakarran people, Malays and Dyaks of Sakarran
and Batong Lupar, upheld him in authority. The
experiment, however, was a failure, for Sheriff Hassim
did not agree with the Sakarran Malays, and he committed several unjust acts, and the consequence was
that the Sakarran Malays came to me to complain,
and requested his removal, or permission to leave the
place.

These people had, I considered, a right to do what
they pleased in the matter, and after inquiry I found
that Sheriff Hassim had behaved badly, and I gave my
consent to his removal, and I left it with the Sakarran
Malays and Dyaks to choose any one they liked to
govern them, and they all said, if I gave them a good
Englishman they would prefer his rule to that of any
native. At their request, therefore, I chose Brereton
to rule over these one hundred thousand people, and I
trust to God he will do it well; and though young, I
have confidence in him, and know that he has many
qualities suited to the task. Mr. Hume himself, must
allow that no better title can exist, and Brereton is now

in Sakarran, supported by the Sakarran people, and not
interfering with them in any manner, excepting to prevent piracy, to encourage commerce, and to do justice.

The Dyaks have come down from the interior, and
occupy all the lands before deserted, and the Sakarran
Malays occupy the town, and farm below the town, half-
way to Linga; or about twenty-five miles, whilst the
Linga people farm up the river, the other twenty-five
miles. The Undop is beginning to be settled once
more by the unhappy tribe of that name, who were
driven out by the ceaseless incursions of the Serebas;
and Sakarrana will become a place of importance in
a commercial point of view.

These are the grounds upon which I have acted, the
results are yet to be seen; but if I succeed, if the
Sakarrans support their ruler, peace and security will
succeed to piracy and insecurity, and the first object
of Brereton, is to put an end to intertribal war, and
to reconcile the Linga Dyaks with those of Sakarran.
Had I not been so great an invalid, I should myself
have gone to Sakarran to establish them in the right
path—and I esteem it *most important* to establish
similar governments along the entire coast, wherever
the population desire it, to establish security for life
and property, and I doubt not we shall see results,
which, when I am passed away, will be a blessing to
Borneo, and a substantial commercial advantage to

England. It would indeed be lamentable, if this miserable system of tampering with all subjects under the sun, and reducing all distant measures to the level of Parliamentary faction, should impede a great substantial and practical good—but I will not believe that such a thing is possible. Let me say then—

1st. That Sakarran is governed by Sakarran people, and Brereton placed there by their choice.

2nd. That our Government has been acquainted with the establishment of a fort, and my intention of its becoming a nucleus for a trading town.

3rd. That the Sultan of Borneo, whose territory it originally was, has given his consent; and it is clearly for the advantage of the Borneo Government, for it may derive a revenue in time from a river, which, for half a century, has disowned its authority.

The establishment of this fort has cost me some money, and I shall derive nothing from it. Brereton in undertaking the charge, lives at his own expense, and is entirely dependent on the Dyaks for the amount of revenue it may please them to give; but from what I know of them, I do not doubt of their giving what has been an immemorial custom. No government, however simple, can be sustained without some expense, and the labourer is worthy of his hire; but I have arranged with Brereton, that, if the revenue ever rises from the increased prosperity of the place, that the rights of the Borneo rajahs, (and these rights are very doubtful) are to be fairly considered.

With Brereton is Mr. Lee,* an independent gentleman; and Mr. Chambers, the missionary, when he becomes a little acquainted with the language, will take up his abode amongst the Dyaks, and we may expect great things from his labours.

1st April, 1851.—I add a line, to say that I have made up my mind to go by sea, to Naples, Civita Vecchia, Leghorn, and Genoa, visiting the capitals from the respective sea points, and giving up Switzerland. I shall proceed from Genoa, to Marseilles and Paris, and be with you by the end of June. I only wait here, till I get a circular letter of credit from Coutts's, which I have asked Mr. Cameron to send.

Malta is a cheap place, and I have given myself an outfit here at half the price, it would have cost in England.

Lord and Lady —— were going to Sicily, and they have asked me to go with them for a few days' trip, which I shall do, if they hold to the purpose.

Give my love to all your party, children and all. Farewell.

Yours, ever affectionately,

J. BROOKE.

---

* This gentleman was afterwards killed in a most gallant and determined attack on a fleet of the Sakarrans, to prevent their putting to sea for piratical purposes.

To arm you more completely, I may further mention, that with Brereton, at Sakarran, is firstly, the aged Laksimana Minudeen, and his active and intelligent son, Abong Aim, both natives of Sakarran; who left it in the troubled times. The Laksimana was the last officer appointed by the Bruné Government, whose authority was superseded by the father of Sheriff Sahib and Sheriff Mullah. The Laksimana was then a young man, and the Sakarran Dyaks did not, in his time, pirate, nor, as I before said, do the Dyaks of Batong Lupar, pirate now. Besides the Laksimana, is his connexion Abong Kapi and his people, whom I before induced to locate, *without a fort*, at the same place. Sheriff Mullah, who before ruled, has likewise promised never to pirate again, and lives there; and Sheriff Sahib's widow and her family prefer it to any other place, because they are sure to be well treated. This lady sent her son to Sarawak, with Grant, and the boy lived with me for a fortnight, just before I left. This does not look like persecution or aggression on my part, or distrust on theirs. I ask but one thing from them, that is, to renounce piracy; and if I am not prevented, and my life be spared, I do not doubt being able to extend the benefits of good government along the entire coast. I have power, great power, but I maintain, that I use it for the benefit of the mass of the people, for the benefit of the miserable Bruné Government, and for the extension of our national commerce.

Ask Mr. Cobden whether this is not better than insecurity, and bloodshed, and piracy, and intertribal wars? And whisper in Mr. Hume's ear, that what I have done for Sakarran, I intend doing for other rivers, and that I am proud to see my own countrymen ruling a willing people; and that I don't suspect every Englishman of being a rascal; nay, I am inclined to believe that Joseph himself is not a bad fellow, barring his obstinacy and suspicious turn of mind. I have written so much, that I must close, and

Believe me,

J. BROOKE.

When you have done with this letter, I want you to show it to Mr. Brereton. You are mistaken about Colonel Butterworth having made a judicial inquiry on piracy. The inquiry he made, was to satisfy himself as Governor of Singapore, of the propriety of Capt. Keppel's measures; and he reported very strongly on the subject to the Government of India in their favour.

———

No. 147.

JOHN C. TEMPLER, Esq.

Malta, April 17, 1851.

MY DEAR JACK,

I RETURNED from Sicily yesterday, after a week's cruise, and received your letter. The blow will keep, and my last letter on Sakarran will thus have time to take the field, as well as the address from the merchants of Java, which I now forward, and which is signed by all the English firms, some Dutch, and one Major of Chinese.   You will see the ravages the pirates are committing near Labuan, and the measures forced on the Government there, to protect the island, and reinforce the north points—the natives being panic-struck at a report (by no means improbable) that the island was about to be attacked. That it might be assaulted any day there is no doubt. We ought to have a steamer, always at the disposal of the local authorities; and there are three or four lying here, which would sail as well.   How stingingly this may be retorted on Hume and Cobden.

Parsimony has led to the danger of the island: and if taken by the pirate force, let the nation thank these her *patriots.*   If the English flag be insulted, who is to blame?   The lives now sacrificed at Gaza, the slaves taken, the trade interrupted, are the consequences of the outcry made by Hume and his party.   This outcry has checked the course of measures for the suppression of piracy.

The exertions of the navy have been damped, and obstacles thrown in our way.

The pirates are daily gaining strength and courage, whilst I am employed answering my calumniators.   .

I forward you likewise, as I promised, a correspondence with Colonel Butterworth, arising out of these calumnies. You will please observe, dear Jack, what a resolute rascal I am, and how determined to fight this battle to the knife.

I know not what the Government may think : but I know that they ought to support me, for I am the person wronged ; and really they had better put a vituperative editor on the bench, to keep him silent.

The story pretty well tells itself, therefore will keep till we meet, which, when you receive this, will only be a few days. You know that I am a bungler, and a mere child in arrangements and parliamentary conflicts ; but the approval by the House, of the policy would be admirable ; and if you can, pray obtain Lord ——'s assent.

I shall leave this on the 25th at latest, therefore, should arrive at Southampton on the 5th or 6th, if not the 4th.

Now for lodgement. I suppose I must be in London, or at any rate with you at Greenwich, till Hume's motion comes off. Where shall I lodge? If you judge London to be the best place, see if you can get my old lodgings, if not exorbitantly dear—otherwise with you at Greenwich, till I can look about me. I enclose a note for Channon, whom I have just sent home ; will you add a line, telling him

where to meet me. Say the Railway Hotel, Southampton, or your own house, Greenwich. He is near
Southampton, at Portsmouth. Charlie Grant can
always shift for himself; he is hard at work on the
papers, and making a capital chart of the coast of
Borneo.

Believe me, &c.,
J. BROOKE.

I say nothing of your meeting me, for I know you
are busy; but I shall go to the hotel close to the ter-
minus and the docks.

18th.—Since writing, I find my note to Channon
must go home through Cameron, as I do not know the
direction, and I have told him to meet me at Southampton. I think, likewise, my best plan will be to go
to Warren's Hotel, Waterloo Place, which is but a
step from the club, and where I shall be in the very
focus of news. I have, therefore, written to Mundy to
take me rooms.

If I do not arrive at the time I have mentioned, you
must attribute it to my not having found room in the
" Euxine," from Constantinople; you may look for me
in the next packet, or viâ Marseilles. I have only now
to mention, that Sir Thomas Cochrane has written to
Lord John Russell, about Borneo and myself, which
letter you should get. The Bishop's letter, likewise,

to the committee, should be in your hands; and of course you will get Captain Wallage's letter to me complaining of being tampered with, if you think necessary. It is in the Colonial Office; and at any rate ——· will use it. The history of Butterworth's report to the Supreme Government of India is as follows :—

Keppel reported his attack on Sheriff Sahib and the Sakarrans to Butterworth, as Governor of Singapore; but the evidence of piracy was with me in Borneo. Butterworth on this, set to, in Singapore, to obtain evidence of piracy, in order to satisfy himself of the propriety of Keppel's measures; and having done this, he reported to the Supreme Government on the subject, at the same time forwarding the affidavits he had taken from inhabitants of Aya and Muka, on the north-west coast, who were trading in Singapore. These affidavits are strong; and he says in his report, that they are the *most desperate pirates*. He read me the report, &c., the very last morning I was in Singapore, but refused to give them to me.

On this, I applied to the Government of India, requesting copies might be forwarded to the Foreign Office. If the Government has complied with my request, the papers may have arrived by the last mail, or they may come by the next mail (24th or 26th May), if Hume's motion be postponed so long. In urging the approval of the policy by the House of Commons, the great injury done, is the main argument; measures impeded, pirates gaining courage, our national character lowered, &c.   2nd. The unjust persecution of me, &c.

My kind love to all your party; I long to be with you

J. BROOKE.

Perhaps the papers from India are directed to me, in which case, they will be signed on the envelope by one of the secretaries of Government, and may be opened at once.

Sir Thomas Cochrane writes me, that Hume sent him a book of letters, written by Scrutator (—— by report), called " Borneo Revelations,"* which he is going to produce, or argue from.   The letters are ingenious; but written in the worst spirit; and by tearing passages in my Journal from their context, and perverting their meaning, and placing them in juxtaposition, they make apparent contradictions, such as may be made even from the New Testament.

———

MY DEAR JACK,

I ADD a line at the last moment to say that we are well, and shall positively come by the " Euxine " steamer, which at the latest leaves this on the 26th.

I got up at daybreak yesterday and wrote in haste

* A pamphlet that had appeared in Singapore.

the accompanying hints, some of which are new to you. When I arrive it will be time to scrutinize " Scrutator " briefly ; not that it deserves such scrutiny, but only because it is as well to meet everything alleged against me, and because Hume means to make a flourish about it. I have shown the Butterworth correspondence to Lord ——, who quite approves of what I have done, and thinks the Government must support me. Adieu.

Ever yours,

J. BROOKE.

CHAPTER III.

JANUARY 31, 1851, TO FEBRUARY 20, 1851.

THE CORRESPONDENCE WITH THE GOVERNOR OF SINGAPORE.

No. 148.

LIEUT.-COLONEL BUTTERWORTH, C.B., Governor of the Straits Settlements and Presiding Judge of the · Court of Singapore.

Singapore, January 31, 1851.

SIR,

I AM anxious to call your attention to the recent appointment of Mr. Woods, the editor of the " Straits Times " newspaper, to be the deputy sheriff of Singapore.

I am aware that this appointment was not made by your Honour, but that owing to a delay on the part of the gentleman selected by you, you permitted the sheriff to nominate to this office.   I am aware, likewise, that it would have been invidious (however objectionable the appointment might be on general grounds) to refuse your sanction to the sheriff's nomination, without some specific proofs, that Mr. Woods was an unfit person to hold any public situation whatsoever.

Appreciating your Honour's motives and feelings, and knowing that you were imperfectly acquainted with Mr. Woods' character, and in ignorance of the proofs of this person's moral turpitude. it becomes my duty to offer for your consideration the following statement :—

Mr. Woods, as editor, advanced charges in the "Straits Times" newspaper, of the 23rd May, 1849, relating to the expedition up the Kaluka River, for the suppression of piracy in Serebas.

I have the honour to enclose three extracts from the article in question, but I must refer to the paper itself (and to numerous other papers) for the details of these and many other statements of a similar character, worked up with every circumstance of horror, which malignity could devise; and you will permit me to add that the effect produced by these unprecedented slanders is still in force, and still exercises such an influence on the minds of some statesmen, that the matter will, in all probability, be again discussed in Parliament during the course of the approaching

session. The charges brought forward so distinctly by
Mr. Woods, are of such a nature, so deeply affecting
the character of the officers of Her Majesty's service,
of the officers of the Honourable Company's steam-
vessel " Nemesis," and of the other gentlemen present,
that the only alternative, is to pronounce the persons
engaged in the expedition, to be murderers and felons,
or the deputy sheriff of Singapore to be a gross slanderer. Although these statements have been repeatedly
pronounced false, although publicly challenged to give
up his infamous informant, the deputy sheriff has
declined doing so, and has thus made himself responsible, for the falsehood and infamy, of being the
promulgator, if not the inventor of these monstrous
calumnies.

Your Honour, and the Judges associated with you on
the bench, are aware that the criminal law affords no
redress for this heinous moral offence ; and I would be
clearly understood, that my objection against this
appointment, is not urged on the ground of personal
injury, but on the broad principle that a man notoriously and absolutely, violating the obligations imposed
by society, and the precepts inculcated by religion,
cannot be permitted, under any circumstances, to fill a
respectable public office, without danger and disgrace
to the Government under which he serves, and the
community in which he lives.

The charges of murder and felony publicly advanced by the deputy sheriff against his fellow-citizens, must by the first principles of equity be held to be false, until they be proved; and it is left for society, and for Government as the organ of society, to mark its sense of a heinous deviation from the path of rectitude, and a glaring outrage on public morals.

Lord Coke has declared " that those things which are of the highest criminality, may be of the least disgrace," and, reversing this proposition, your Honour will, I feel sure, agree with me that there are misdemeanors in law (which money cannot compensate), which are in the highest degree disgraceful and degrading, in a moral point of view. In the present instance, the moral degradation of the deputy sheriff, is not confined simply, to giving currency to a calumny furnished by an informant, who might have deceived him; and had the deputy sheriff been misled, or unable subsequently to advance proofs of his allegations imputing felony and murder to public officers, an atonement might have been offered for inflicting so deep an injury on society and on individuals.

The enclosed copies of documents will prove, however, that Mr. Woods did not receive the information contained in his editorial article, from any source on which an honest man ought to have relied; and as every respectable person present during the expedition, as

E 2

well as every respectable person within 300 miles of the
scene of action, has positively and solemnly denied all
knowledge of these statements, and the only conclusion
therefore to be arrived at, is, that Mr. Woods derived
his information from a seaman or native, (which supposition is highly improbable); or that he invented the
falsehoods which he promulgated as truths. In whatever light the conduct of the deputy sheriff may be
viewed, there can be but one opinion of a moral delinquency so serious and so apparent; and I will content
myself, therefore, after offering a few remarks, with
leaving the principle for your Honour's consideration,
and for the consideration of the other Judges of the
Court, whether it be consistent with the character of
the East India Company's Government, with the purity
of the Court of Judicature in Singapore, or with the
duty which Government owes to society, to permit a
person to hold a responsible situation, who has been
guilty of a crime, too heinous to stigmatise in appropri-
ate terms, in an official document. On the score of
public morality, I would represent the danger, and
worse than danger, of intrusting judicial functions to a
man, who, (if he be the editor of the newspaper in
question) is undeniably guilty of the gravest moral
offence against his fellow-men, against society, and
against the principles of virtue and religion. On the
score of public morality, I would represent that if there

be a duty incumbent on an upright man to guard his own character, or the character of his family, from moral contamination, it is a more imperious duty of Government, especially in the judicial department, to select agents for the public service, untainted by moral baseness.

It appears to me, that the foundations of society, the stability of institutions, the standard of morals, depend on the character of those who administer justice, dispense the offices of religion, and execute the laws; and that to countenance a gross departure from rectitude in a public officer, be he high, or be he low, is to strike a blow at the highest interests of mankind. It is separating Government from morality, and avowing to the world that the rewards of office may be conferred as the wages of sin.

A notorious gamester—a notorious profligate—a man degraded by any notorious public vice, could not be selected to exercise the functions of a Judge, without disgrace to the bench and danger to the people. Can, therefore, a sheriff, or a deputy sheriff, or any other functionary attached to the judicature, be a falsifier and a slanderer without disgrace, and without danger to the administration and the dignity of the Court? Is it in his want of truth, in his blindness to moral obligations, or in his defiance of those precepts of duty which regulate the conduct between man and man, that the Court over which your Honour presides could look, for the conscientious discharge of his present official duties by the deputy sheriff?

The purity of the higher offices of the State is regarded with scrupulous care—are the lower offices to follow another rule? Is there no moral standard by which public functionaries are to be judged? Is there no moral delinquency, abhorrent to the upright mind, which should incapacitate the perpetrator, for the duties and rewards of judicial office? Are deliberate falsehood and malevolent slander in future to be excluded from the category of vices? Can they ever become recommendations or matters of indifference within Her Majesty's dominions?

On the score of public morality I have thus strongly, though with every sentiment of respect to your Honour, and your brother Judges, insisted upon a principle, sacred in my opinion, even to its minutest details, and altogether independent of personal considerations—a principle, in my view of the subject, on the due maintenance of which, rest the moral character and the moral power of all free governments.

Having fulfilled the obligation imposed upon me by a sense of duty, I submit to your Honour, together with your colleagues on the bench of Judges, whether the deliberate, if not venal imputation, of such heinous crimes, falsely charged on public officers, be a moral offence, and whether such an offence ought to be rewarded, by permitting the offender to become associated with the Judges, in their official duties? The decision, with all its consequences and responsibilities, rests with your Honour and your colleagues: it is sufficient for me, to express the principles I hold, and to place on record the character of the deputy sheriff of Singapore, and his defamation of public officers bearing Her Majesty's commission, when acting under orders, and carrying out measures, subsequently approved by Her Majesty's ministers.

I herewith publicly denounce Mr. Woods, the deputy sheriff of Singapore, with wilful, malicious, and unretracted falsehood, in having charged Her Majesty's officers, and the officers of the East India Company, with knowingly invading the peaceful marts of commerce, and slaughtering the innocent inhabitants; with being principals or accessaries in the death of four prisoners, "at first treated in a friendly manner," and afterwards "treacherously set upon and brutally murdered;" and with a felony, in allowing an elderly woman and her two children, to be retained by their native captor, or, in other words, with having reduced those persons to the condition of slaves. I herewith publicly brand Mr. Woods, the deputy sheriff, with these and other malignant falsehoods, and with being the author of the foulest slanders that ever disgraced

the character of a Christian man; and I appeal to the
Judges, in the name of religion, of virtue, and of public
morality, solemnly to weigh the consequences of re-
taining in a court of justice, a vicious and degraded
servant, publicly branded, as I have branded the
deputy sheriff, with falsehood and with infamy. I
appeal to the Court over which your Honour presides,
to mark its sense of such unheard-of, such unprecedented social crimes; and to rescue the community of
Singapore from the contamination of such an example.
There is another view of Mr. Woods' appointment,
though of far minor importance, to which I would
direct your Honour's attention. Mr. Woods, as a
newspaper editor, has expressed strong opinions relating to Her Majesty's Court of Judicature in Labuan;
thus may be established a precedent, that a functionary
of one Court of Judicature, may publish matter derogatory to the dignity of another Court of Judicature.

Mr. Woods, likewise, since his appointment as
deputy sheriff, has been actively engaged in obtaining
signatures to a memorial addressed to a Member of
the Legislature (his own signature being affixed),
recommending a Parliamentary investigation upon a
case, already decided by the Court over which your
Honour presides, and calling in question measures,
approved by Her Majesty's Government. Thus is
established a precedent of an inferior officer attached

to the Court, expressing a public doubt on the decision
of the Judges, and taking a prominent part in a local
agitation, calculated to embarrass Her Majesty's service.   In his character of editor of a newspaper, there
could be no objection to the course pursued by Mr.
Woods; but for the deputy sheriff to become an
active partizan, on questions relating to the public
service, and a hostile critic of the judgments of the
Court, appears highly reprehensible.

The actions and opinions of the deputy sheriff and
the newspaper editor are inseparably combined; and it
is to be feared that the Court of Judicature will be
considered responsible for the deeds and sentiments of
its subordinates.   The enmity of the deputy sheriff
may be held in contempt, by those whom he calum-
niates in his editorial capacity; but his connexion with
your Honour in public life, his official intimacy with
the Judges of the Bench, his introduction by one of
the Judges to the Right Reverend the Bishop of
Calcutta, as a respectable person, his influence with
the other subordinate officers of the Court (especially
the native officers), and the impression produced on
the native population—are just causes of apprehension,
whether viewed as an example, or dreaded as a contamination.   The deputy sheriff's active partizanship
in obtaining signatures to the memorial before alluded
to, further establishes a precedent, that a functionary

of the Court of Judicature of Singapore, can not only vilify in his newspaper; but whilst in office, assail the reputation of the Presiding Judge of the Court of Judicature of Labuan.

I need not point out the serious inconveniences certain to result from the establishment of such precedents, and it will be apparent to your Honour, that if the Court of Singapore combines the functions of deputy sheriff and newspaper editor, and allows its officer to become an active agent, in political proceedings, directed against the Presiding Judge of the Court of Labuan; the Court of Labuan, exercising a like authority, and acting upon the same principle, may likewise unite the judicial and editorial functions in a subordinate, and permit the same license of conduct, in reference to other jurisdictions. Thus might be witnessed the unseemly spectacle of two of Her Majesty's courts of justice, through their official and responsible functionaries, waging a war of newspapers, and calling in question the characters of their respective Judges. That such might be the consequences, resulting from the appointment of a newspaper editor to an official situation, can scarcely admit of a doubt; and it is a duty incumbent on the higher functionaries, to preclude the remotest chance of such an occurrence; but I am bound to say, that so long as the two characters are united, so long is the danger of retaliation; and if the license assumed by the deputy sheriff be permitted, the danger of evil passions being aroused on both sides, and of the worst confusion.

I can imagine no danger more imminent to the administration of justice, than combining the base calumniator, the violent political partizan, and the newspaper editor, in the person of a judicial servant, who is expected to discharge the calm and dispassionate functions of an office under the Court.

If by possibility it should be held that functionaries of a Court of Justice are to be permitted to treat on political subjects through the press, under their own unlimited control; actively to engage in gaining signatures to memorials relating to subjects to be debated in Parliament; to sit in judgment, and to publish opinions on the conduct of public affairs, and on the character of Her Majesty's servants; the extent of such privileges should be clearly defined: as heretofore, it has been generally understood that a discreet silence, and a discreet forbearance on subjects unconnected with the functions of office, is the duty of all persons employed under the Crown, whether in the executive or judicial departments of Government.

The obligation imposed upon me has now been fulfilled, and though the prudence of reserve and decorum dictates silence in some circumstances, in others prudence of a higher order may justify us in speaking our thoughts.

The task has been an unpleasing one to myself, and I may not expect that it can prove agreeable to your Honour, or to your colleagues, but the principle at issue is of vital importance, and in my regard should be maintained as a sacred duty; for in the words of the great statesman I have before quoted, it is to be feared that "those who are bountiful to crime will be rigid to merit."

I have, &c.,

J. BROOKE,

Governor of Labuan, Presiding Judge of the
Court, and Her Majesty's Commissioner
in Borneo, &c., &c., &c.

P.S. Since the conclusion of the despatch I have learned that Mr. Woods, the deputy sheriff, holds, likewise the appointment of messenger of the Bankrupt Court, and of course every objection which applies against the one office, applies likewise against the other, nor have I in writing supposed the possibility of the sheriff maintaining in office, an infamous person whom the Judges desired to remove.

J. B.

Enclosure, No. 1.*

EXTRACTS from the Editorial Article of the "Straits Times" Newspaper, of May 23, 1849.

1. IF the expedition failed to discover pirates, peaceable traders were found, who, perhaps, were more acceptable victims, as lacking the means and courage to resist aggression.

2. The spy boat was in advance, in which we believe was the "Datu Patinghi," and came across a small boat containing four men, apparently Serebas traders; these men had no arms on them, and none in their boat; the latter contained a quantity of seree, a native luxury, and a staple article of trade throughout the Indian Archipelago. These four men were at first treated in a friendly manner, and taken on board the "Ulai" spy boat, their own frail vessel being towed. After remaining on board the spy boat some time, they were treacherously set upon, and most brutally murdered; their heads after being cut off, were subsequently smoked.

3. At one of the five villages, were taken captives—yes, reader, allowed to be retained by the Rajah's allies as captives—an elderly woman and her two children; the husband and son of this woman were slain before her face, and their heads smoked in her presence.

This is no exaggeration, we are dealing with facts.

* There were six other enclosures, showing, that none of the officers engaged in the expedition, nor any of the European inhabitants of Sarawak, were the authors of the above statements.

SIR JAMES BROOKE, K.C.B.,

Singapore, February 5, 1851.

SIR,

I HAVE had the honour to receive and submit to the Honourable the Recorder, and the other Judge of the Court of Judicature at this station, your Excellency's letter dated the 31st January, which reached me yesterday afternoon.

I confess that I was much pained by that communication and its enclosures, but it will be evident to your Excellency, that I could only view it in my judicial capacity, in conjunction with the highest legal authority in the Straits.

If your Excellency intends, that the charges advanced against the deputy sheriff, should be put in a train of legal investigation, then it would be necessary to place these documents in the hands of Mr. Woods, and to call upon him to take such proceedings as may be required, for disproving the charges brought against him.

If, on the contrary, it was your Excellency's desire that the Court should assume all these charges to be correct, without other proof than the voluntary affidavits enclosed in your letter, and that the Court, acting upon that letter, and those affidavits, should dismiss from office, a public officer, without affording him an opportunity of disproving the charges brought against him, or of being heard in his defence, it would be impossible for the Court consistently to comply with such a request.

The very first principle of common law and common justice is, that a man should not be condemned before he is heard in his defence, and as Mr. Woods has been nominated to his present office by a gentleman of the rank and character of the high sheriff of this settlement, the Court are bound to presume, until the contrary be proved, that a fit person has been appointed.

Under all these circumstances, it does not appear to the Judges, that there is sufficient before the Court to comply with your Excellency's request, but should your Excellency desire to institute any charges against Mr. Woods, the Judges are of opinion that recourse should be had to the usual judicial proceedings to which all persons resort in libel cases, and to which there appears to be no legal impediment.

I have, &c.,

W. J. BUTTERWORTH.

No. 149.

Lieut.-Colonel BUTTERWORTH, C.B.

Singapore, February 6, 1851.

SIR,

I HAVE to acknowledge your Honbur's reply to my communication of the 31st ultimo, relative to the appointment of Mr. Woods to be deputy sheriff, and messenger to the Insolvent Court of Singapore.

I am informed, that although *de jure* the appointment of his deputy rests with the sheriff, it is *de facto* an appointment of the Court, an arrangement being usually made to that effect, the present appointment, however, being an exception to the general rule.

I am likewise informed that the appointment of messenger to the Insolvent Court, is in the direct gift of the judge.

In either case, it will be apparent to your Honour that an appointment, if objectionable on moral grounds, is not less objectionable, from being made by the high sheriff, and that an injury to public morality is not less injurious, in consequence of the quarter whence it proceeds.

It is true, as stated by your Honour, that by the first principles of common law and common justice, a man, if he be tried, should be heard in his own defence, before he is condemned; and it is true, likewise, that by the first principles of common law and common justice, that charges must be held to be false, until they be proved. It is a notorious and undeniable fact, that Mr. Woods has brought charges against Her Majesty's officers, which he has not proved. I, in the name of these officers, have branded him with infamy for so doing, and demanded whether he be a fit person to hold any public situation whatsoever.

Your Honour in stating, that without other proof than the voluntary affidavits and the charges contained in my letter, it would be impossible for the Court, consistently to comply with a request, to remove a public officer, must surely have totally mistaken the question at issue. I have made no request to the Court, but I have stated that an outrage on public morals has been committed, by the appointment of Mr. Woods to be deputy sheriff. The voluntary affidavits are not intended to be proofs offered, but statements to show the extent of infamy, already sufficiently known and sufficiently public. If we discard these extra-judicial affidavits, the fact remains, that Mr. Woods is the editor of the " Straits Times " newspaper, and is the author, or the original promulgator, of slanders as infamous as ever disgraced a man.

This single fact, and the nature of these statements, require no elaborate or refined consideration; the fact is within the personal cognizance of the judges of the Court, and as certain as any fact can be in the world. It is the character of the Court, of the public service, and the rights of honest men, that are at stake; and the conversion of the accuser into the accused, cannot avail the defamer who has been raised to office.

A systematic course of shameless defamation has been pursued in the "Straits Times" for three years, and is rewarded with public office, where public office was never conferred before. I must repeat, therefore, that it is separating Government from morality, and bestowing the emoluments of office as the wages of sin. Mr. Woods is bound to prove what he has advanced; if he does not prove it, he is infamous and degraded in the eyes of every upright man. This is my view of the real question under discussion.

By the custom of society and for the maintenance of private morals, a menial must have a previously good character, before he can be admitted into a respectable family, and would not be permitted to retain his place, if discovered that he was of bad repute, and has been guilty of immorality. I ask, therefore, whether a man notoriously guilty of a great moral offence, the offence of charging murder and other crimes on his fellow-men, and not proving these charges, is to be maintained in office; and whether a Government can dispense with a good previous character in its servants?

I repeat, again and again, that by the first principles of common law and common justice, the deputy sheriff must prove his charges, or that the Court is bound to hold them to be false, and their inventor or original promulgator to be infamous and debased.

Is it not notorious, that for years the deputy sheriff has been an habitual calumniator of Her Majesty's officers? that he has publicly made assertions which cause a man to shudder?   Whether they be true or whether they be false, has he ever offered a proof?   Is he not bound, legally and morally, to offer proof when he charges murder; to prefer a judicial accusation to a malignant slander?   Is this his recommendation for office?

My duty has now been fulfilled, and the principle maintained, that moral turpitude, not to be exceeded, incapacitates a man for public employment.

The duty of the Court, I am not sufficiently presumptuous to point out, nor the particular steps by which public morality may be vindicated, the dignity of the judicature maintained, and society rescued from the contagion of vice and evil example, set up in high places.

I have already informed your Honour that I act upon public principles, and not on private grounds, and although the falsehood and the slander be not the less infamous, there has been, thanks to the right moral feeling of our countrymen, no personal injury from the diabolical attempt of this calumniator to ruin Her Majesty's officers. It is this moral feeling, which has been outraged by his appointment; and another objection sufficiently obvious to the course recommended by the Court is, that an action for personal wrongs received, would not vindicate the general principle, that a notorious vice incapacitates for public office. If such a principle be a theory not carried into practice, it is to be lamented, and should be removed; and if the innocent Woods can, with propriety, grace the sheriffalty, the religious —— and the moral —— are worthy of higher station. I should hope, however, that the principle I advocate, is acknowledged in action, and not held to be a romantic delusion.

Your Honour has further affirmed, that as Mr. Woods has been nominated to his present office by a gentleman of the " rank and character of the high sheriff, the Court are bound to presume that, until the contrary be proved, a fit person has been appointed."

Of the rank or character of the high sheriff I know nothing, but I do know that rank and character are ill associated with falsehood and slander; and in direct contradiction to the doctrine laid down by your Honour, I maintain that such charges as Mr. Woods has advanced in a newspaper against innocent men must be proved, or otherwise held to be false and infamous; and their author, or general promulgator, considered unfit for public office, or for the company of honest men. I cannot consider either, that the Court is bound to presume anything, contrary to self-evident and notorious facts; nor does there appear any necessity for a presumption so unreasonable; as summary dismissal from the magistracy, from the sheriffalty, and even from the lord-lieutenancy of counties, is a practice by no means uncommon when rendered necessary for the good of society. Should your Honour contend that the infamous slander, promulgated by Mr. Woods was prior to his appointment, I would beg to reply that this fact is an additional reason for his removal, as it proves neglect in the selection for office, as well as being an injury to society.

The Court is not to be considered in this case as a Judge, before whom legal proceedings are to be opened, but as a party deeply interested in preserving public morals, and maintaining its own character. If the deputy-sheriff be the editor of the " Straits Times " newspaper, the conclusion is unavoidable, and the Court should hold him guilty. If he be not the editor of that newspaper, or if he can prove his charges, then the Court is bound to affirm his innocence, but a middle course cannot be consistent with justice, as on one hand, or the other, a wrong is permitted.

I show, likewise, that the rule of procedure, in conferring this office, has been departed from, in this single instance, to admit Mr. Woods to become deputy sheriff, and that his appointment of messenger of the Insolvent Court has been confirmed by the Court.

On the score of religion, virtue, and morality, I have brought to the notice of the Court, the infamous character of the person now in the public employ, and if, after a reperusal of the single article, quoted in my former letter, (one amongst many such), the Court cannot perceive the consequence of upholding and justifying the appointment, the difference between us must be decided by a competent authority, and, I doubt not, will be decided on the general ground of public morality, and not on the limited base of legal form.

I beg to assure your Honour, that, whilst I continue to discharge the duties of Governor of Labuan, and President of the Court established in that island, no immoral person, polluted by vice, and shameless in want of truth, shall, under any circumstances, be appointed; or if appointed (through inadvertence), continued in office; and that a defamer of the innocent shall be called upon to prove his accusation, before he be rewarded, or before the public service be polluted by such association.

Reserving to myself such future measures, as I may deem necessary to establish the vital principle of the moral responsibility which the Government of Singapore owes to society, and to absolve the public service from the imputation cast upon it, by the appointment of a notorious slanderer to be deputy sheriff and messenger of the Insolvent Court,

I have, &c.,

J. BROOKE,

Governor of Labuan and Presiding Judge of the
Court, Commissioner of Borneo, &c.

SIR JAMES BROOKE, K.C.B.,

Singapore, February 20, 1851.

SIR,

I HAVE the honour to acknowledge the receipt of your Excellency's letter, dated Singapore, the 6th instant, which reached me from Penang, by the Honourable East India Company's steamer "Hoogly," on the 18th inst.

The Judges adhere to the opinion given in the concluding paragraph of my communication to your Excellency, under date the 5th instant, viz., that there is not sufficient before the Court to warrant its interference.

I refrain from making any comments on the tone of your Excellency's communication, or on the threat you hold out to the Court, as the whole correspondence will be forwarded to the Right Honourable the President of the Board of Control, for the information of

Her Majesty's Government, and to the Government of India, by the Honourable the Recorder and myself respectively.

I have, &c.,

W. J. BUTTERWORTH.

Thus closed this remarkable correspondence, and the following high legal opinion, which has been taken on the case, will show how right Sir James Brooke was in his view, though opposed to that of the authorities in Singapore.

Your Opinion is requested :

1st. Are not the passages extracted from the "Straits Times," marked 1, 2, and 3,* libellous *per se,* and would not Sir James Brooke have been entitled to a decision in his favour, in any legal proceeding he might have taken against Mr. Woods, by merely showing that Mr. Woods was the editor of the "Straits Times," at the time those articles were published, unless Mr. Woods had justified the charges, by proving their truth ?

2nd. Was the communication to Lieut.-Colonel Butterworth a privileged communication ?

3rd. Generally to advise Sir James Brooke in the matter, so that he should be prepared to take the proper and best course on his arrival at Singapore, and particularly as to his right of appeal, should the Court there, come to a wrong judgment.

* See *ante*, page 85. Enclosure 1.

Answers.

1st. I am of opinion that the passages extracted from the " Straits Times," marked 1, 2, and 3, in the enclosure, are libellous *per se*, and that Sir James Brooke would have been entitled to a decision in his favour, in an action for libel against Mr. Woods, by merely showing that Mr. Woods was the editor of the " Straits Times" at the time those articles were published, unless Mr. Woods had justified the charges, by proving their truth. Those passages charge piracy and murder, aggravated by treachery, and barbarous cruelty. A man who publishes such charges without being able to establish their truth, is beyond a doubt, guilty of libel. Tried even by the test of verbal slander, the passages are actionable, because they charge a crime; and as printed libels, they are calculated to bring, not only the persons immediately concerned in suppressing the pirates, but, indirectly, Her Majesty's naval service, into public hatred and contempt. The passages are, therefore, libels, and libels of an aggravated character.

2nd. I am of opinion that the communication to Lieut-Colonel Butterworth was a privileged communication. It was a communication respecting the propriety of an appointment to a public office, addressed to the person, in whom the power of appointment was, or was supposed to be, by one who, as a subject of Her Majesty, had an interest in the matter, containing charges of unworthy conduct, against the person who had been appointed to the office, which charges the person making the communication had good ground for believing, and, indeed, knew to be true. Charges brought forward under such circumstances are privileged, unless they can be traced to a malignant feeling, or, in other words, actual malice against the accused, *and proved* to have been made without reasonable or probable cause. In the present case, there seems to be no pretence for imputing to Sir James Brooke private malice against Mr. Woods, and, even if it could be imputed, still there can be no doubt, that there was reasonable and probable cause for the communication, because, in point of fact, Mr. Woods had published the libellous matter complained of. I may cite, by way of illustration, the case of Fairman *v.* Ives, 5 Barnewall and Alderson, 643, where a creditor of an officer in the army, presented a memorial to the secretary-at-war, with a view of obtaining payment of his debt, which memorial contained statements derogatory to the character of the officer, but which the creditor believed to be true, and the memorial was held not to be actionable. It was considered immaterial that the secretary-at-war had no direct control over the officer. In recent cases, the law of privileged communications has been upheld by the Courts with a high hand, and I have no doubt that, in any Court in Westminster Hall, the communication of Sir James Brooke to Lieut.-Colonel Butterworth, would be held to have been privileged by the occasion, and not to be actionable.

3rd. I advise Sir James Brooke, in case of proceedings being taken against him at Singapore, to resist them on the grounds above suggested. In case of a judgment against him, I advise him to petition for leave to appeal.

As the damages, if any were given, would probably be small, the case would not fall within the limits of ordinary appeals, which is 10,000 Company's rupees: but under the circumstances of this case, I think an appeal would be allowed, though the damages were under that sum.

31 March, 1853. Jas. S. Willes, Inner Temple,

I have read and concur in the above opinion.

April 1, 1853. Hugh Hill, Liverpool Northern
Circuit.

I also concur in Mr. Willes's opinion.

April 20, 1853. Frederick Thesiger, Temple.

CHAPTER IV.

AUGUST 31, 1851, TO DECEMBER 27, 1852.

SIR JAMES BROOKE arrived in England on the 6th
of May, and was at once engaged in meeting the
attacks on him, which were urged with great perse-
verance, both in and out of Parliament. On the
10th of July, Mr. Hume brought forward his motion
for a Commission of Inquiry into the proceedings of
Sir James Brooke on the coast of Borneo; and it was
felt that, under the mask of inquiry, Mr. Hume's real
object was censure. An elaborate debate, of seven
hours' duration, followed; every accusation was urged—
that Sir James Brooke had destroyed the Serebas and
Sakarrans as pirates, when they were not pirates, but
merely indulging in harmless intertribal wars—that
he had exercised unduo influence over the officers of
the navy to aid him in his designs—that as a Government servant he had been improperly engaged in

trading speculations—and that he had used his de-
puted powers as Consul-General, to the detriment
rather than the advancement of British commerce.
The decisive majority of 230 to 19, by which Mr.
Hume's motion was rejected, sufficiently marked the
sense of the House of Commons; and, as far as could
be gathered from the tone of the public journals, the
nation unanimously approved the judgment of the
House. (See the report of the debate, "Hansard,"
vol. 118, p. 436; "The Times," July 11th and 12th.)

In the month of April, the news of the death of the
old king of Siam arrived in this country; and it was
proposed to renew the negotiation, for a treaty of amity
and commerce between Great Britain and Siam, and
again to intrust this delicate mission to the hands of
Sir James Brooke. The intention was, however, abandoned, and Sir James was enabled to continue his
stay in his native country. On the 13th of May he
received the following generous communication from
Captain Hastings :—

Union Club, May 12, 1851.

DEAR SIR JAMES BROOKE,

I HARDLY know how you will receive a letter
from me, but at any rate I venture to write, as I think
it due to you, hearing you have just arrived in this
country, to send for your perusal, a note I received

from Mr. Hume, upon the subject of his intended motion in the House of Commons.

The enclosures which he alludes to, were copies of your letters to Mr. Wise, and the late Sir R. Peel's observation on the subject of my refusing you assistance in the year 1844, which by-the-by, at the time, did me some harm in the Admiralty, as well as showing me up in Keppel's and Mundy's books; but of that I have long since ceased to think of, and only remember the many acts of kindness and friendship which I received from you in the East.

I refused any information to Mr. Hume, and referred him to the Admiralty; but if I can be of the smallest service to you, in giving any assistance to avert the cruel and unjust persecution which some evil-disposed persons are waging against you, I beg you will command the services of,

My dear Sir James Brooke,

Yours faithfully,

GEO. HASTINGS.

Sir James Brooke, K.C.B.

———

(Enclosure.)

Bryanston Square, February 13, 1851.

Sir,

It is my intention to bring before the House of Commons the conduct of Sir James Brooke on the occasion of the massacre of the Dyaks, on the 31st of July, 1849; and as your conduct has been reflected upon in several public letters and papers, which I must refer to in the course of my statement (one of which letters I enclose for your information), I hope you will not object to state the circumstances that induced you to refuse compliance with Sir James Brooke's request; as it is important that the truth (as regards your refusal, and the facts of that important transaction) should be known.

I remain

Your obedient servant,

J. Hume.

The Honourable
  Capt. G. F. Hastings, R.N.

P.S. Oblige me by returning the enclosure with your answer to

J. H.

No. 150.

CAPTAIN THE HON. G. HASTINGS, R.N.

Maurigy's Hotel, 1, Regent-street,
May 14, 1851.

MY DEAR HASTINGS,

How should I receive a letter, and so generous a letter, excepting with the liveliest pleasure?

That you should at the time have felt hurt by the
remark (foolishly made public) I am not surprised to
hear; and the reason I did not notice it sooner, was
the hope that you might never see, what had been
written.

It appears to me that there can be but one construction put on the passage referred to.—I, from my
position, was eager to attack the pirates, whilst you,
being under orders, could not, in your opinion, do so
consistently with your duty; I was disappointed, and
the reflection of this disappointment appears in the
remarks made at the moment, but our difference was a
difference of opinion, only as to whether you ought, or
ought not, to act with the orders you had received.

Under this impression the entry in Mundy's Journal,
and the remark in my letter to Mr. Wise, were made;
I was irritated and harassed by circumstances, and if
anything I said caused you pain, I am sincerely sorry
for it, and you have truly heaped coals of fire upon my

head, but there is no gentleman will believe for a moment, that I deliberately intended *to reflect upon you.*

I do not dwell further on your kind letter, or on the *Senator's* attempt to beat the bush for *low game.* I am too good a quarry to be struck down by a kite, and you too honest a man to resent a casual remark, at the expense of truth.

Where shall we meet ? let it be by appointment.

Believe me, my dear Hastings,
Yours, very sincerely
J. BROOKE.

P. S. Am I at liberty to use Mr. Hume's letter ?

No. 151.

REV. CHARLES JOHNSON, M.A.

Maurigy's Hotel, May 20, 1851.

MY DEAR CHARLES,

EVERYBODY must see the Exhibition, it is so wonderful and so beautiful. I was grieved to hear that our dear Georgey* was ill.

Do come up, for I long to see you again. Hume's motion comes on to-night, and I am all bustle and business. Yesterday I received most satisfactory

* A daughter of Mr. Johnson.

F 3

letters from Brooke, and good news from all quarters. The storm is passing over, and few men who have been assailed as I have been, have come out so free of damage.

Love to dear Emma and the girls; and believe me,

Yours affectionately,

J. BROOKE.

P. S. Of course, Stuart shall have a holiday. I bought a very pretty thorough-bred mare for forty guineas yesterday, at Tattersall's.

No. 152.

JOHN C. TEMPLER, ESQ.

White Lackington, August 1, 1851.

MY DEAR JACK,

I ARRIVED quite safely, yesterday afternoon, with my mind released by the prospect of being clear of the horrid town for a couple of months.

How are you, dear Jack? and what are to be my plans? As I think at present, I propose staying here about a week; by which time Johnson, who is now convalescent, will be strong, and they can take flight for Lyme. Then I will come to Downe Hall, with my *big box* and horses. You must tell me about a stable—a good one—as near the mansion as may be:

and the men can find lodgings attached or near.   Then I shall live on the road between the two places.   Prior told me you were thinking of taking a house at Bromley for the winter.   Where is Bromley?

Give me a line to say that you are all well; and if you are ailing, and want me, I will come over.

My best love to all.

Ever yours,
J. BROOKE.

No. 153.

JOHN C. TEMPLER, ESQ.

White Lackington, August 3, 1851.

MY DEAR JACK,

I WILL come on Friday next; but though our party here is anxious to see you, yet you must not overdo the drive, if it be inconvenient.

Will you come, as you propose, on Friday, and drive me back? or will you meet me at Beaminster, at 4 o'clock P.M., to which I shall ride?

Here is a plain question, to which I want a plain answer.

We can go and look for a house at Charmouth or Lyme, as my sister will follow me in a week's time. Johnson is better; Charlie's leave, I am sorry to say, drawing to a close.

I am delighted to hear that you are better; you are not meant to be ill.

I feel very gay and happy. We dine at three, and ride afterwards. Twenty-five miles, by Shrewsbury clock, the night before last, as I am a sinner. My love to all.

Ever your friend,
J. BROOKE.

Many thanks for the stables.
The nags flourish.

No. 154.

JOHN C. TEMPLER, ESQ.

White Lackington, August 31, 1851.

MY DEAR JACK,

LORD —— approves, nay, is eager for my departure for Siam; so I have just written to say, that I shall be ready for the October mail, orders being sent to have the requisite vessels ready.

It is of such importance, in a public point of view, that there ought to be no private regrets; and I shall stipulate for my return, when the mission is accomplished.

I do not think it is ungrateful to Old England, but my heart throbs with delight at the prospect of seeing them again in the East; the unpleasant passage is lost sight of; and thus, the ills of this life should be forgotten in the prospect of arriving at a better. I go to town on Tuesday next. I shall then visit Norfolk till the 15th September, and return to London, which will be the best time, if you are stout, to come house-hunting. I shall curtail my Scotch trip, and be ready, as I said, by the 20th October for a start to Siam.

I forgot to bring with me Mr. Wise's public letter to Lord John Russell, denouncing my proceedings. It is in *the box;* will you send it to the United Service Club? Of course, I shall come for a few days to Downe Hall.

Yours, very affectionately,

J. BROOKE.

No. 155.

JOHN C. TEMPLER, ESQ.

United Service Club, September 8, 1851.

MY DEAR JACK,

I LEAVE town to-morrow morning for Norfolk, but shall be back on the 14th or 15th. Will you meet me at Greenwich, look out for a house, and take a real good opinion on your own case. I had a long and comfortable conversation on the subject of cod's liver oil with Dr. Beith, of the hospital, who is an able man, and I have been longing that you should take three doses per diem.   On Saturday I despatched a box of toys, for the little ones.   I was first going to make them into four parcels, directed one to each, but the selection puzzled me, so that I resolved to leave the distribution to papa and mama.   Of course, Dora won't wish for the " Lady Carolina Wilhelmina Furbisher's" company ! but nevertheless I meant it for her.

In great haste, ever yours, my dear friend, affectionately and sincerely,

J. BROOKE.

No. 156.

JOHN C. TEMPLER, ESQ.

9, Croom's Hill, September 16, 1851.

MY DEAR JACK,

I AM delighted to hear of your improvement, and I am not selfish enough to enforce what I wrote last night.   My plans are as follows.   I shall stay in town till the 22nd, by which time my Siam business will be nearly completed.   Till the 26th, I shall stay at Worsley, and then go to Kilgraston, and be in town again on the 2nd or 3rd October, pack up and finish all that is to be done, and start about the 7th or 8th for the Isle of Wight, and thus give a day or two to

Downe Hall and White Lackington, before embarking.

Respecting the Eastern Archipelago Company; the inefficiency of the Company, as well as the truck system, is fully proved by Coulson. Again, touching the grant of the sultan of Borneo, it is clear that it was obtained in order to develop the resources of Borneo, and cannot be held as an instrument of obstruction.

Will you read my last journal, which is in the box, and show such parts as you like to ———. Love to the dear children.

Ever affectionately yours,

J. BROOKE.

With regard to the grant of the sultan of Borneo, mentioned in this letter, a most interesting question had arisen between Sir James Brooke and the Directors of the Eastern Archipelago Company, and a long correspondence with the Colonial Department of Government ensued upon it. Sir James Brooke submitted a literal translation, (for the original was in the Malayan character,) and stated that in obtaining the grant from the sultan, he always understood it to convey a right to work the mines only, and that it did not confer any exclusive privileges, and that such was the true interpretation of the instrument. On the other hand, the Directors submitted a free translation, and contended that its proper construction, gave them the exclusive right to the mines, and that they might work them, or keep them closed as they pleased, and the Colonial Department of the Government eventually arrived at this conclusion. It appears, however, that Sir James Brooke's view was the correct one after all, for after the official correspondence had closed he submitted the Directors' translation and his own to two eminent counsel, and received the following opinion on the interpretation of the instrument.

The documents with the queries referring to them, were stated as follows.

———

The following is a free translation of the Malayan grant—

> State Seal
> of his
> Highness
> the
> Sultan of
> Borneo.

This memorandum of agreement is recorded by Sultan Omar Allie Saferdin, son of Sultan Mahomed Jarmarhar Allum, deceased, of Borneo, by which the whole of the coal found in the country, extending from Mengkabong as far as Tanjong Barram is granted to James Brooke, Esq., the rajah of Sarawak, the coal to be considered at the entire disposal of Mr. Brooke, and his assigns, without any interference whatever on the part of the sultan, but on the distinct understanding that the sultan is to receive, two thousand dollars for the first year the mines are opened and worked, and ever after the annual sum of one thousand dollars.

August 23, 1846.

The following is a literal translation of the grant :—

"This is an agreement of Tuam Sultan Omar Ali Saerfidin, the son of Sultan Mahomed Jarmarhar Allum, deceased, of the country of Brunie, promises to give Tuam Sir James Brooke, Esq., rajah of Sarawak, coals from the country of Mengkabong, as far as Tanjong Barram.

" Whatever may be the spot he may work (the mine) or whoever of his relations (agents) Tuam Besar (Sir James) may authorize (to do the work), Tuam Sultan will not interfere. However, if Tuam Besar has worked at the commencement of the work, we Sir James are to give to **Tuam** Sultan two thousand dollars, the season following (he is) to give Tuam Sultan one thousand dollars (more), and (at every) each (succeeding) season (year) the same. Written on Saturday the 30th of the month, Shaham, at four o'clock, in the Hejira, 1262."

A question has arisen—

1st. Whether the grant is exclusive, so as to confer

the right to all the coals found within those limits, so that whether the Eastern Archipelago Company work the mines or not, they may exclude any third party from the field.

2nd. And also as no limits landward are assigned by the grant, what limits would the law assign, and subject to what terms, if any.

Your opinion is requested on each of the above points.

OPINION.

1. We are of opinion that the grant in the literal translation is not exclusive, but that as made to appear in the free translation, it would, if valid in other respects, be exclusive.

2. We are of opinion that no limits landward can be assigned, and that the grant would according to the law of England, be void for uncertainty.

At all events the grant does not, in our opinion, include veins or beds of coal, not as to some parts of them lying or being upon a line drawn from one of the given points to the other.

(Signed) HUGH HILL.

     JAMES S. WILLES.

Inner Temple,

February 22, 1853.

No. 157.

JOHN C. TEMPLER, Esq.

9, Croom's Hill, September 20, 1851.

MY DEAR JACK,

IN consequence of news just received, that the king of Siam wished to burn his brother, before treating with us, the mission is postponed. I am glad of it; and it gives us breathing time. I start to-morrow to Lord ——'s, where the case will follow me; and from that, I shall go on to Scotland, and be back by the 8th or 10th of October. Will this suit you? or will you come up, and look for a house before my return? I am all abroad, as this palace of Miss ——'s only holds me till October. I think I shall take the cottage in the Park by the month; but if you are not at Greenwich, my inducement to be here is gone.

I have been dining regularly with Sir James Gordon, when disengaged; and to-day St. John comes to me.

Direct to me, Worsley, near Manchester, till the 25th. Kind regards to your party.

Ever affectionately yours,

J. BROOKE.

Delightful accounts of Sarawak and Lundu.

No. 158.

JOHN C. TEMPLER, ESQ.

Kilgraston, Bridge of Earn, Perthshire,
October 3, 1851.

MY DEAR JACK,

SCOTLAND is delightful, and Kilgraston a charming place, whether as regards nature or society. I shall stay here till to-morrow week, as I am commanded to dine with the —— of —— on Wednesday.

Let me hear from you about your movements; and if your house is not ready, pray take possession of the sylvan retreat in the Park, till it is.

Ever your affectionate friend,

J. BROOKE.

No. 159.

JOHN C. TEMPLER, ESQ.

Kilgraston, October 11, 1851.

MY DEAR JACK,

I HAVE been waiting to hear from you, but no news,* they say, is good news; and I hope you are strong and able to face the coming winter.

I have been enjoying myself here, and to-day leave

* The illness of the Editor is here alluded to.

for Keir, which Walter Scott calls the "princely." On Monday I go to Edinburgh; and then, after a visit or two, make my way to London, to my damp little cottage. Will you let me have a line from you, at 6, Duke-street, Edinburgh?

Charlie Grant is in high feather; and there is no end to dancing. The Scotch really dance. My kind love; and, believe me,

Ever your affectionate friend,

J. BROOKE.

During the winter of 1851, Mr. Hume continued to reiterate his attacks through the press;* and upon the opening of the session of 1852, renewed his efforts in the House to bring on a fresh motion for inquiry. The subject, however, was considered as fairly met, by the repeated decisions of the House; and Mr. Hume's attacks savouring of persecution, the merchants of the city of London, to mark their sense of the high services Sir James Brooke had rendered his country, and the unworthy return he was receiving at the hands of a very small but persevering party, determined to give him a public dinner; and this was carried into effect on the 29th of April, 1852. The proceedings at this dinner will be found in Appendix No. 2. It was a

----

* These led to some vigorous letters from Sir James Brooke, which appeared at the time in the columns of the "Times."

great and glorious triumph.   Sir James Brooke delivered a speech which, for truth and feeling, language and action, will never be forgotten by those who had the privilege of hearing him.   It created a general expression of regret, amongst a very select audience, that he had not made England, rather than Borneo, the field of his ambition; and the feeling was current, that should a crisis ever arise in the fortunes of this country, he would be the man of action, who ought forthwith to be called to the councils of the nation.

No. 160.

REV. RICHARD COXE.

White Lackington, January 22, 1852.

MY DEAR RICHARD,

I HAVE taken the advice you gave me, in your last letter in very good part, and commenced my assault on the Eastern Archipelago Company, by moving Government to take some decided measure with respect to it.   This failed of producing any effect, which was not surprising, considering the expedient policy pursued in these latter days; but nothing discouraged, I called to mind Mr. Lindsay's challenge to Mr. Drummond, to allow an inspection of the books and accounts of the immaculate Company, and I resolved to examine how it really stood.   After a world of trouble I have, with the assistance of Templer, laid the whole case bare, and a more rotten company is not to be found. We must now be guided by good counsel, either to file a bill in equity, or apply for a *scire facias*, which is the mode of proceeding in the Queen's Bench, and will give us the power of a *vivâ voce* examination.

I have already had the best opinions on the legal question, which are decided, that the Charter cannot stand, and that a full exposure may render the directors liable for the entire amount received from the shareholders.

I believe the game is now in our hands, and it only remains, to use it justly and moderately. To me it is a matter of surprise, how I have bent myself, for the last three months to trace, step by step, all the doublings, through the intricacies of accounts and counter-accounts —deeds of settlement—shareholders' lists—balance-sheets—and the like. We began by a cold scent, but now it has warmed, so that we shall soon run into our game, be he lion, or be he fox. I wanted to give you this history, which will account for my time, since you heard last; and now that I am going to Oxford, I want to know, where your brother Henry is to be found, when he is out of that vast library?

I am going, for the benefit of the air, to take up my quarters in Brighton, which will allow me to run backwards and forwards to London, whenever it may be requisite, and at the same time, to enjoy my sister's society. I have been staying here for the last three days, trying to induce this party also to pass a couple of months there. I hope, my dear Dick, you and yours are quite well. Write when you have time and inclination, and with kind regards,

Believe me, ever your sincere friend,

J. BROOKE.

P. S. I shall be in town to-morrow.

No. 161.

THE RIGHT HON. SIDNEY HERBERT, M.P.

Maurigy's Hotel, Regent Street,
June 22, 1852.

SIR,

FROM the lateness of the hour, my friends in the House of Commons were unable to offer any reply to the statements made by you, on the Labuan estimates on the 15th instant. I feel assured that it was not your intention to inflict an injury, and that you would not wish that I should submit in silence, to imputations, so unfounded and so derogatory to my reputation, as you have thought fit to advance.

In all courtesy, therefore, I ask, and as an act of

justice I trust you will not object to declare, on what grounds this statement rests, and that you will permit me to afford such explanations as may be requisite, not only on my own account, but on yours.

You, Sir, would not desire to maintain a false accusation, and, on my part, I am anxious that the truth should be made known to yourself and to the world.

According to the report in the "Times," you affirmed, on the occasion referred to, that I was a merchant whilst holding an office under Government, and that my "mercantile speculations" were opposed to the public interests.

On this statement I beg to remark, that if by a merchant is meant a person who buys and sells for his own advantage, that I have never been a merchant at all; and I most distinctly contradict the assertion that I have ever been engaged in "mercantile speculation" or pursuit since my appointment to office in 1847.

In the year 1845 I was the unpaid agent of the English Government.   In 1847 I was appointed Commissioner, and in January, 1848, became Governor of Labuan.

With these dates the following brief narrative will be better understood.

In September, 1841, it became necessary that a revenue should be raised to support the expenses of the new government of Sarawak, and this revenue was realized with the consent of the native chiefs. Owing, however, to the depressed condition of the population, the expenditure considerably exceeded the income; and in order to supply the deficiency of the public revenue, I (through agents appointed for the purpose, and in accordance with the custom of Malayan rulers) purchased the produce brought by the natives for sale.

The entire proceeds derived from this expedient, were applied to defray the charges incurred by my unprecedented, but public position; and the deficiency of the revenue, year after year, was made good from my private fortune.

I leave you, Sir, to decide, whether in the ordinary application of language, it can be said I was trading at all, or trading for profit to be devoted to my own advantage; but there is ample evidence (at all times at your command) to prove that, from the first hour I undertook the government, my desire was to place the revenues of Sarawak upon a secure basis. After encountering many obstacles, I succeeded in carrying out my views on this subject, and in 1846, the antimony mines, the opium farm, and other inconsiderable items of revenue, were leased for five years, and, at the same period the trading operations on the public account were finally terminated.

In 1849, in consequence of the bankruptcy of the lessees, this lease reverted to Government, and in 1850 the antimony mines were again let, whilst the opium farm has since continued to be managed by an officer of the Sarawak government.

I should be happy to explain to you the system of revenue pursued in Sarawak; but to avoid prolixity, I will content myself, on the present occasion, with the mention of the two principal sources whence it is derived, and upon which the question at issue between us, may be judged. The antimony mines are analogous to the Crown mines of any other country; the revenue from them accrues from the annual sum paid by the lessees; the rights of individuals, whether European or native, are not violated, nor is the freedom of commerce in any manner infringed by the appropriation of these mines for public purposes; and instead of being, as formerly, a forced labour monopoly for private use, they are now applied for the benefit of the people, by free labour supply.

The opium farm is identical in principle, and not materially different in its operation, from the opium farm in the British settlements. It is a farm for the purposes of revenue on the retail sale of opium, and the right of retail sale rests in the Government, and is let to a farmer, or if a farmer cannot be found, is superintended by a Government officer.

I may add to this brief explanation, that the revenue system of Sarawak, (although probably not the best that could be devised in theory, is suited to the state of society,) is, conjointly with myself, administered by the native chiefs, and is not complained of by the people; and it must be with you, Sir, to show how a public revenue, realized as I have described, and applied to public purposes, can be termed a " mercantile specu- lation " in which I am personally engaged.

If the revenues of Sarawak cover the annual ex- penses of the government, I am content; and if at any time one branch of the revenue should be su- perseded, the deficit would be supplied by some other tax imposed on the people; but it could in no way affect my personal interest, excepting as it affected the prosperity of the country.

I have expended a very considerable sum from a limited private fortune, to maintain the government of Sarawak, and to relieve the sufferings of its people. I boldly affirm that the security and happiness of a large population, now depends upon that government. I have refrained from imposing taxes, even to repay the sum I have laid out; and at this present moment the revenue barely meets the expenditure, and the country is burdened with a debt. I have expended the greater portion of the salary I have received from the English Government to advance public objects; I have made sacrifices in which I glory. I have gained nothing but the love of a rude and noble people, and the abuse and suspicion of my own countrymen.

I blush to write this, but you force me to do so, when, after a life of danger, privation, and pecuniary sacrifice, you call me a trader—one engaged in " mercantile speculations," contrary to duty and to honour. and contrary to the interests of the public.

I repeat that I am convinced that you did not desire to injure me, or to misrepresent the facts; but I will now ask you, as a man of honour (whose opinion I do not undervalue), to inform me on whose authority these charges are made, and by what evidence they are supported.

I, on my part, will make good what I have now advanced whenever I am called upon, and prove that a public revenue cannot be confounded, without injustice. with private trade ; and that I have never been engaged in any " mercantile speculation " or pursuit, since my appointment to office in the year 1847.

I have the honour to be, Sir,

Your obedient and humble servant,

J. BROOKE.

The Right Hon. Sidney Herbert,
&c.   &c,

P.S. The trial in the Queen's Bench will explain my not having addressed you earlier on the subject.

Belgrave Square, Thursday night,
June 24, 1852.

SIR,

I FOUND, on my return from the House of Commons yesterday morning, the letter which you have done me the honour to address to me.

I regret that the observations, which I thought it my duty to make, on a question of public policy, should be considered by you to be injurious to yourself.

I certainly am not conscious of having in any way impugned your motives. It was not my intention to do so.

The question which I raised was this :—Whether your engagements and interests at Sarawak are of a nature to justify your appointment as governor of the neighbouring island of Labuan? and whether your selection for that office is conformable with the principles, which are understood to regulate the choice of civil servants of the Crown in our colonial possessions?

I must confess that your letter has by no means tended to satisfy me on that point.

I understand that the occurrences in Borneo and Labuan will shortly be the subject of an investigation, in which the particular point to which I have referred would necessarily be included.

Under these circumstances I am sure you will feel

that I should not be justified in entering into any correspondence on the subject.

I have the honour to be,

Your obedient servant,

SIDNEY HERBERT.

Sir J. Brooke, K.C.B.

No. 162.

THE RIGHT HON. SIDNEY HERBERT, M.P.

Reigate, June 26, 1852.

SIR,

I BEG to acknowledge your reply of the 24th instant to my letter.

It would have afforded me satisfaction, had you either denied the charge which you have not supported, or supported the charge which you have not denied.

I am sorry that this point still continues in some degree of obscurity.

If you used the expressions attributed to you, of which I had so just a right to complain, I beg once more to offer a positive and unequivocal contradiction to them; but if, as I infer from your note, you did not use those expressions, you must regret even more than I do, that the "Times" newspaper, instead of reporting the simple question you raised, should so have perverted your speech in the House of Commons, as to make it appear a charge, alike injurious and derogatory to my reputation.

In justice to yourself, some precaution should be taken to prevent the recurrence of a similar error in Hansard's report of the debate referred to.

My motives you are at liberty to impugn at all times according to your pleasure; but what I cannot permit to pass in silence is a misrepresentation of the truth, resting on your authority, or appearing to do so, from a newspaper report.

The question which you acquaint me you raised in the House of Commons, was entirely different from the statement you are reported to have made, in the course of your speech; and as you appear averse either distinctly to affirm, or distinctly to deny, this statement, I will not press the subject further.

" Whether " (as you state) " my engagements and interests at Sarawak are of a nature to justify my appointment as governor of the neighbouring island of Labuan, and whether my selection for that office be conformable with the principles which are understood to regulate the choice of civil servants of the Crown in our colonial possessions," I leave you, Sir, and others whose duty it may be, to discuss and to decide; but it is certain that the position I occupied was known previously to the year 1847, and since that year it has remained unchanged.

In 1845, although cognizant of the circumstances, the Government of the late Sir Robert Peel, of which you were a member, conferred upon me a public office. In 1848 Her Majesty's late Ministers not only selected me for the appointment of governor of Labuan, but they thanked me for the services I had rendered, and placed on record that my position at Sarawak was advantageous to the interests of this nation; and now, should Her Majesty's present Government think fit to reverse the policy or the appointment of their predecessors, it may be done without difficulty, and without acrimonious feelings being excited on a public question.

I hold my appointments for the public good, and only so long as I possess the confidence of the Queen's Government and of the country; and you may rest assured that so long as I continue in office, I shall never shrink from the responsibilities of a stern duty, whether it be to punish a pirate or expose a fraud.

I shall await with calmness the investigation which you inform me is about to take place. I was previously as ignorant of the fact, as I still am (though a party somewhat interested) of its nature and object: but I shall offer no objection to it, should it be consistent with the principles of justice and the dictates of honour; but you must permit me to add that the revival, year after year, under unaltered circumstances,

G 3

of the same charges, is as little in accordance with right principle, as it is with the English character.

Having attained the object I had in view, I shall now lay the truth before the public, as fearless of consequences, as I am unchangeably impressed with the proper course of public duty and of private rectitude.

I have the honour to be, Sir,

&c. &c. &c.

J. BROOKE.

The Right Hon. Sidney Herbert.

Wilton House, July 1, 1852.

SIR,

I WISH that there should be no misunderstanding, as to the observations made by me in the House of Commons.

I have stated in my previous letter, what was the question which I raised to your position in Borneo, in the debate to which you have alluded.

In raising that question, I stated that the perusal of public documents left an impression on my mind, that you were engaged in trading at Sarawak, and I appealed to the Government to institute an inquiry into the matter, as such an engagement on your part could not be otherwise than prejudicial to the interests of the Crown at Labuan.

Your letters to me have strengthened this impression.

I beg, therefore, to decline any further controversy, on a matter which will again be a subject of discussion in Parliament, and where it will be my duty to show the grounds, on which my opinion rests.

I have the honour to be,

Your obedient servant,

SIDNEY HERBERT.

Sir James Brooke, K.C.B.

No. 163.

THE RIGHT HON. SIDNEY HERBERT, M.P.

Reigate, July 2. 1852.

SIR,

In order to avoid controversy, I had the honour to inform you in my last communication that, as you appeared averse either distinctly to affirm, or distinctly to deny, the statement made by you in the House of Commons, that I would press the subject no further.

Your note of yesterday removed the ambiguity which previously existed; and as you now grant the report in the "Times" to be correct, I must remind you, that when stopped by Sir John Pakington, you were supporting your allegations from a private paper, and not from a public document.

I desire that the truth should be made known; and when you bring the subject once more before Parliament, I trust that an opportunity may be afforded to my friends in the House, to offer a reply to your statements.

The question has been repeatedly discussed during the last three years; and having been before one Committee of the late House of Commons, it appears from your letters that it is again to be discussed and referred anew, to a Committee of the Parliament not yet elected.

The Parliament will doubtless require at your hands, such grounds in support of your opinion, as will warrant a new inquiry, and clearly mark the distinction between justice and persecution.

* The public will now be enabled to weigh the facts I have advanced, against the impressions you have received, and to decide whether a public revenue is to be treated as a " mercantile speculation."

I have the honour to be, &c.,

J. BROOKE.

The Right Honourable Sidney Herbert,
    &c.   &c.

---

* This correspondence was intended for publication in the daily papers, but it was withdrawn in consequence of the general election engrossing the public attention.

No. 164.

REV. RICHARD COXE.

Reigate, July 3, 1852.

MY DEAR RICHARD,

I AM pretty well, spite of my labours and trial, and these, too, are drawing to a close. I came to issue with the Eastern Archipelago Company, and commenced proceedings in the Queen's Bench, upon which the directors, a powerful body, from their *rank, position, and character*, abused me in every possible way, and moved heaven and earth to change the trial from the Queen's Bench to the House of Commons; they petitioned Parliament against me, and on the 15th, on the Labuan estimates. Wilson Patten and Sidney Herbert urged the Government to interfere; on the 16th and 17th, they used every interest to stop the legal proceedings, but failed; and on the 19th I got them into the Queen's Bench, face to face; and the "Times" of yesterday will tell you, with what result.

I have since had a correspondence with Sidney Herbert, which you will read and judge of for yourself. I have played a bold game with great caution, and have proved successful against long odds; but right, was in the scale against wrong, and Old England is Old England still. I shall be moving to Scotland in August, and will stop with you on the way.

I have taken a house here for three months, and though, as yet I have not had much of it, enjoy the repose more than any one, less jaded, can understand. After the elections, I shall seek a final explanation with the Government. If I possess their confidence, and an efficient course of action promising good results, is entered on, I will continue in the public service—if not, I shall seek that repose and that independence, which I prize above ambition, and above silver and gold. I met —— the other day, when pressed with business, and had only time to shake him hurriedly by the hand. My kind regards to them all, and believe me,

Your affectionate friend,
JAMES BROOKE.

No. 165.

MISS DORA TEMPLER.

Reigate, July 25, 1852.

MY DEAR MISS DORA,

I HAVE a great secret to tell you, which you must not tell to anybody, excepting to Jemmy, and Jemmy can whisper it to Harvey, and Harvey can inform Freddy, and Freddy can bawl it into Georgie's ear—if you find it very difficult to keep this secret, tell it too, to papa and mamma.

The secret is this—papa is going to pass a month in

Scotland, and mamma wishes very much to go with him, but she is not able, because she has five children to take care of. Now, I think, as you are all very good, that you might each take a basin of gruel and go quietly to bed, for a whole month, and be quiet until mamma comes back. Is not this a nice plan? You may tell mamma about it, and ask her advice whether you may not go to bed for a month.

With my best love to the dear boys. Believe me, my dear Dora,

Your affectionate friend,
J. BROOKE.

No. 166.

REV. RICHARD COXE.

Reigate, August 14, 1852.

MY DEAR RICHARD,

I HAVE had several interviews with ministers, and crowned them all with one with Lord ——: but, as yet, there has been no result. They were all very polite, I may say kind, and appear to enter into my views; but the groundwork of my position was, that they might avail themselves of my services if they choose; and if not, that I would be obliged to them to make up their minds, and let me take an independent course. If employed, I insisted on confidence and efficiency—reality and not pretence—and a remedy for the anomalous position in which I was placed by my being Consul-General, with plenipotentiary powers, &c., &c. They will soon give me an answer, and I will let you know, what it is. At the same time I offered, for the good of the public service, and to set the question at rest, to submit to a committee of the House of Commons; this ministers will likewise consider. Yesterday (10th) there was a long correspondence of mine with the judges of Singapore, published—all very wrong and shameful in the opinion of the " Daily News," because the shoe pinches on that quarter; but I believe that you, and every other high-minded and honest man, will commend me for the principles I asserted, at no small personal inconvenience. On Wednesday I am going to Scotland, and, as I come back, I shall stop with you at Newcastle, giving you due notice—but do not bother yourself about my accommodation. What about our dinner? I should like it early in October.

Farewell. My kind regards to all your party, and believe me, my dear Richard,

Your affectionate friend,

J. BROOKE.

No. 167.

JOHN C. TEMPLER, ESQ.

Newcastle, September 14, 1852.

MY DEAR JACK,

I HAVE postponed my return from Tuesday to Wednesday, that I may enjoy the society of Coxe and his family a little longer.

I hope you got home safely and comfortably. I found a supper and hot negus awaiting me at Newcastle, and thought of you during the watches of the night, and of your release at ten. Kindest regards,

And ever affectionately yours,

J. BROOKE.

No. 168.

JOHN C. TEMPLER, ESQ.

Reigate, October 7, 1852.

MY DEAR JACK,

THE weather has been, and is so wretched, that I the less regret my not having been able to get westward for the present. The Ministry will be in town the end of this week, and my affairs will then be decided; I have sent in a long report of the details for the suppression of piracy, and I have now a translation of a letter from the Government of Bruné, which proves

Mr. Burns' and Mr. Motley's joint letter to Mr. Hume, to have been a fabrication. How are you all? and when do you return?

Farewell. I do not bother you, or myself by writing at large, for you ought to enjoy yourself, and I am going driving in my pony chaise. Love to your party; and,

Ever your affectionate friend,
J. BROOKE.

P. S. I am expecting Grant; but for the last week I have been out of spirits, from the intelligence of the death of my poor friend Elliot—whom you knew—a fine, true-hearted fellow.

No. 169.

REV. RICHARD COXE.

Reigate, November 9, 1852.

MY DEAR RICHARD,

I SHALL positively be in town on Friday. Will Philip* and yourself come and dine with me, at the hotel on that day at half-past seven?

The pinch of my political existence is at hand; next week, the argument and decision on the Charter of the Eastern Archipelago Company, will be over—it will be

* A brother of the Archdeacon.

in my favour, and terminate in the repeal of the charter. Then comes the question, whether Government will grant these convicted directors a new charter? If it does, of course I retire. This keeps me busy, but, having made up my mind, not anxious. Certainty is a comfortable thing. In haste.

Ever affectionately yours,

J. BROOKE.

No. 170.

REV. RICHARD COXE.

Hillingdon Grove, near Uxbridge,
December 27, 1852.

MY DEAR RICHARD,

How are you this season, which should be a cheerful one? I shall be rejoiced to hear you are enjoying it.

For myself, I have been much troubled by the ceaseless fluctuations of the political world, which reflect their uncertainty upon me. I am now all abroad, as to my future course; but I day by day gain the experience required, and learn how little dependence can be placed on the English Government, or on English politics. I shall not, therefore, regret parting company, on my own account, or on account of Sarawak, but at seeing a rational and noble policy thrown away, amid the contentions of faction, and popular institutions.

I have been here for the last week, and confined to my couch, or nearly so, with influenza and other ills. I am, however, better, but in no mood for writing, and I only scrawl these lines to tell you my news, and to wish you happiness and health, present and future, at this season.

My kind regards to Mrs. Coxe and your family circle, and believe me, my dear Dick,

Yours ever effectionately,

J. BROOKE.

CHAPTER V.
FEBRUARY, 1853.

THROUGHOUT the winter of 1852 the persecution of Sir James Brooke continued, led by Mr. Hume and the Directors of the Eastern Archipelago Company, whose charter by the judgment of the Queen's Bench had been declared to be repealed; against this judgment, the Directors appealed to the Court of the Exchequer Chamber,* and were thus, under the name of the Company, still enabled to gain access to the Government departments. At the commencement of the session of 1853, a change of ministry took place; and Mr. Hume, who had met with no encouragement from its predecessor, apparently obtained the ear of the present Government, with reference to Sir James Brooke. His mode of attack, however, was as novel, as it was unconstitutional, and consisted in writing vituperative letters to the heads of the departments, and then moving in his place in Parliament, for the

* The judgment of the Queen's Bench in Sir James Brooke's favour, has been confirmed by a majority of seven to one of the judges in the Exchequer Chamber.—See Editor's note, p. 175, post.

printing of such letters. This was generally granted, apparently without much examination or knowledge of what the letters contained, and in this way libel upon libel on Sir James Brooke was printed at the expense of the nation, while it was difficult to prosecute Mr. Hume, by reason of his privilege of Parliament. At length, however, Mr. Hume printed and caused to be privately circulated, some copies of a pamphlet, containing all his charges against Sir James Brooke; and one of these falling into Sir James's hands, he took the opinion of counsel upon it—That opinion is given in the note to p. 196 (*post*). Sir James Brooke acted upon it, and, instead of taking any legal proceeding against Mr. Hume, for the libellous matter contained in the pamphlet, he addressed to Mr. Drummond the following four letters, numbered 171, 172, 173, and 174, as a vindication of his character and proceedings.

(No. 1.)   No. 171.

HENRY DRUMMOND, ESQ., M.P.

MY DEAR SIR,

MR. HUME has printed a pamphlet containing a repetition of all the charges which for several years he has preferred against me; and although I had resolved no further to notice what this gentleman might either say or do, I have, on reflection, changed my mind, in the hope that my present labour may tend to my future ease ; and that it may afford to all those who really desire to make themselves acquainted with the subject, an easy reference to the documents connected with it.

It is however necessary, in the first place, to explain the circumstances under which this discussion arose, and whence it has since been protracted to an interminable length, and a perplexing entanglement to the cursory inquirer.

In 1848, I was encouraged by the public approbation, by memorials from the principal commercial associations in the kingdom, and by the express sanction of the Government of the country, to undertake a decisive course of policy for the suppression of piracy.

In 1849, in pursuance of this duty, the punishment of the Serebas pirates—a measure both previously and subsequently approved by Her Majesty's ministers—was successfully accomplished. Mr. Hume then, for the first time, stepped forward as my public accuser in Parliament. Ample time was afforded him to collect all the evidence on the subject which could be procured; and no effort was spared, to render it of a sufficiently condemnatory character, to justify a demand for inquiry. Mr. Hume's motions were fully and solemnly discussed in 1850 and 1851, and on both occasions they were rejected by nearly unanimous majorities, conclusively demonstrating the sense of the House of Commons and of the country.

It appears to me a grievous injury inflicted on an individual and on the public interest, to repeat the same charges with the same absence of testimony; and, in order to prove the injustice of the course pursued by Mr. Hume, I need only recapitulate, the accusations which, session after session, and year after year, he has heaped upon me. The first grave charge which Mr. Hume advanced, was to the effect, that *I had massacred innocent people, falsely asserting them to be pirates.* This charge having for a time been dismissed, he endeavoured to prove that I was a merchant whilst engaged in the public service. He next asserted that an unnecessary loss of life had been inflicted in the action of July 1849; he afterwards cavilled at the title by which I hold Sarawak; he has accused me of cold-blooded murders; he has denounced me for neglect of public duty; for abuse of official power; for impeding the progress of commercial enterprise; and for establishing a trading monopoly; and added to this frightful category of crime and of misdemeanour, he seeks to convict me " out of my own mouth " of bad motives, ambitious designs, violence, tyranny, falsehood, injustice, and petty larceny.

Never probably before has a civilized man been so unfortunate as to have charged upon him, at one and the same time, so varied a list of offences; and yet a repetition of these charges is to be found in the pamphlet, *privately printed, and privately circulated, with letters of recommendation* from Mr. Hume, addressed to exalted personages, whose ill opinion would most injure me, and best advance the object at which he aims.

I will leave it with impartial persons to decide whether such a course can be reconciled to the principles of justice, to the maxims of English law, or to the sense of English fair play; and I shall content myself with the remark that, in my opinion, Mr. Hume impedes his own success, and prevents the possibility of a fair inquiry by the indiscriminating extravagance of his assertions, and by the virulence with which he urges them against me.   It is true that he has, with a clumsy solemnity, staked his reputation on the purity of his motives; but in doing so, he has overlooked what others cannot fail to perceive, namely, the *deep personal interest he must have in establishing the charges he has preferred; for if I be innocent, then Mr. Hume is guilty*—guilty of the serious offence of repeating accusations, alike the most grave and the most trivial, against his fellow-man, upon evidence which has been twice weighed by Parliament, and twice rejected.

I am desirous, however, of avoiding Mr. Hume's acrimony of expression.   I am not unwilling to give him credit for being ignorant of the real motives which actuate him : and I am inclined to plead in his favour *that pertinacity of will* which is too often the misfortune, and not the fault, of advanced age.

I propose referring, in the Notes, to the sources for procuring complete information on the various subjects under discussion ; and in refutation of the first charge of the massacre of innocent people, I shall content myself with an array of the positive testimonies, to establish the piratical character of the Serebas community, and the specific acts of piracy committed by it.*

1. Mahomed Kassim—Piracy thirty years ago.

2. Mr. Windsor Earl, 1836.

3. Monsieur Cornet de Groot, 1839—Secretary-General to the Netherland Colonial Minister.

4. Sir James Brooke, 1839, 1840.

---

* Papers presented to the House of Commons relating to Piracy; Foreign Office, 5th Feb., April, 11th June, 15th August.—Notices Historiques sur les Pirateries, 1816 to 1845—Presented to both Houses of Parliament, July 1851—Additional Papers respecting the operations against the Pirates, presented to both Houses, 1851—Borneo Piracy: Further Correspondence, presented to the House of Commons, 30th June, 1852—In continuation of Papers presented 23rd March, 1852—Colonial Office: No. 378, 6th June, 1851—Admiralty: presented to the House of Commons, 11th Feb. No. 53; 15th April, No. 239—Vide Note signed D. B. Woolsey, 1851; 15th November; 16th November, 1852—Hansard's Reports, 10th July, 1851—Edinburgh Review, July 1852—" Visit to the Indian Archipelago," by Captain the Hon. Henry Keppel, R.N., Chap. ix. to xiv.

5. Captain Keppel, 1843, 1844.

6. The Rajah Muda Hassim, 1843, 1844.

7. Mr. Church, 1843— Resident Councillor of Singapore.

8. Tay Song Que—Commander of a Chinese vessel.

9. Colonel Butterworth, 1844—Governor of Singapore.

10. Dawich   ⎫ Commanders of prahus from the
11. Mahdout ⎬ N.W. coast of Borneo.

12. Admiral Sir Thomas Cochrane.

13. The Sultan of Borneo ⎫ Subsequently to the
14. The Pangeron Makoto ⎬ action of 1849.

15. Mr. Louis Jackson—Civil Service of Bengal, 1849.

16. Mr. Urban Vigors, 1852.

17. Siup—captured after the action.

18. Abang Bit   ⎫
19. Abang Buyong ⎬ Serebas Men.

20. Asin—a Chinese, formerly of Sambas.*

21. The decision of the Court of Admiralty in Singapore.†

To this list I may add, that in 1850 I received the

---

* The Parliamentary Papers will furnish more depositions than are here noticed.

† If the decision of a Court of Justice on a simple matter of fact is not conclusive, where is the safety of the subject ? where the right of property to be insured ?

approval of Her Majesty's Ministers, with instructions from Lord Palmerston to repeat the same measure when it should again become necessary.[*]

I need scarcely tell Mr. Hume that *a fact cannot be more than proved*, and if this fact be not established, there has not been, nor can there ever be, an established fact in the world.

On the second charge, of the unnecessary sacrifice of life, I reply :—

That there is no testimony whatever in support of it; as Mr. Urban Vigors, who was formerly asserted to be an evidence in its favour, has now stated as follows : " No man " (writes this gentleman) " can entertain a greater horror of unnecessary bloodshed than I do, and yet I do not for one moment hesitate to express my most unqualified approbation of all that was done in that expedition ; the lesson was a severe one, but I am satisfied that it was necessary."[†]

It is proved that I was several miles from the scene of action—that the following morning I stopped the pursuit, and rejected a proposal to effect the destruction of the pirates ;[‡] that rewards were given for prisoners ;

---

[*] Parliamentary Papers: F. O. Moved for, but not yet presented to the House of Commons, 1853.

[†] Parliamentary Papers: F. O. Moved for, but not yet presented to the House of Commons—" Visit to the Indian Archipelago," Appendix.

[‡] Statement of Captain Farquhar.

that they were well treated, and after a time, dismissed to their homes.

I was not a witness of the action, and had no control over it; how then could I, in any case, be held responsible for what occurred?

The third charge is for murder.

Crimes were committed in Sarawak of the most aggravated character,* causing a loss of life, and threatening the peace of society, by the defiance of a humane law, forbidding bloodshed. The criminals were tried and executed, after the deliberation of several days; and *this*, because the trial was not specifically mentioned in a desultory diary, has been termed "*murder*," with a view to my ruin, under circumstances of peculiar and premeditated treachery! †

Mr. Hume has still another story, advanced on the authority of a Singapore paper: "that in 1846 "by uttering the words, *let them die*, I ordered, or caused to be put to death, without any form of trial, three prisoners taken in the attack on Bruné." I do not envy Mr. Hume *the authority* on which he has advanced so grave an accusation, and he must surely himself allow, that if a public man were on

---

* Parliamentary Papers: Colonial Office, presented to the House of Commons, 17th May, 1852, No. 357, pp. 117, 118.

† Idem, p. 117.—Letter from Mr. J. A. St. John and the Rev. Francis McDougall.

every occasion to resort to a legal remedy to acquit himself from the imputations thrown out against him, that the business of the country would be impeded, and the Courts of Law kept in constant employment. The editor in question has been repeatedly challenged to produce proof, or to name his informant, but has never done either—and yet this barren assertion, contained in a newspaper, Mr. Hume considers a sufficient ground to warrant him in demanding a Parliamentary inquiry!

The real circumstances I must briefly relate. The men mentioned were not made prisoners by the English force, but were subsequently arrested by the order of Pangeran Mumein, and others, who were administering the government of the city, whilst it was occupied by the naval Commander-in-Chief.

The fact was notified to Sir Thomas Cochrane, who declined interfering with the administration of justice; and the criminals, who had been actors in the murder of a branch of the Royal family, were executed, we may presume in accordance with the usual procedure in that country.

For myself, I may say, that I knew neither the names nor the persons of the men mentioned, and neither uttered the words, "let them die," or "let them live;" being ignorant of the circumstances which induced the arrest or the execution.

(No. 2.)   No. 172.

HENRY DRUMMOND, ESQ., M.P.

MY DEAR SIR,

On the fourth charge, namely, that I have been engaged in trade whilst holding a public office, I must dwell at somewhat greater length.

If by a merchant be meant a person who buys and sells for his own profit, then I have never been a merchant at all.

In the year 1845 I was the unpaid agent of the English Government; in 1847 I was appointed Commissioner, and Consul-General; and in 1848 became Governor of Labuan.

With these dates, the following brief narrative will be better understood.

In 1841, I stated that the yearly expenses attendant on the government of Sarawak would be from 4000l to 5000l. I disclaimed all personal views of advantage, and offered the country to the English Government, or to others, able, if willing, to enter on the task: I declared that I sought to advance an object, which I considered to be recommended both by policy and humanity, and " after devoting time and fortune," I hoped that " having borne all the brunt, I should not be left to bear the burden likewise."

Should I, however, fail in arousing sympathy, I professed my readiness to proceed without help, although, as I then wrote, "*I must seek to raise the necessary expenses by entering into trade, in which case my position would be less influential, and less useful, than it would otherwise be, and my attention distracted, by details foreign to my principal object.*"*

In this early stage of my undertaking, I might have been justly styled a merchant ruler (no uncommon character in those countries), resorting to trade in order to supply a deficit in the public revenue; but I could never, in the received acceptation of the term, be called a merchant, engaged in trade on my own account, or for my own profit; for, on the contrary, so late as the year 1851, there was *an excess of expenditure over receipts, which I willingly made good from my private fortune.*

Before confidence was established, and the measure could be justified by the general increase of prosperity, the imposition of additional taxes would have disturbed the population of the country; and the trading on Government account, for the same reason, was left entirely to the option of the natives, who were always permitted to dispose of their produce to the highest bidder.

* Letter addressed to James Gardner, Esq., published in 1842, pp. 5, 6, 36, 37, 38, 40.

. There is the clearest and fullest testimony of my reluctance to avail myself of this means of defraying a portion of the inevitable expenses of the Government, and of my efforts to absolve myself from the responsibility, by placing the revenues of Sarawak upon a more permanent basis.*

This object was finally accomplished on the 1st September, 1846; the trading operations on account of Government were finally closed, and the antimony mines, and opium farm, &c. leased for five years.

I cannot close this portion of the subject better than by quoting three short extracts from the correspondence at that time carried on between my agent in England and myself. The first bears date the 4th December, 1845, when I wrote as follows:—

"At the same time you must bear in mind that if you endeavour to keep me mixed up in trading matters, that you cannot expect success, for you must work with the grain and not against it, and *you well know that from my temper, habits, and education, I am averse to and incapable of all matters relating to commerce. I assure you I would rather return to England, and live in poverty and retirement, than continue subject to the fluctuations and anxieties of commerce. You may*

* A voluminous private correspondence, a small part of which has been published in the Appendix to the Report of the Army and Ordnance Committee.

n 3

be sorry for this, but you cannot alter my nature or my feelings, and you will therefore, I am sure, seriously put your shoulder to the wheel to clear me from my present position."

What that position was may be judged from the following extract, dated on the 16th March, 1846.—"I consider myself" (I wrote) "representing the Government of Sarawak, and a Government with a moderate sufficient revenue, is more stable, than with a larger one, subject to fluctuation."*

* The following extracts from my correspondence with my agent will further prove my views and sentiments.

15th October, 1845.—"I cannot soar about money matters, and my mind is seriously disturbed and injured by the fluctuations, and even the *very discussion of commercial matters*, in which I am mixed up. This then my desire should be effected as soon as possible."—My desire was to be relieved from responsibility, by the lease of the mines, &c.

10th February, 1846.—"I am not blind to the advantages that might accrue to myself, nor do I undervalue riches, but I cannot be swayed by them. Did such considerations sway me, I should be unfit to be where I am, and had they swayed me, it is most probable I should not be here at all. All the advantages which may accrue from farming of antimony ore, &c. you can share with others, who are capitalists. I want nothing beyond what I have stated at present—the due reward of my labour—and I look forward to increase *my revenue, together with the prosperity of Sarawak*." I had stated the rental for the antimony mines, opium farm, working diamonds, &c. &c. at 2,500*l.* per annum.

No man relinquishes the golden dreams you have held up to my eyes without a sigh—no man would relinquish them, excepting from a sense that he was doing right.   [Then

To this communication my agent replied on the 24th June, 1846. "The accomplishment of your wishes" (he stated) "on this subject *will I trust terminate the anxiety you have so frequently expressed, to be clear*

Then again, on the 1st March, 1846, after alluding to the proposed Company, by means of which I was to become "*one of the wealthiest commoners in England*," I wrote as follows :—

"You may rightly reap an advantage from this, or any other enterprise of a similar nature, but so essentially different is the position in which I am placed, that I could not do so without the loss of reputation, not only in the opinion of the world, but likewise in my own estimation.—*I am pledged to the good government of Sarawak, and I am bound not to risk the welfare of this people for any motives, whether of cupidity or ambition.* I repeat again, I can in no-wise participate in profits which may arise out of the formation of a company, or any other project, which may be started in England, *for it is incumbent upon me to remain independent.*"

The truth is, that previously to these projects being started, and the offer made me of realizing vast wealth— "*a princely fortune*"— by my participation in them, I had never seriously considered the duty which I had to perform towards Sarawak—and, I may add, towards England—circumstances altered with a rapidity unknown under established governments—to afford protection to Sarawak, and to save myself from the ruin which threatened, I would, in 1842 or 1843, have made over the government, which had cost me thousands, to a Company, for a few shares in the scheme ; but in 1846 I would not have done so, for the people were happy ; difficulties and dangers had been surmounted, and there was an approach to the permanency which I desired in the state of things. The difficulties of my position, with the change of circumstances, should be borne in mind, when a judgment is formed of any particular event, as separated from the general course of my career. I leave these extracts—a few amongst many of the like tenor in my correspondence—to the consideration of the candid reader.

*of all matters connected with trading, as you can now
pursue, with undivided attention, the measures you may
consider best calculated to benefit your adopted
country ! !"*

The revenues of Sarawak are distributed amongst
four different departments, administered by three
native Datus or Chiefs, and myself: they are derived
from a fixed rice-tax, the lease of the antimony mines,
an opium farm, a spirit-farm, a tax on killing pigs, a
tax on working gold, ground-rents, fisheries, fines, and
other small items; and that portion of this revenue,
with the disbursement of which I was formerly intrusted, amounts to about 5,000*l.* per annum.

To raise Sarawak to its present prosperous condition,
I have expended from my private fortune a sum
certainly not less than 20,000*l.*; and my relations,
therefore, with the country are twofold, firstly, as its
ruler, and secondly, as a public creditor.

Previously to the year 1848, I received from the
revenues a yearly sum for my personal expenses,
varying from 300*l.* to 500*l.*; from the commencement
of 1848 to October, 1851, I took nothing; and from
October, 1851, to the close of 1852, I have drawn at
the rate of 1,000*l.* per annum.

This is substantially the state of affairs at the
present time: as a public creditor I have not been
hard, I have never desired to charge interest on the

money I have advanced; and when the country can afford to repay it, I shall have no claim on its revenues, and shall be content with such a sum as may be yearly apportioned, to maintain the position which I now hold.

Having premised thus much, I shall confine the explanation, with which I must still trouble you, to the departments of Government, which I once superintended, in Sarawak, but which, since I accepted an appointment in the public service of England, has been more efficiently superintended by my relative, Captain Brooke.*

The charges to be defrayed are similar to those in other countries. Payment of interest on the public debt—*excepting what is due to me*—public establishments and salaries, charities, improvements, public buildings, roads, army,† navy, police, &c. &c.; and the amount, I have before mentioned, of 5,000*l.* per annum, is mainly derived from the opium farm and the antimony mines.

A brief detail, therefore, of these sources of revenue will enable you to judge whether a monopoly exists, in the legal and injurious sense of that word, or whether I can justly be said to be engaged in trade

* A portion of the time by another gentleman.

† The full complement of the standing army is twenty-four men.

whilst holding office under the Government of this country.

1stly. Opium. This branch of the revenue is superintended by an officer appointed for the purpose, and is a fiscal regulation for the retail sale of opium. The farm is leased to responsible persons for a stated monthly sum, or should such persons not be found to undertake the entire management, there are one or more farmers who receive opium from the Government officer, which they are licensed to retail, and which they account for at a fixed price. I must add, that the opium farm in Sarawak is identical in principle, and nearly so in details, with the same farms in Singapore, Malacca, Penang, and Labuan; that the Governors of these settlements have never been accused of trading, and that this fiscal arrangement in no manner interferes with the wholesale import, export, or sale of opium.

2ndly. The antimony mines. It will be at once evident, that a *proprietary right to the mineral productions must exist in every country.* The antimony ore of Sarawak does not belong to private individuals, and has, since its first discovery, been treated as the property of the State.

The merchant, formerly wishing to purchase the ore, dealt with the ruler of the country, and it was for this ruler that the population were once *forced* to procure it. *They were driven to labour,** and very inadequately remunerated—trade, as I declared in 1841,† was a "curse instead of a blessing," and led only to the oppression of the poorer classes. When I took charge of the government of Sarawak, I retained the antimony ore as a means of revenue, but I freed the people from compulsory labour, and quadrupled the price paid for the article. The antimony mines have been leased since the year 1846,‡ and the only right, claimed for the Government of Sarawak, or for the lessees, is, that they may be permitted to dispose of the ore in the market, where it will fetch the highest price.

Antimony is the produce of other places in Borneo. The freedom of trade is guaranteed by treaty, and I possess no power to prevent the natives working the mines, should they desire to do so. My character would be sunk in European estimation by any such attempt, and my influence over the native mind destroyed by it, and there could be no temptation for me; for should the ore of another locality, supersede the ore

* Keppel's Narrative, vol. ii., pp. 204, 205. " The Dyaks were compelled, amidst their other wrongs, to labour at the ore, without any recompense. Many died in consequence of this compulsory labour." This is what some persons are pleased to describe as Free Trade ! !

† Letter to James Gardner, Esq., p. 21.

‡ With a brief interval only.

of Sarawak, the loss, in the first place, would fall on the lessees, and the revenue now derived from that source, which amounts to 2,000*l.* per annum, would be as readily obtained by the imposition of a tax upon salt, by an additional tax upon rice, or by many other means. Sarawak, from the increase of its population and its trade, and from the increased confidence and prosperity which reigns, would yield a revenue far exceeding what is now collected—it is, *because I have refrained from imposing burdens on the people which they would bear without complaint—because I have expended a large sum to advance the welfare of the country—because my habits, temper, and education, render me averse to all matters connected with commerce —because I have never kept a private account in my life —because I have but rarely and cursorily looked at public accounts—and because the surplus revenue (when it shall accrue) would not belong to me personally, but to the State of Sarawak—it is because of these things that I am accused of engaging in trade, whilst holding a public appointment in the service of England.* You may, my dear Sir, now decide whether a monopoly has been established,* or whether the indirect administration of

---

* The following is an extract from a letter from Messrs. Shaw, Whitehead and Co., the Agents in Singapore, to Messrs. Melville and Co., the lessees of the antimony mines in Sarawak, 14th June, 1847:—" We note your *remarks on the subject of raw sago; it might*

a public revenue, can with justice be confounded, with the personal obligations of trade.

(No. 3.)   No. 173.

HENRY DRUMMOND, Esq., M.P.

MY DEAR SIR,

THE fifth charge urged by Mr. Hume rests on a complaint made by Mr. Burns, of my having impeded his trading operations in the Bintulu river. Mr. Nicol (a partner in the firm of Messrs Hamilton, Gray, and Co.), the employer of Mr. Burns, has stated that, " as the speculation was a mere delusion, he made up his mind to have nothing more to do with it," and " he emphatically denied that I ever, to his knowledge, evinced the least jealousy of the undertaking, or attempted to thwart it; but, on the contrary, that I was willing to promote it as far as lay in my power."*   It will be necessary, however, for me to dwell briefly on some of the allegations made by this unfortunate young man, in order to show the nature of the charge, which rests on his authority, as opposed to that of his em-

be against the principles of free trade established in Sarawak to make a monopoly of the article."

* Borneo.—Further papers respecting Mr. Burns, presented to the House of Commons, 25th June, 1852, pp. 1, 2.

ployer, Mr. Nicol.   He stated, in a letter addressed to
Lord Palmerston, dated June 28, 1851, that during
my absence in England, a letter had been sent from
Sarawak, menacing *the chiefs of Bintulu, should they
permit a white man to reside in their country.** This
letter Mr. Burns stated that *he heard read* early in the
year 1848, although no complaint was made relative to
it until June 1851, whether to his employer or to Her
Majesty's Government.   So important was this letter
considered, that *a sum of eighty pounds was offered for
a copy,*† by Mr. Motley, the superintendent of the
Eastern Archipelago Company, and Mr. Burns subsequently offered money for it, when in Bruné for the
last time.   Whether they succeeded in obtaining the
information which they sought must continue a matter
of doubt ; but the truth of Mr. Burns' statement may
now be judged, by *the copy of the letter which has been
forwarded from Sarawak.*‡

It is further asserted that a second letter was sent
by me to Bintulu, in the " Phlegethon " steamer, which
Mr. Burns *heard read*, and which ordered the chiefs to
turn him out of the country.   In reply, it is enough to

---

* F. O. Borneo.—Correspondence respecting Mr. Burns, presented
to the House of Commons, 23rd March, 1852, pp. 1, 2.

† Idem, p. 19.

‡ F. O. Parliamentary Papers moved for, but not yet presented
to the House of Commons. 1853.

say, that in 1848 when *the events occurred they were not mentioned;* in 1849 they were stated to be *"rumours"* *which Mr. Burns "was led to believe,"* and in 1851 *are discovered to be facts, all along well known to this same person !**

I am obliged, however reluctantly, to notice another subject connected with a statement referred by Mr. Hume to the Earl of Derby, on the 28th February, 1852.†

On July the 30th, 1851, Mr. Motley joined Mr. Burns aboard the " Dolphin " schooner off Labuan : it is probable that on the following day the " Dolphin " sailed for Bruné, a distance of fifty miles, the last fifteen being a difficult river navigation.   On the 4th of August, Mr. Burns and Mr. Motley were in the palace of His Highness Omar Ali, and on the 5th, at anchor below Palo Chermin, having left the city, *whence they addressed to Mr. Hume a statement of the complaints alleged to have been made by the sultan against my proceedings,*† in the presence and hearing of Pangeran Mumein, prime minister of Bruné, Pangeran Makota, &c.

The dates will prove that trade was not the object of the visit.   Mr. Burns proceeded on a trading voyage to Malludu Bay, where his vessel was captured, and he

* Borneo.—Correspondence respecting Mr. Burns, 23rd March 1852, p. 5.
 † Idem, p. 19.

himself was murdered by Lanun pirates; and on the recovery of the vessel, amongst the papers aboard, were the two following extracts from a journal kept by the deceased :—

"July 30, 1851. Mr. Motley came (from) Coal Point to-day, and wishing to go to Bruné with me, said he offered the sultan two hundred dollars for the Bintulu letter."

"August 4th.—*Got the Sultan and Mumein, &c., to promise to write to the Queen about Sir James Brooke and Sarawak in two or three days.*"*

Having become acquainted with these facts, I addressed the sultan and rajahs of Bruné on the subject, omitting the names of the parties concerned, and their reply demonstrates, that they had *been instigated* to make complaints, and that the *statements forwarded to Mr. Hume were fabricated to injure me.*

I am content to draw a decent veil over these intrigues, and to expose them only so far as it is imperatively necessary in my own defence.

The sixth and last charge urged by Mr. Hume, rests on the unsupported allegations of the directors of the Eastern Archipelago Company, and is, that "I made a most unscrupulous use of my high position in the service of Her Majesty, to obstruct by every means in my power a company chartered by the Crown, which I was

* Borneo.—Correspondence respecting Mr. Burns, 23rd March, 1852, p. 19.

ordered by Her Majesty and the Government, to assist
and protect."*

I may first state, in reply, that every step which I
have taken during the last five years, has been regularly reported to the Government, without a single
instance of its disapproval; and that the above accusation was advanced, when with *the writ of the Attorney-General, and with the knowledge both of Earl Grey
and Sir John Pakington, I had taken proceedings to
vacate the charter of the Eastern Archipelago Company
on the ground of fraud!*†

The following summary of the transactions of this
Company, since its formation, are at once curious and
interesting, and merit attention, as relating to a subject
of national importance.

The Eastern Archipelago Company was incorporated
by the Government of Lord John Russell in 1847,‡
for the avowed purpose of *rapidly developing the resources of Labuan, and of taking advantage of the relations which existed between myself and the Government
of Sarawak, for the establishment of new branches of
British commerce with the island of Borneo.* The settlement of Labuan was so materially injured by the

---

* F. O.—Parliamentary Papers moved for, but not yet presented
to the House of Commons. 1853.

† Appendix to the Fourth Annual Report of the Eastern Archipelago Company, p.p. 20—42.

‡ Eastern Archipelago Company, ordered by the House of Commons to be printed, 3rd April, 1848. No. 227, p.p. 6—9.

dilatory operations of the Company, that I considered it my duty on various occasions, to report the circumstance to Government; and so desirous was I, of advancing the objects contemplated by the charter, that in a despatch addressed to Earl Grey, bearing date the 9th January, 1850,[*] I stated, " that I attached so high an importance to the efficient working of the coal-mines, that *I urgently recommended that, if feasible, Her Majesty's Government should afford every encouragement to the Company, in order to enable it to fulfil its agreements.*"

In November, 1851, being then in England, I complained officially, of the misconduct of some of the directors, and of the intrigues carried on by the Company's agents and servants in Borneo.[†]

At the commencement of 1852, I resolved to make myself fully acquainted with the affairs of a Company which had caused, and was likely to cause, such serious detriment to the public interest in general, and to the settlement of Labuan in particular: and on referring to the deed of settlement, the facts I shall now narrate came to light.

For the attainment of the objects above mentioned, namely, the rapid development of Labuan, and the establishment of new branches of British commerce in

---

[*] Colonial Office, ordered by the House of Commons to be printed, 17th May, 1852. No. 357, p. 86.

[†] Idem, p.p. 113—131, 132.

Borneo; Her Majesty's Government intrusted the formation of this Company to Mr. Henry Wise, who, besides the Royal Charter, had obtained a lease of coal in Labuan, and a grant for working coal on the mainland of Borneo. It became necessary that Mr. Wise should find persons to assist him in forwarding this important undertaking, and he fixed upon five gentlemen, whose names I am reluctantly obliged to mention in connection with the transaction.

A legal instrument was drawn out and signed on the one part, by Mr. McGregor, Mr. Hugh Hamilton Lindsay, Sir John Pirie, Mr. Alexander Nairne, and Captain Drinkwater Bethune; and on the other part by Mr. Henry Wise. This instrument was executed previously to the formation of the Company, and was subsequently incorporated into the deed of settlement, and contained the following clauses :—

1st. "Mr. Wise to be one of the managing directors of the Company, irremoveable, except by a general meeting of the shareholders, for misconduct or incapacity."*

2ndly. "Mr. Wise to be paid 6,000l. within four calendar months after the complete formation of the Company."

3rdly. " And also, the annual sum of 3,000l. every

* Deed of Settlement to be seen at the Enrolment Office in Chancery Lane.

year, during the first ten years of the existence of the said Company."

4thly. " Mr. Wise to receive one hundred shares (*i. e.*, shares of 100*l.* each), in the Company, to be paid up out of the capital of the Company."

5thly. " Mr. Wise, also, to receive 2*l.* 10*s.* per cent. on the amount of all dividends, and every bonus, to be made by the Company, provided that no such per centage should be payable in any case, or at any time, where, and when, the amount of such dividends and bonus should be less than 7*l.* 10*s.* per cent. of the Company's capital.

" The above monies, shares, and per centage to be considered *as in payment of the purchase of Mr. Wise's interests in the Charter*, and for the grant to Mr. Wise for the said term of twenty years (out of thirty years' lease), as before mentioned, of his interest in the said agreement, with the Crown, and the said right of working coals on the mainland of Borneo."

And further, " as a remuneration for his services and the premises already rendered, as before stated, Mr. Wise to receive (over and above the before-mentioned monies, shares, and per centage) as his salary, as one of the managing directors, 800*l.* per annum, and 2*l.* 10*s.* per cent. on the amount of all dividends, and of every bonus to be made by the Company, such per centage not exceeding in any one year, 1000*l.*; so that

Mr. Wise's salary in the whole, over and above the first-mentioned monies, shares, and per centage, shall not in any one year exceed 1,800*l.*"

I cannot suppose that these five gentlemen, accustomed to business, and aiming at the direction of a public Company, could have been so negligent as to affix their signatures, without being fully aware of the purport of the instrument, conveying to Mr. Wise such enormous sums ; and I must leave it to persons better acquainted than myself with commercial transactions, to understand the motives which actuated them, in thus raising so serious an impediment, to the success of a national undertaking.

The fate of the Company was decided by this bond, entered into, before its commencement : and the gentlemen who had signed it, having become Directors, obtained no support from the public, and possessed no means to carry out the important objects for the accomplishment of which the Charter had been granted.*

By a cursory inspection of the Registered List of Shareholders in August 1851, it will be seen that the undertaking had little reality, excepting upon paper. Out of the 2,000 shares into which the Company's

---

* Captain Luard of H.M.S. "Serpent," in a report dated March 1852, the Reverend Francis McDougall, in the middle of the same year, and the "Singapore Free Press," so late as November last, confirm the inefficient working of the Company's mines in Labuan.

capital was to be distributed, Mr. Wise, the irremoveable Director, held 728 shares; Mr. Lindsay, the Chairman (with two relatives), possessed 713 shares; and the remaining Directors 274 shares: thus making a total of 1715 shares in the hands of the direction.*

I thus, for the first time, became aware of the true cause, which had defeated an object I had been striving to advance, and I had long before perceived and represented the danger of coal from other places superseding the coal of Labuan, and thus sealing the ruin of a settlement which deserved a better fate. I was resolved to remedy this state of affairs; I reported the circumstances officially; and with the knowledge of ministers, I took proceedings in the Queen's Bench to vacate the letters patent.

---

* The accounts relative to the Company's capital are perplexing:—

The list of Shareholders, as per Register of the 9th of August, 1851, shows the amount paid up on the shares at　-　-　-　-　-　-　£33,835

The abstract of general account of the Company, obtained from the Directors by Mr. Macgregor, June 28th, 1852, gives the paid capital as　-　29,825

Paid up capital in 1852, minus　£4,010

thus demonstrating that the amount paid up on the shares was £4,010 less in 1852 than what it had been in 1851—and as there is an annual decrease in the sum already paid up, we may in time, arrive at the true amount paid by the shareholders—*i. e.* the Directors.

One of the conditions of the Charter was, that the Company should not commence business until three of its Directors had given a certificate to the Board of Trade,* which certificate they were to endorse on the Royal Charter, that 100,000*l.* had been subscribed for, and 50,000*l.* at the least paid up of the capital of the Company.   Whether this condition had been complied with was the main issue in the Queen's Bench, and in June last, the verdict given by the special jury was, *to the effect that five of the Directors had given a false certificate to the Board of Trade, knowing it to be false.*†

This verdict placed the merits of the question beyond dispute, and beyond appeal, and I must again affix the names of the Directors to this false certificate, lest the gentlemen, who have since joined the Company, and are not implicated by the verdict, should be confounded with their associates.

The certificate, pronounced to be false, and endorsed on the Charter, runs as follows:—" *We, the Directors of the Eastern Archipelago Company, hereby certify, that the sum of 100,000l., being half of the capital of the said corporation, hath been subscribed for, and that*

---

* Board of Trade, ordered by the House of Commons to be printed, 3rd April, 1848. No. 227.

† That the 50,000*l.* had not been paid up, as they well knew, when they gave the certificate that it had been paid.

the sum of 50,000*l. hath been paid up.   Dated this* 25*th day of July,* 1848.

    (Signed)   " J. McGREGOR, *Chairman.*

             CHAS. D. BETHUNE, *Dep. Chairman.*

             H. H. LINDSAY.

             ALEX. NAIRNE.

             HENRY WISE."

The Directors set up in their defence, against the verdict of the jury, that *they had received permission from the Board of Trade, to endorse this false and illegal certificate on the Royal Charter !* It is replied, that the nature of the transaction cannot be altered— *that the crime of falsehood must rest upon those who commit it,* that the guilt of the Directors, has been proved by the verdict of a jury; and that the permission, pleaded as an excuse, could neither be given nor accepted.   In the second place it is shown, that the Board of Trade was deceived by the Directors, *who requested permission to substitute property for capital, when in truth the Company had no such property as they represented it to have.* This is clearly demonstrated by Sir Stafford Northcote's letter[*] addressed to Captain Bethune on this subject; one or other of the Directors called upon me (writes Sir Stafford Northcote) and inquired, whether it would be correct to include *the value of the Company's property* in the return—this

[*] The whole of this letter ought to have been printed.

permission was granted,—but "whether we were right or wrong" (continues Sir Stafford) "*in allowing the property to be reckoned as part of the paid-up capital, we certainly did it with our eyes open.*"*

The representation, however, that the Company was possessed of property was *a false representation, as the certificate founded upon it was a false certificate; for having run into debt to the extent of 46,000l., and in return having acquired a nominal property, asserted to be worth that sum, this nominal property which had not been paid for, was substituted for the paid-up capital required by the Charter; and the Board of Trade, having been deluded by this pretext, the false certificate was given that 50,000l. at the least had been paid up.*

Sir Frederick Thesiger declared in the Queen's Bench, that "the 46,000l. *only represented, in fact, a debt of the Company to that amount; they had not paid one farthing for the 46,000l. worth of value.*"† And Lord Campbell from the Bench, in adverting to the proper exercise of the Attorney-General's discretion, stated that "it was possible that in this case evidence was laid before the Attorney-General, of the *gross fraud respecting the false certificate;* 'that the capital of 50,000l. had been paid up,' which is suggested in the *scire facias,* and *which was proved to the satisfaction of the Jury,* whereby there was a failure of consideration,

* Fourth Report of the Eastern Archipelago Company, p.p. 24. 25.

† Short-hand Writer's report of the trial, *Times,* 28th June, and 1st July, 1852.

and the *objects of granting the Charter to work mines abroad*, with capital to be subscribed at home, will have been entirely defeated."*

* Lord Campbell, in his judgment, further stated that "the "*scire facias* suggested *gross misconduct* on the part of the Directors, that they knowingly signed a false certificate," and "that *the alleged misconduct* must be considered as established by the verdict of the jury."—*Short-hand Writer's Notes.*

Other serious charges of misconduct have been proved. Lord Campbell, in summing up for the Jury, asked, "How is that (capital) made up? Not of the result of calls, but of some *imaginary value* put upon the coal-mines in Labuan, and the coal-mines in Borneo."—*Short-hand Writer's Notes.*

Earl Grey considered the rental of 100*l.* per annum, as representing the proper value of the property leased to the Company in Labuan previously to the application of the capital stipulated by the Charter; the rental of the coal-mines on the mainland was about 220*l.* per annum, payable only when they should be worked, and with the rental of 320*l.* per annum as the test of value antecedent to the development of the mines, (which at twenty years' purchase would give 6600*l.*,) the Directors of the Company, without *any warrant whatever*, stated this property to be worth 46,000*l., that being the exact sum wanted to meet the condition in the Charter, and therefore likewise the exact sum owing to Mr. Wise for the transfer of the property.* Thus a year afterwards, in the account rendered to the Board of Trade, appeared a credit in favour of the Company for 51,455*l.* (including 46,000*l.*, the imaginary value of the property) to satisfy the stipulation of the Charter; and on the other side a debit against the Company for 46,000*l.* to satisfy Mr. Wise!

Here is the account as it stands:—

Balance Sheet of the Eastern Archipelago Company for the Year ending the 30th day of June, 1849.

Dr. Ledger folio.	£.	s.	d.	Cr. Ledger folio.	£.	s.	d.
4 Royal charter, Crown lease, and coal grant	46,000	0	0	1 Capital	51,455	0	0
6 Founder's original grant	4,200	0	0	46 Henry Wise	574	1	6
With other items of expense	3,829	1	6	56 Loan	2,000	0	0
	£54,029	1	6		£54,029	1	6

Examined and approved.
(Signed)   J. H. GLADSTONE, Auditor.
        J. MACGREGOR, Chairman.

[Was

Thus, these five Directors, having substituted *no property, in the place of no capital*, endorsed a false certificate, *knowing it to be false*, upon the Royal Charter, and the legal* question at present pending, solely relates to whether the revocation of the Charter

Was the Board of Trade cognizant of *this fashion of substituting property for capital?* Until it be avowed, I do not believe it!

---

* This refers to the appeal in the Exchequer Chamber against the judgment of the Queen's Bench, which has, as before stated, been decided in favour of Sir James Brooke, by the majority of seven of the judges to one. In his judgment, Mr. Baron Martin says, "The real question in the present case is, does there, or not, appear on the record, that there was such conduct on the part of the Directors (being the managing body of the Company), as amounted to a misuser or abuse of the charter? . . . Now the record shows, not merely that this sum was not paid, when the Company began to trade, but that the Directors knowingly delivered to the Board of Trade a false certificate, that it had been so paid. In my opinion, such conduct amounted to a gross abuse and misuser of the privileges conferred by the charter. And that quite independent of the form of language in which it is framed, the corporation so conducting itself by its governing body, forfeited the franchise conferred upon them. It was a proceeding in direct defiance of the provisions of the charter, accompanied by a wilful false statement to the President of the Board of Trade, in regard to a matter which the charter required to be stated with truth." And C. J. Jervis in his judgment says, "I agree that the falsehood vitiates the certificate, but in my opinion, it has another and more serious effect upon the charter itself. It is a falsehood stated to the Crown by the Directors in their corporate capacity, professing to act under their charter, and is an abuse of their franchise. . . . It is not provided for expressly by the charter, but it is implied, that when the Directors certify, they will certify truly, and, in my opinion, if availing themselves of their corporate capacity, and professing to act under their charter, they certify falsely to the Crown, through its officers, they abuse the franchise, by which they are created, and are liable to a scire facias to repeal their patent upon that ground."—*Short-hand Writer's Notes.* Thus nothing that Sir

[James

should proceed from the Crown, under the sign manual, or from the subject, by *scire facias.*[*]

You will, I am sure, absolve me from any desire to injure these unfortunate gentlemen, who have placed themselves in a position so derogatory and so painful; but after a prolonged silence, when an accusation is advanced against me, upon *their authority*, I am bound to explain the circumstances which preceded and which gave rise to it.

--- --- ---

(No. 4.)   No. 174.

HENRY DRUMMOND, ESQ., M.P.

MY DEAR SIR,

   I APPROACH the conclusion of a weary task, by noticing briefly that portion of Mr. Hume's pamphlet

James Brooke has said or written of this Company (which now appears to have done no act as a corporation, save through its Directors, to sign a false certificate) but what is borne out by the judgments from the Bench. And the argument of counsel on the demurrer before Vice-Chancellor Turner is confirmed that the Company never had a legal corporate existence at all. In law a false certificate was no certificate—and without a certificate there could be no corporation. The 50,000*l.* paid up in money, and the true certificate to that effect, were of the essence of its existence—a striking proof of how right Sir James Brooke has been in all his dealings with this pseudo-Company from first to last.—*Editor's Note.*

---

[*] The total expenditure of the Company up to the 30th June, 1351, is alleged in the Third Annual Report, p. 7, to amount to - - - - - - £10,819
Receipts - - - - - - - 3,786

       Loss - - - - 7,033
Exclusive of the expenses in England, comprising interest upon
                  [the

which he supposes will "*convict me out of my own mouth*," but which, in fact, is attempted by resorting to a vulgar artifice to pervert the meaning of a narrative sufficiently clear to any candid reader; it consists in extracting particular passages from a desultory and broken diary, which being torn from their contexts, and placed in unwarranted juxtaposition, without reference to dates, or to the change of circumstances, by altering the sense, by suppressing words, and by drawing false inferences, are made to appear of a condemnatory character.

It is an amusing supposition that I should have published my guilt to the world, and that during a series of years my confessions should have escaped the attention of the best critics, to be discovered by Mr. Hume when he was seeking some plea for his threatened attack in Parliament. "Books do not ruin characters,"* and if Mr. Hume desires to effect such a purpose by such means, he will be bound to accept the entire testimony which my written works will afford, and not by partial quotations to make the worse, assume the semblance of the better, cause.

the debt due to Mr. Wise, of 46,000*l.*, his salary of 800*l.* per annum, &c., &c.

The scale of the operations may be judged from the fact that the Company's superintendent in 1849 was obliged to borrow 130*l.* from the Labuan Treasury to prevent the stoppage of the works.—Par. P. Admiralty, printed 24th June, 1851, No. 428, p. 5.

* Colonial Office.—Ordered by the House of Commons, 17th May, 1852. No. 357, p. 121.

I shall content myself with a reference to the Parliamentary Papers,* in order to prove the unfairness of Mr. Hume's relation, of what really occurred ; and a perusal of the diaries, will at once confute the laboured perversion of their meaning, and the disingenuous distortion or suppression of their words.

I offer a brief, and unavoidably an imperfect summary of the narration contained in the works of Captain Keppel, and of Captain Mundy, where facts will be found interspersed with opinions, and where the hopes, fears, or conjectures of the hour were noted down, amid the occasional record of passing events.

I visited Sarawak in my yacht.† I was unconnected with commerce. I met a native prince involved in difficulty. I assisted him. He offered me the country. I at first declined, as it would have been ungenerous to accept.‡ I was not eager to embrace the offer. The war was terminated successfully. Muda Hassim made out an agreement,§ purporting that I was to reside at Sarawak, "to seek for profit."|| I *objected*, and was assured that *this was not the agreement* understood between us. Trusting to the good faith of the

---

* F. O.—Parliamentary Papers moved for, but not yet presented to the House of Commons, 1853.
† Keppel, vol. i. pp. 7, 73, 142, 146, 177, 208, 209.
‡ Idem, p. 210.   § Idem, p. 213.
|| By carefully suppressing the context, which mentions my objection, and the assurance given, Mr. Hume makes this appear to be the *only* agreement.

Rajah, I purchased a vessel. I loaded her with cargo.*
I made this cargo over to him. I was detained month
after month, at a ruinous expense. I requested repay-
ment, or the fulfilment of his promise. I remonstrated.
The Rajah allowed the justice of what I urged, and
again pledged himself to give me the country.†
Delays followed—poison was attempted. I resolved
to bring matters to an issue.‡ I loaded the guns,
obtained an interview, and *with many protestations of
kindness* towards the Rajah,§ I threatened *Makota* with
attack, as neither he, (the Rajah) nor myself were safe,
whilst Makota continued practising those arts. The
Rajah then fulfilled his repeated promise. The Sultan's
signature was freely obtained to the same grant of
Sarawak ; and I declined the government of all the
rivers along a coast line of three hundred miles.‖

Early in the year 1845 arrangements had been
made¶ to obtain a fixed yearly revenue from the possessions of Bruné, which contributed nothing, or next
to nothing;** and at the same time to commute the
tribute paid by Sarawak for a stated sum††

(These arrangements were not carried into effect,
in consequence of the treacherous murder of the
princes who held the reins of government, and sub-

---

* Keppel, vol i. p. 214.   † Idem. p. 243.
‡ Mundy, vol. i. p. 270.   § Keppel, vol. i. p. 251.
‖ Mundy, vol. ii. p. 323.   ¶ Keppel, vol. ii. p. 158.
** Mundy, vol. i. p. 189.   †† Idem, vol. ii. p. 26—39.

sequently, when order was restored, the sultan, through his ministers, ratified his violated engagements with England, and confirmed the cession of Sarawak on the terms previously agreed upon; the only difference being, that the sum to be paid was devoted to the support of the Rajah Muda Hassim's unhappy family, instead of being given, as it would have been, to that prince himself had he lived.)*

This relation may be verified by a reference to the published works; but in order to prove the studied manner in which Mr. Hume suppresses the relative positions of the princes and parties in the city of Borneo, and the circumstances connected with the death of the one, and the defeat of the other, the continuation of this summary will best explain.

I described the Government of Bruné to be in the last stage of decay. There was no sovereign, but two claimants to the throne; namely, Omar Ali, called the Sultan (which is not the sovereign title), and Muda Hassim, called the Rajah. The claim of the rajah was as valid as that of the sultan†—he possessed the *de facto* power, (which the sultan could not exercise) before he quitted Bruné for Sarawak.‡

---

* I mark by a parenthesis the circumstances not mentioned in the journals.

† Letter to James Gardner, Esq. p. 30.

‡ Mundy, vol. ii., p. 39.

The sultan was imbecile and wicked, "with the head of an idiot and the heart of a pirate."[*] The rajah was an amiable prince, his brother Budrudeen, an able and noble gentleman—they supported the cause of good government, desired to suppress piracy, and to advance commerce, they sought a friendly alliance with the English, and had always in the capital been the protectors of European merchants. With the aid of Sir Edward Belcher, these princes returned to their native city of Bruné, and were reinstated in the authority they before possessed, *because the people in general, sided with Muda Hassim, and were decidedly opposed to the rule of Pangeran Usop, who had frightened the Sultan into a show of hostility.*[†]

On the other hand, exercising an evil influence over the weak Sultan, was Pangeran Usop (an illegitimate son of the former sovereign or Iang di per Tuan), and connected with him, a *piratical party*, which not long before had committed an outrage upon British subjects [‡] *This piratical party* was violent, difficult to

---

[*] Mundy, vol. i., pp. 356—357.

[†] Idem, vol. i. pp. 380, 381.

[‡] Here is a fair example of Mr. Hume's process of arriving at a conclusion to suit his purpose. A reference to Captain Keppel's work, vol. i., pp. 237, 238, will show that in January, 1841, the English ship "Sultana" had been burned at sea, and her crew plundered, and imprisoned by the Sultan and his Minister Pangeran Usop. Mr. Hume accuses me of having deliberately contemplated

restrain, opposed to commerce or good understanding,[*]
and an obstacle alike to progress and to improvement.
In 1843 the dissensions in the capital were serious,
and the reason was, that Pangeran Usop aimed at

the Sultan's dethronement, and quotes as follows from my diary,
in support of his assertion.   *Vide* Mundy, vol. 1, pp. 274, 275,
276.

Mr. Hume's version.

"Feb. 2, 1842.—I some months ago suggested to N—— the
advantage of raising Muda Hassim to the throne, or placing him as
Bandharra (first minister) in a position to govern the Sultan."

Sir James Brooke's Diary.

"Feb. 2nd, 1842.—It appears that the Bengal Government has
determined to resent the conduct of the Sultan of Borneo and his
profligate Pangerans, to the crew of the Sultana."

       *   *   *   *   *

"The increasing interest in China, owing to the war in that
quarter, has induced the Government to act ; *and foreseeing the
possibility of such an event,* I some months ago suggested to N——
the advantage of raising Muda Hassim to the throne, or placing him,
as Bandharra, in a position to govern the sultan : *and it now seems
that Mr. ——* is rather inclined to adopt this suggestion, he having
inquired how far such a step would accord with my views."

The annals of controversy cannot furnish a more deliberate and
mischievous suppression.   It is not done by Mr. Hume ; but can
he read its exposure without a feeling of shame ?   Placed in juxtaposition to the above is a passage from the Diary of 1845.

It is true that I recorded my opinion that the Sultan was unfit
to reign, and that it would be advisable to place Muda Hassim on
the throne.   Muda Hassim's return to Borneo had no connection with
this opinion, which was opposed to his own views. Mundy, vol. ii.,
p. 75.   Mr. Hume suppresses my reasons for the opinion I entertained.

[*] Mundy, vol. ii., pp. 11, 12, 14, 15.

acquiring power, and *ultimately gaining possession of the throne.**   Such was the state of parties when Muda Hassim regained his influence in Bruné.   There are in my Diary many conflicting statements, made at different times, in regard to the relative positions and claims of the sultan and the rajah, but the fact really was, as may be gathered from a fair comparison of these conflicting passages,† that the Rajah acknowledged the Sultan, and forbore urging his claim to his prejudice, whilst the Sultan, with the single interval of his uncle's absence in Sarawak, acknowledged him as the prime minister, which he was, by hereditary descent.‡

The Rajah Muda Hassim, on his again assuming the reins of government,§ offered, in conjunction with the Sultan, to enter into relations to advance trade and to suppress piracy.

The English Government accepted these offers, and dispatched a mission to Bruné to encourage the good resolves of the princes.

The sultan and the rajah conveyed renewed assurances of friendship to the Queen of England, and

---

* Mundy, vol. i., p. 355 ; vol 2, p. 20.   † Idem, vol. ii., p. 75.

‡ The difference between an hereditary prime minister of the royal family in an Asiatic State and a prime minister in an European one should be remembered.

§ Mundy, vol. i., p. 187.

" *expressed their hope that through her assistance, they
should be enabled to settle the government of Borneo, to
suppress piracy and to foster trade ;*"* and on the faith
of the encouragement they had received, they resorted
to measures for attaining the objects arranged between the two governments.†

It further appears, that in February, 1845,‡   I
had succeeded in reconciling the rival parties—that
Muda Hassim was in power, and Pangeran Usop
friendly and quiet—that in May, affairs had retro-
graded—that doubts had arisen in the minds of the
well-disposed, from the continued absence of our
support—and that Pangeran Usop disbelieved our
power, and disturbed the public opinion.§   In August
of the same year, Sir Thomas Cochrane visited Bruné,
to improve the good understanding which existed, and
in accordance with the intentions of his own government, as well as with the view of supporting the authority of Muda Hassim, demanded reparation *for the
detention and confinement of two British subjects, subsequently to the friendly engagements entered into with
England.*‖   The act, however, was Pangeran Usop's ;
he was too powerful for the sultan and rajah to con-

---

* Mundy, vol. ii., p. 15.   † Keppel, vol. ii., p. 165.
‡ Mundy, vol. ii., p. 10.   § Mundy, vol. ii., pp. 32, 33.
‖ Keppel, vol. ii., pp. 170, 171.

trol, and the measure, with their consent, was left in
the hands of the naval commander-in-chief. " I was
in hopes that when he saw the overwhelming force
opposed to him, his pride would yield to necessity."*
Usop was punished; the government of Bruné supported in its object of suppressing evil, and the two
British subjects, confined and enslaved, were liberated.
I advised reconciliation; the Rajah Muda Hassim
made every effort to bring Pangeran Usop over to the
side of order.† He was offered pardon, which he refused to accept.‡ He attacked the city of Bruné,
was defeated, and fled to Kimanis, where, after my
departure, in obedience to a written mandate, signed
by the sultan and the rajah, he was put to death
(without indignity and without bloodshedding, according to the prescribed form of executing members of
the royal family).§

The Rajah Muda Hassim and the Pangeran Budrudeen became *the de facto rulers of Bruné*, which the
sultan could never be, on account of the imbecility of
his mind; and these princes, who had been encouraged
by the British Government in a worthy course of policy,

---

* Keppel, p. 171. † Idem, vol. i., p. 180.
‡ Mundy, vol. ii., pp. 37—74.
§ This mandate was, and probably still remains, in the possession
of the Orang Kaya of Kimanis. I have marked in a parenthesis
some particulars not mentioned in my Diary.

were fully aware of the danger to which they were exposed, should they not be supported by their ally.[*] So imminent was this danger, that they urged upon the English ministers their claim to protection, or otherwise demanded a release from their engagements.[†] I pleaded the same cause, and pointed out the peril. The Pangeran Budrudeen applied to the naval commander-in-chief for aid, and in my Diary of 21st May, 1845, will be found the following sad entry: *" Budrudeen says he knows not the day when his own life and the rajah's may not be sacrificed. Delay is our ruin."*[‡]

The tragedy, which had cast its shadow before it, was consummated; a conspiracy was formed with the knowledge of the sultan; in the dead of the night their houses were fired, and these amiable princes, the friends of the English Government, who trusted to its support in taking measures for the suppression of piracy—these princes were treacherously assaulted and foully murdered.

There are crimes at which humanity revolts; the treacherous and indiscriminate assassination of our nearest relatives is one of these crimes. The wild and untutored savages of Borneo expressed their in-

---

* Mundy, vol. ii., p. 14.
† Foreign Office Correspondence, 1845.
‡ Mundy, vol. ii., p. 33.

dignant abhorrence, and it was left for the liberal and civilized gentleman to declare that *it was an act which the sultan was entitled to commit without rendering him responsible to his own subjects.** There are crimes hateful to God, and which should ever be hateful to man, and I have never hesitated to avow, that had the necessity arisen, I would have led the thousands of Borneo, who felt as I felt myself, to punish the perpetrators of this bloody tragedy, and to save the remnant of the royal family from the fury of their treacherous relative and sovereign. The necessity did not arise. Sir Thomas Cochrane proceeded to the entrance of the Bruné river, *and* " *sent an amicable message intimating his intention of visiting the sultan; the simple inquiry to be made was, whether the sultan adhered to his former engagements, to which Muda Hassim had been a party.*"† *After three days' detention, the answer was an unmeaning letter, bearing a forgery on its face, with an insolent verbal message, conveyed in a manner, which all men, acquainted with native usage, would consider a gross insult. The admiral proceeded up the river as he had intimated, it was open to the sultan, to receive his Excellency, if he thought fit, but instead*

---

* Mr. Hume's letter to the Earl of Malmesbury, p. 10.

† Mundy, vol. ii., pp. 324, 325.

of doing so, the English flag was fired upon, directly it came within reach of the Bruné guns."

Here the information contained in my Diary concludes, and in offering this *entire testimony* to Mr. Hume for his consideration, I cannot better conclude than by a brief quotation from it. " Now I have brought up my Journal to the close of the year 1844; and written as it has been at various intervals, and amidst manifold discomforts, it will probably be very disconnected and badly arranged."*

Mr. Hume has asserted, that there is a law against a subject of England becoming the ruler of a foreign country. I know no such law, and supposing such a one could be discovered, and could be enforced, of what practical use would it be? Would such a law preclude a British subject becoming the minister or the adviser of a native chief? And supposing Mr. Hume's objections to the tenure of Sarawak to be valid, what practical result could follow? Would he deny the right of a free people to re-elect the ruler of their choice?

The people of Sarawak *are a free people, free in the truest sense of that term, free to frame their own government, and free likewise to administer it,†* and any encroachment on this admitted right, common to all

* Mundy, vol. i., p. 385.

† F. O.—Parliamentary papers moved for but not yet presented to the House of Commons, 1853; and Despatch, November, 1852.

communities, whether large or small, would be a
wrong, only to be effected by violence and an infringe-
ment of the principles upon which every free government rests.

Mr. Hume, however, is ignorant of the true position which I occupy; he is ignorant that, in 1846, the
Earl of Aberdeen expressed to the Netherland Minister his "satisfaction that the Netherland Government
should be disposed to do justice to Mr. Brooke's conduct, since *his possession of Sarawak;*" that every
precaution should be taken to prevent the occurrence
of the complications apprehended by the Netherland
Minister; but that "Her Majesty's Government could
not allow the apprehension of their possibility to interfere with their duty to protect *the rights and interests*
of Her Majesty's subjects;" but should any proposition be made, "showing a due regard for the *natural
and acquired rights of third parties, and of Her Majesty's subjects,*" such a proposition should be taken
into the most favourable consideration. Mr. Hume is
ignorant that Lord John Russell, as the Prime Minister, knowing the position I held in Sarawak, thanked
me, in the name of Her Majesty's Government, for the
services I had rendered to my native country; that
the flag hoisted at Sarawak was sanctioned as a commercial flag by the English Government, which had
previously declared that it sought to avail itself of

" *my relations* " with that country. He is ignorant
that the President of the United States addressed me
as the ruler of Sarawak, proposing a treaty of friendship and of commerce with America; that Lord Palmerston, being previously informed, offered no objection
to the contemplated treaty, when the subject was mentioned in Parliament;* and, lastly, my position in
Sarawak has been known and tacitly acknowledged
during the last ten years, by England, and by the other
countries of Europe.

I lay no great stress upon these formal or informal
sanctions from without. I have the support of the
people to confirm such a cession made by Bruné, as
England might formerly have made of France, or that
the Two Sicilies might now make of Jerusalem. I
insist upon the practical question: a government has
been established which is administered by the chiefs
and people; the scanty population has increased to
sixty thousand or more souls; and security, order, and
prosperity, have succeeded to rapine, oppression, and
famine. In 1842 the trade of Sarawak was conveyed
by a few native prahus, and in 1852 it employed
twenty-five thousand tons of shipping; from a strag-
gling village Sarawak has increased to a considerable
city—a busy and thriving mart, where the European

* *Times,* 28th March, 1851.

mixes on kindly terms with the native ; where crime is infrequent, and where authority is supported by the people.   Could such success spring from a narrow and sordid policy ?

The tree must be judged by its fruit, and when the question has been divested of passion and of prejudice, men will wonder that such notorious facts, were not believed upon testimony, and could not be verified, without inflicting an individual injury.

The government of Bruné has long since lost all command over its subordinate possessions ; they have cast off their allegiance, and for years past have paid little or nothing towards the support of the sovereign or of his court.* Where there is no power to restrain, there is a tendency towards lawless excess, in many of the communities ; and though the establishment of the government of Sarawak has in a great measure checked this downward tendency, and has encouraged the well-disposed, it has not resulted in the formation of similar governments in the other rivers.   This is to be attributed to the want of confidence in their chiefs, to the incapacity of the chiefs themselves, or to their unscrupulous use of power ; so that the numerous communities of the coast live in a state of internal distraction or depression, and the countries they inhabit, are

* Mundy, vol. i., p. 189.

not developed to commerce, or to the application of European capital, merely from the absence of good government.

In 1845 I had arranged to apply a remedy to this state of affairs,* and with the consent of the Bruné rulers, I was to have commuted all claims for a revenue† (which they could rarely obtain without coercion, if they obtained it at all),‡ for a fixed yearly sum to be paid, on the condition that each subordinate government should be left to regulate its internal administration. I have ever since adhered to the proposed arrangement, *for I possess that power, and that influence from my position at Sarawak*, and from the success attendant on the government established there, which would enable me to form inexpensive establishments in the various localities; and either to make over the surplus revenue, whenever it should accrue, to the Bruné Government, or to commute the taxes, which should be justly paid according to former custom, for a fixed sum, as previously proposed. Some plan of this sort would be a great benefit to the sovereign and to the nobles of Bruné; it was proposed by them

---

* Vide note at the conclusion.

† Mundy, vol. ii., p. 26.

‡ The more powerful communities resist the authority of Bruné, whilst any attempt to coerce the weaker ones or to oppress them would lead to their taking refuge in Sarawak.

recently to the English Government, and it would afford them an interest in the advancement of their dependencies. It would likewise be a blessing to the various communities, by affording them security, permanency, combination, and increasing prosperity; and it would, by the progress of good government, and by the development of the richest countries in the world, become in due time an object of great national importance to England. *There can be no trade without government;* and trade must always be confined to its lowest limit, where the producing classes are not remunerated for their labour, or where there is insecurity for life or property. Such has unfortunately been the case, throughout the Eastern Archipelago for very many years past. England is content with an emporium where trade is free; but the trade sold in the market of Singapore, is often wrung from the toil of the starving Dyak, or is stained with the blood of the peaceful trader. We have no knowledge; we have no influence; we make no exertion; we shrink from interference in native states; we effect no good, because we fear a possible difficulty: substantial advantages are lost for want of action; and the fairest lands are abandoned to piracy, barbarism, and the worst evils of misgovernment. Let any man consider what would be the result on English trade, should such a state of affairs accrue. Let him reverse the picture, and consider what the commerce of the Eastern Archipelago might become, under the same circumstances of security and of peace, which England has so long enjoyed. This is no visionary dream of improvement—it rests on the simplest principle of political economy, and has been *practically demonstrated in Sarawak.* Let similar governments be established; let a similar kindly development follow; let a yearly increasing trade spring up, and the north-west coast of Borneo *alone* will become of importance to the commerce of Great Britain. This is no sinister project of mine, but one which has been recorded since the year 1845; and if there be some who will give me credit for evil motives, there are others, and, I trust, a far larger portion of my countrymen, who will agree with me that this measure is for the benefit of the native princes, for the happiness of the native population, and for the advantage of England. For myself *I might gain increased power, with the increased burden of responsibility and misconstruction.*

Mr. Hume has said that I have been supported in Sarawak by the navy of England; but I believe that this will be found as little consonant with fact as his other allegations. The naval officers have, under orders from their own government, on several occasions, acted against the piratical hordes which infested the coast; but the suppression of piracy is a treaty obliga-

tion imposed upon this country, and can only affect
Sarawak, as it affects the rest of the world in a greater
or lesser degree; beyond this, a man-of-war has occasionally visited Sarawak, in the same manner as they
visit the ports of other countries, without any interference with the internal affairs of the government, and
with the real object of protecting British subjects and
British commerce. I plead guilty to having availed
myself of *the prestige* of such visits to advance the cause
of order, although I never claimed any authority in
consequence of them;* and I have on all occasions
found a sincere desire on the part of the naval officers
to advance what they considered for the interests of
their own country, or of mankind. They have most of
them enjoyed ample opportunities of forming a judgment from local knowledge and experience, and on this
account, have ever been the most consistent, in denouncing the mischief and the injustice of the course,
which Mr. Hume has pursued.

I have little more to add. Mr. Hume can gain
nothing by his persevering abuse of me; he cannot
even accomplish so paltry an end, as my ruin. If to-
morrow I retire into private life, the relative positions
of Sarawak and of Bruné would not be changed; the
former would maintain the independence it has

---

* Keppel, vol. i., pp. 320—326.

were fully aware of the danger to which they were
exposed, should they not be supported by their ally.*
So imminent was this danger, that they urged upon
the English ministers their claim to protection, or
otherwise demanded a release from their engagements.†
I pleaded the same cause, and pointed out the peril.
The Pangeran Budrudeen applied to the naval commander-in-chief for aid, and in my Diary of 21st May,
1845, will be found the following sad entry: *Budrudeen says he knows not the day when his own life
and the rajah's may not be sacrificed. Delay is our
ruin.*‡

The tragedy, which had cast its shadow before
it, was consummated; a conspiracy was formed with
the knowledge of the sultan; in the dead of the night
their houses were fired, and these amiable princes, the
friends of the English Government, who trusted to its
support in taking measures for the suppression of
piracy—these princes were treacherously assaulted
and foully murdered.

There are crimes at which humanity revolts; the
treacherous and indiscriminate assassination of our
nearest relatives is one of these crimes. The wild
and untutored savages of Borneo expressed their in-

---

* Mundy, vol. ii., p. 14.
† Foreign Office Correspondence, 1845.
‡ Mundy, vol. ii., p. 33.

dignant abhorrence, and it was left for the liberal and civilized gentleman to declare that *it was an act which the sultan was entitled to commit without rendering him responsible to his own subjects.** There are crimes hateful to God, and which should ever be hateful to man, and I have never hesitated to avow, that had the necessity arisen, I would have led the thousands of Borneo, who felt as I felt myself, to punish the perpetrators of this bloody tragedy, and to save the remnant of the royal family from the fury of their treacherous relative and sovereign. The necessity did not arise. Sir Thomas Cochrane proceeded to the entrance of the Bruné river, *and " sent an amicable message intimating his intention of visiting the sultan; the simple inquiry to be made was, whether the sultan adhered to his former engagements, to which Muda Hassim had been a party."*† *After three days' detention, the answer was an unmeaning letter, bearing a forgery on its face, with an insolent verbal message, conveyed in a manner, which all men, acquainted with native usage, would consider a gross insult. The admiral proceeded up the river as he had intimated, it was open to the sultan, to receive his Excellency, if he thought fit, but instead*

---

* Mr. Hume's letter to the Earl of Malmesbury, p. 10.

† Mundy, vol. ii., pp. 324, 325.

on the throne, and thus to save the sovereignty from extinction. I am bound to the son of Muda Hassim by every sentiment of honour. I would save him from the fate of his unhappy father and uncle, and I would teach him by precept and by example to govern his people justly.

The peace, the progress, the prosperity of Sarawak are the best assurances of what may be done on that coast by a just maintenance of power, combined with a kindly influence over the native mind. I have desired, to reconcile the progress of good government among the natives, with the advancement of the commerce of England. I still desire to serve my country, with honour to myself, and with usefulness to her, and it is only when this can no longer be done that I shall assert the independence I feel, and which I prize above all other earthly distinctions. To you, my dear Sir, I owe a debt of gratitude, which I am proud to acknowledge, and which I will repay in the manner most pleasing to your feelings, by the defence of the cause of truth, and of justice, of the injured, and of the innocent.

I long to escape from these ceaseless heart-burnings and vain contentions. It is with pleasure, mixed indeed with some regret, that I shall leave this country ; and whether in public or in private life, I can find a home in the land where I am respected and beloved; and whatever may be the course of events, whatever the progress of time may bring me, of evil or of good, I can calmly appeal from the present to the future, and from the judgment of man to the justice of his Maker.

Believe me,

&c. &c.

J. BROOKE.

P.S.—Since concluding my task, I have been informed that there are some gentlemen who, allowing the piratical character of the Serebas community, and the justice of the punishment inflicted at sea, entertain a doubt whether the expedition *on shore*, to the places they inhabited, can be justified.

I pointed out this mode of proceeding to Her Majesty's Government in 1845, and it may be presumed that it met with their concurrence, or it would not have been permitted in action. This course is recommended by common sense, as the most effectual way of protecting the innocent from the depredations of the guilty. It is supported by the opinions of the ablest jurists. I may instance the opinion of Chancellor Kent, viz., that "pirates are *everywhere pursued and punished with death*," Commentaries, vol. i., p. 183, ed. 1844; and of Sir Stephen Lushington—"Nor is it to be supposed" (he observes) "that *the name of pirate does not attach to persons on shore, but merely to persons at sea, who must have some residence on shore.*" Vide Keppel's Visit to the Indian Archipelago, vol. i., pp. 226, 227. Further than this, it has been practically acted upon by all nations, at all times. By the English, Americans, Spanish in the West Indies, by the English in the Red Sea, and by the Dutch, and Spaniards, and English in the Eastern Archipelago; viz., by the Dutch, the inhabitants of the islands of Vordate and of Flores were severely punished for their piracies. Two piratical retreats were burned and destroyed on the south-east coast of Saleyer; at Sekana the houses were fired as well as the prahus, &c. &c. &c. By the Spanish the island of Balanini was utterly destroyed, and every inhabitant, of the pirate community that escaped the attack, was carried away. Sulu was likewise attacked, and the city burned for piracies alleged to have been committed, &c. &c. By the English the city of Sambas was attacked and destroyed. Captain Chads, of the "Andromache" frigate burnt and destroyed some piratical haunts on shore. Captain Keppel, in 1843-44, destroyed and burned Serebas and Sakarran. Sir Thomas Cochrane, in 1845 and 1846, destroyed Malludu, &c. In 1849 Captain Farquhar repeated the punishment of the Serebas; and on all these occasions the proceedings were approved by Her Majesty's Government.

NOTE to Page 192.

THE reasons which induced me to attempt the settlement of the coast are expressly recorded, Mundy, vol. ii., p. 26 ; but, in spite of this, Mr. Hume urges the accusation, that *I designed to subjugate the rivers contiguous to Sarawak.* He does not instance a single hostile act unconnected with the suppression of piracy, and the only expression he can find in support of his accusation, is that I desired " to establish Sarawak influence and rule." Mr. Hume, however, as an acute literary critic, must be prepared to weigh the sense of a single form of expression, with parallel passages in the same writing, and I shall not despair of convincing him, that the words he has quoted will not fairly bear the sense he wishes, or warrant the accusation he has advanced.

The following extracts, as exhibiting Mr. Hume's ordinary mode of reaching the goal for which he strives, are interesting, and on any less serious subject would afford amusement.

Mr. Hume's version.	*Sir J. Brooke's text, with its context and explanatory passages.*
Borneo Papers, 1846, p. 59.	Letter to James Gardner, Esq., 1841, p. 30.—" From the imbecility of his nephew, Omar Ali, the affairs of Borneo are *entirely in the hands of the Rajah Muda* " (Hassim). Page 27.—" The Rajah Muda Hassim came from Borneo to suppress it " (the rebellion). Pages 32, 33.—" I pro-

Mr. Hume's version.	*Sir J. Brooke's text, with its context and explanatory passages.*
Borneo Papers, 1846, p. 59.	pose the following steps," 3rdly, " To return with the Rajah Muda Hassim to Borneo Proper, and through his means to *establish an English influence."* Keppel, vol. i., p. 320, 1842.—" The Sultan, Pangeran Usop, Pangeran Mumein, and others, declared ' Borneo would never be well till he (Muda Hassim) came back.' "
	Borneo Papers, 1846. p. 59.—" This Pangeran (Muda Hassim) and his brothers, do no actual mischief, but there is a slight tendency to petty intrigue, and a great drawback to trade whilst they are present, for no native will trust himself within reach of his rajahs if he can help it.
" It is highly desirable, therefore, to remove Muda Hasssim and his suite to Borneo Proper, not only from his being mischievous here [at Sarawak], but from his presence being necessary in the capital, to uphold our influence there. I hope to effect this through Keppel's kindness, &c." (Thus it would appear that the rajah, Muda Hassim, a prince of the blood royal, uncle of the imbecile sultan, who managed entirely the affairs of Borneo, was about to *return home to his native city* in 1844, according to arrangements made in 1841.	" It is highly desirable therefore, to remove Muda Hassim and his suite to Borneo Proper, not only from his being mischievous here, but from his presence being necessary in the capital to uphold *our influence* (*i. e.*, British influence) there. I hope to effect this through Keppel's kindness, &c."
Borneo Papers, 1846, p. 59.—With the neighbouring rivers our grand struggle is now approaching, and I am rejoiced that it is so, for it will at once bring about what otherwise might have cost us years to effect, *viz.*, the removal of all the bad	Borneo Papers, 1846, p. 59.—" With the neighbouring rivers our grand struggle is approaching, and I am rejoiced that it is so ; for it will at once bring about what otherwise might have cost us years to effect, *viz.*, the removal of all *the bad and pestilent rajahs and their followers, and the establishment of Sarawak influence and rule over the contiguous rivers. Good*

Mr. Hume's version.	*Sir J. Brooke's text, with its context and explanatory passages.*
and pestilent rajahs and their followers, and the establishment of Sarawak influence and rule over the contiguous rivers." (How does Mr. Hume justify the suppression of the context ?) Idem, p. 59.—"The removal of the bad and pestilent rajahs and their followers."	and evil are now fairly pitted against each other, and I repeat again, I am glad of it. Heaven help the right !" Page 60 of the same letter : " *Seriff Sahib marking his course with rapine, retired to Sakarran.*"
(I was not, therefore, writing about Muda Hassim, as Mr. Hume supposes, but the term "rajah" is commonly applied in a general sense to a man of rank.) Idem, p. 59.—"The establishment of Sarawak influence and rule over all the contiguous rivers." (Mr. Hume again suppresses the context to suit his purpose !) There are numerous passages relating to "British influence," "our influence," "my influence," "Sarawak influence," which should limit the sense of the latter expression. *Vid.* Mundy, vol. i., pp. 343, 344—376. Borneo Papers, 1843, p. 12, &c. Mundy, vol. i. 268, 269. Mr. Hume states that the visit of the "Diana" steamer to Sarawak, as I observed, "strengthened my position" and "other-	Idem, 1846, p. 60.—" Linga has, or had its *resident demon,* Seriff Jaffer. Sakarran has a small Malay population, at the head of which is Seriff Muller. The Dyak population is very numerous and *highly piratical.* Seriff Sahib was born in Sakarran ; for many years he was the sole ruler of all the rivers, *destroying the Dyaks, oppressing the Malays, employing the Sakarrans on frequent piratical excursions, and fostering all the Illanun and other pirates.* The influence of these Seriffs must be entirely broken, and their persons banished." Idem, p. 59.—" The establishment of Sarawak influence and rule over all the contiguous rivers." Idem, p. 60.—" *The utmost good will result to every river along the coast, for they will then look to, and appeal to us, and we may gently influence their various governments !*" Letter from Sir James Brooke to Captain Sir Edward Belcher, 1843. " *The virtual ruler* (of Borneo Proper) *would in fact be a British servant in disguise.*" Keppel, vol. i., pp. 234, 244.—" They were therefore excessively frightened when, a week after the " Swift," the " Diana " steamer entered the river. *I had the plea-*

Mr. Hume's version.	*Sir J. Brooke's text with its context and explanatory passages.*
wise did good to my cause, by creating an impression among the natives of my power and influence with the Governor of the Straits settlements." (How does Mr. Hume imagine I can prevent a *popular* impression?)	*sure of calming their fears, and was too generous to push matters to a settlement, during the two days the steamer remained,"* et seq. Relative to the same negotiation, arising out of the detention of the crew of the "Sultana," in Borneo Proper, I stated to the sultan, " *That I was not a man in authority, or belonging to the East India Company.*"—Keppel, vol. i., p. 320.

These extracts afford a fair specimen of Mr. Hume's *honesty* in his *literary character ;* but there are other amusing perversions of facts and of meaning. He asserts that *I took Muda Hassim aboard a man-of-war,* to Brunè (p. 9). How could I take any one on board a ship of war? Again—the native Datus resisted the sultan's authority for several years before my arrival in the country—my interference induced this people to lay down their arms ; that after nine months subsequently passed in vain endeavours to establish the power of Muda Hassim, *i. e.,* endeavours made by Muda Hassim himself, that prince handed over the country which he could not govern, to me ; and the Datus and people accepted my government, as they had before accepted my mediation (p. 6). This Mr Hume declares to be a contradiction !

Page 13 shows that in 1844 I wrote that " I could not sport an independent monarchy," and that in 1852 I declared (the circumstance being altered), that " I held my position at Sarawak as emanating from the will of a free people, to choose its own form of government." Is there anything new or

astonishing in this ?   Do not changes of circumstances beget
changes of government ?   Do not nations progress from
dependence to independence ?   Do not people advance from
slavery to freedom ?   Would Mr. Hume push back the dial of
time, and maintain the divine rights of despots and despotic
governments ?

No man has better reason to complain than myself of the
means which have been used *to make out a case against him.*
A correspondence of eight years (of which I retain no copy)
has been quoted, doubtless in the same manner that Mr. Hume
has quoted from my published Diary.   Another private correspondence with an intimate friend, which was accidentally
obtained, and secretly copied, has been employed with the
same object of injuring me.   The evidences of *two* captains of
the East India Company's marine, have been magnified into
the evidences *of four officers,* to give a *primâ facie* importance.
A memorial addressed to Mr. Hume by fifty-three merchants
—who were not merchants—has been dwelt upon as though
it contained something beyond a desire for inquiry, founded
on a profession of ignorance !   A letter was written, and
" *cooked* " for William Henry Miles, who could not have written
it himself !   Eighty pounds sterling was offered for the copy
of a letter which was supposed would prove injurious to my
cause ! and *the Government of Bruné was instigated to make
complaints to the Queen of England against my proceedings ;*
and this conspiracy not succeeding, a fabricated statement
was made out, which Mr. Hume still parades as an evidence,
though it has been disowned by the princes of Bruné, and by
them exposed.   Mr. Hume ought to distrust the honesty of
his informants, or honest men will distrust him !

So complete and overwhelming a defence was considered the finale to this long contest, and it was felt that with the House of Commons, Mr. Hume, however urgent, would have but little chance of obtaining a hearing. Sir James Brooke was preparing to depart for Borneo, and had signified to the Government his intention of leaving Southampton on the 4th of April for that purpose, when to his surprise and that of every one of his friends, within ten days of his departure, he heard, through an indirect channel, that the Ministry had determined to concede the Commission to Mr. Hume, and that in fact such determination had been come to, fully three weeks before ; and thus either from a combination of party, or some other unknown cause, an inquiry which had been denied by large and repeated* majorities of the House of Commons, and considered unreasonable by the great body of Englishmen, was yielded to the pertinacity of one man, who had fairly wearied the Government into what will ever be regarded, as an act of great personal injustice, without one object to recommend it upon public grounds. It is fit that these truths should be told, as it explains the natural feelings under which the succeeding letters of Sir James Brooke were written. The intention of Ministers to grant the inquiry was followed in the month of July, by the publication of the

* See vol. ii. p. 205, note.

instructions to the Governor-General of India to select the Commissioners. Those instructions appeared so at variance with the known facts of the case, that the Editor considered it his duty to address to Lord Clarendon a protest against them, which, with the letter of instructions, and the correspondence that ensued, will be found in a subsequent chapter in the order of their dates.

.

CHAPTER VI.

MARCH 17, 1853, TO JUNE 28, 1853.

No. 175.

JOHN C. TEMPLER, ESQ.

Ranger's Lodge, Hyde Park,
March 17, 1853.

MY DEAR JACK,

I COULD not manage to get to you to-day.
On Friday (25th) I return to town; on the 31st, I
want to go to Albury to say good-bye to Mr. Drummond and Lady Harriet—could you go with me? The
1st April I am to pass at New Cross and Greenwich,
and will you ask —— and —— to dinner too? I
shall thus be able to say good-bye to two men, whom I
admire. Headlam can't come to dinner, and my engagements have closed in upon me; but if I get off
an engagement for the 28th, which is uncertain, I
should like to go down to Southampton on Saturday,
the 2nd, and we could have all Sunday to ourselves

there.   Perhaps —— would come too, and John Harvey.

John Harvey would, perhaps, come up and meet me at your house on the 1st April. You see the arrangements I am making at Hannah's expense.

Ever affectionately yours,

J. BROOKE.

No. 176.

JOHN C. TEMPLER, ESQ.

White Lackington, March 24, 1853.

MY DEAR JACK,

I SHALL come over and see you on Saturday, either between eleven and twelve, or twelve and one. I have likewise written to Mr. Drummond about our proposed visit. I am getting into that dubious state, to make me believe that I may, by possibility, be walking about on the crown of my head.

The identity of William Henry Miles* has arrived ; —his alias was not Peter Soyd, which we made into Peter Lloyd, but Peter Sidd ;—the circumstances of the police report exactly the same as Mr Adam's

---

* This man Miles was the alleged writer of a letter, produced by Mr. Hume, as a testimony against Sir James Brooke, and read to the House of Commons, as that of a credible, well-informed person. See Hansard, vol. 113, July 22, 1850. Mr. Drummond, by reading a real letter of this person, proved that Mr. Hume's letter was either cooked or forged.

depositions. Mr. Adam saw Peter Sidd once, (as I remember,) and heard of him being at Labuan on another occasion. The police description tallies with the man in age, stature, everything but hair, and he has lost a joint of the fore-finger on his right hand! I hope you will be able to go to Mr. Drummond's on the 31st—I have written to him about it. On Sunday, we can go together to Southampton. I will not sleep at New Cross, but we will make a night of it nevertheless.

Ever affectionately yours,
J. BROOKE.

We are pretty well here; my short stay makes me regret that I have been here so little.

No. 177.

JOHN C. TEMPLER, ESQ.

Steamer "Bengal," off Cadiz.
April 9, 1853.

MY DEAR JACK,

It was twelve o'clock on Tuesday, owing to a fog, before we got through the Needles, and now we are enjoying the most delicious weather conceivable, so genial that it is a pleasure to lounge on deck, or the open air. The "Bengal" is, without exception, the finest vessel of her class that I was ever in; we have tried her on several points, and in a head sea she hardly pitches, from her great length, and though narrow, she rolls easily, and not deeper than other steamers. She has gone, with sails set, fifteen knots and over ; and though two days it was blowing hardish, with a head sea, she will average over ten knots.

Her only defect that I can find, is, that the vibration from her screw is somewhat inconvenient, and, as you may observe, affects my handwriting ; and they say that, in common with other iron vessels, her compasses require attention, which, so long as she does not run ashore, is no business of mine.

As for the proposed inquiry, I can see nothing but good that can result, provided that it be *fair*, and that the Government has no evil design.

I write with great difficulty, my dear Jack ; I am not troubled about myself, but my moral perceptions have been much shocked by the course pursued.

I am much better in health ; the excitement of the last week has passed away, and has not left any remarkable depression. Man and man's judgment is but a little thing, and a struggle against evil, though it be noble, is very disagreeable. It fortifies the character, however, and if rightly used, imparts a degree of charitable feeling, which we too much require. Farewell, dear friend,

Ever yours affectionately,

J. Brooke.

persons on shore, but merely to persons at sea, who must have some residence on shore." Vide Keppel's Visit to the Indian Archipelago, vol. i., pp. 226, 227. Further than this, it has been practically acted upon by all nations, at all times. By the English, Americans, Spanish in the West Indies, by the English in the Red Sea, and by the Dutch, and Spaniards, and English in the Eastern Archipelago; viz., by the Dutch, the inhabitants of the islands of Vordate and of Flores were severely punished for their piracies. Two piratical retreats were burned and destroyed on the south-east coast of Saleyer; at Sekana the houses were fired as well as the prahus, &c. &c. &c. By the Spanish the island of Balanini was utterly destroyed, and every inhabitant, of the pirate community that escaped the attack, was carried away. Sulu was likewise attacked, and the city burned for piracies alleged to have been committed, &c. &c. By the English the city of Sambas was attacked and destroyed. Captain Chads, of the "Andromache" frigate burnt and destroyed some piratical haunts on shore. Captain Keppel, in 1843-44, destroyed and burned Screbas and Sakarran. Sir Thomas Cochrane, in 1845 and 1846, destroyed Malludu, &c. In 1849 Captain Farquhar repeated the punishment of the Screbas; and on all these occasions the proceedings were approved by Her Majesty's Government.

NOTE to Page 192.

THE reasons which induced me to attempt the settlement of the coast are expressly recorded, Mundy, vol. ii., p. 26; but, in spite of this, Mr. Hume urges the accusation, that *I designed to subjugate the rivers contiguous to Sarawak.* He does not instance a single hostile act unconnected with the suppression of piracy, and the only expression he can find in support of his accusation, is that I desired " to establish Sarawak influence and rule." Mr. Hume, however, as an acute literary critic, must be prepared to weigh the sense of a single form of expression, with parallel passages in the same writing, and I shall not despair of convincing him, that the words he has quoted will not fairly bear the sense he wishes, or warrant the accusation he has advanced.

The following extracts, as exhibiting Mr. Hume's ordinary mode of reaching the goal for which he strives, are interesting, and on any less serious subject would afford amusement.

Mr. Hume's version.	*Sir J. Brooke's text, with its context and explanatory passages.*
Borneo Papers, 1846, p. 59.	Letter to James Gardner, Esq., 1841, p. 30.—" From the imbecility of his nephew, Omar Ali, the affairs of Borneo are *entirely in the hands of the Rajah Muda* " (Hassim). Page 27.—" The Rajah Muda Hassim came from Borneo to suppress it " (the rebellion). Pages 32, 33.—" I pro-

K 3

be pleased to see from afar off, the sites of Israel's wanderings—Horeb and Sinai, and the deserts of Sin. I wonder, if this wilderness of Sin is an allegorical, or a real place. Bad as the reality may be, how much worse that flowery wilderness, where we pluck the fruit of Eden (or Aden) amid soft music and sweet sounds— or where the arid rocks of hatred, malice, and uncharitableness look black in the wilderness of life! However, we must flounder through the desert, before we arrive at the land of promise, and if we find a shady nook by the way, we must in our allegory, compare it to a good wife, merry children, and warm friendship. Charlie Grant, like myself, returns with pleasure to the East, and he enjoys himself vastly aboard. —— too has become used to his new element, and the cockatoo has safely performed his land journey, and is in good health.

Do not be afraid, my friend, to act, for really after two years' daily discussion, we have not yet disagreed on a single course of action. Be bold—for that is the temper of my mind, and if I am cautious, it is only to help me to strike the harder. Farewell, with my kind love to all your party at Hatcham,

Ever your friend,

J. BROOKE.

No. 179.

John C. Templer, Esq.

"Oriental," Point de Galle,
May 5, 1853.

My dear Jack,

Our voyage progresses favourably, and of course I have nothing to tell you. We have had a few days hot weather, but the monsoon came last night in torrents of rain, with thunder and lightning to cool the atmosphere, and the rest of the way will not be disagreeable. We shall to-day make the Lacadives—the specks on the ocean in Sanscrit antiquity and name—and the day after to-morrow shall change our steamer at Ceylon.

I hope there to get news of all being right in the Sakarran and Rejang; if it be so, I can take the rest quietly enough.

6th.—Nothing to add, but I shall try to convey the news from Sarawak to-morrow.

I wrote to Keppel not to forget to give Tilsey, my little dog, to Mrs. ——, whenever she sent for it. I hope she has got it. Pray remember me most kindly. Love to Hannah and the children.

Galle, May 7th, 1853.—I add these few lines in the midst of bustle, to say that, as far as I can learn from the vessel on the China line, there is no news of importance from Singapore or Sarawak ; so far so good, and you may conclude it to be favourable news, unless I send you a second letter.   Farewell.

Ever dear friend,

Yours affectionately,

J. BROOKE.

No. 180.

JOHN C. TEMPLER, ESQ.

Singapore, May 15, 1853.

MY DEAR JACK,

WE arrived yesterday, and my mind was much relieved by the Sarawak accounts, offering nothing fresh to deplore.   Since the news* I forwarded from Aden, the material events, so far as I can learn, have been, that a bala of forty prahus have put out (from Serebas probably), and after killing some of the Sarawak people, fishing at Sumpideen, near Tanjong Datu, have proceeded on the prosecution of their intertribal war against the Netherlands, to ravage the coast of Sambas.   Brooke was at sea, in the hope of intercepting this fleet, and I pray, he may make mince-meat of them after the manner of 1849.

I had a long letter from Brereton, dated 26th April, downcast by Lee's death, and his first reverse, but written in an admirable spirit, and begging me

* This was contained in a letter from his nephew Captain Brooke.

not to judge his conduct or policy, by recent events, or rumours. I gather from his letter that the mass of the Dyak population are in his favour, and sincerely desirous of abandoning piracy; and our friend Gasim, without even mentioning to Brereton his intention, walked away into Runtap's country, and destroyed twenty villages. Now that we have begun in earnest, you will see, my dear Jack, that we will humble these pirates by a course of strong-handed measures. I may not be a clear-sighted statesman, but I will cut any man's throat, that asserts that I am not a general. You know how tender I have been, in avoiding occasion of raising up internal strife amongst these communities, and this evil has been brought about by the English Government. There need, however, be no complaint, where there is no redress required. I shall devote myself, with a single heart and mind, to the suppression of this piracy, and the protection of Sarawak. I know, that the energies and the heart of every good man, woman, and child, will be with me, and I shall not be misled again by lukewarm politicians. I wish I had time, and I would give you a sketch of my measures, but it will be better from Sarawak, and it shall be accompanied by a chart on a large scale.

The news from China is startling, we shall soon be disgraced there, or obliged to spend another million or two in a war. The rebels are said to be ill-disposed to foreigners. The Burmese war is beginning, and the admiral is obliged to leave it, to take care of itself.

It is a great truth, as yet undiscovered by the politicians of Europe, that a body of a certain size, requires a government in proportion—and decency forbids that we should only cover half at a time. I am too lazy to write to anybody else, but my sister; so pray do you, dear Jack, tell Cameron that Ruppell is safe and well at Sarawak, and that he has only to say the word, and he shall start for England. The required information shall be sent, so as to arrive by August next. I shall write to the Breretons by the next mail, but will you either send them this letter to read, or extract what I have said of their son? I have written to give him every encouragement. Love to Hannah. My kind regard to Mr. Drummond and Lady Harriett. Adieu—Charlie Grant sends regards too, and is quite well.

Ever yours, dear friend,

J. BROOKE.

No. 181.
JOHN C. TEMPLER, ESQ.

Singapore, May 25, 1853.

MY DEAR JACK,

To-MORROW I sail in a small merchant-craft for Sarawak, and Labuan, and Bruné, to strengthen my relations with the government of the latter place, in whatever hands it may be. There is no doubt but that Mr. Motley has been intriguing largely in Bruné against me, but I shall, perhaps, not only have to undo, but to expose his machinations.

The premature announcement of the Commission has called for another letter from me to Government, as it has given rise to attempts to get up evidence in this place, which will now continue till the Commissioners arrive, but which will be of no avail; and the plotters know not the danger they incur of being convicted of the fact of suborning false evidence. I know nothing more of the Commission, as it puts me in a fever of indignation; for though reason comes out in the market-place, and convinces me that it is the best thing that can happen for myself, and perhaps for the poor people, yet men are blessed or cursed with feelings and passions, and an injustice is hard to bear, and hard to forgive, particularly when it is accompanied, as in this case, by every circumstance of concealment, and of needless disgrace, and pain—disgrace so far as the opinion of the world can inflict it. Hume wrote a letter to the editor of the "Straits Times,"* which was published yesterday, and which I will enclose, if I can get it. This shows suffieiently the communication between the Government and Mr. Hume. I have written to Keppel to send me his orders to Captain Gordon, of the "Royalist," relating to Mr. Burns, and do not forget to send me Miles's jail description.

I am very glad to tell you, that by the last accounts we hold quite firm in Sarawak, and the Dyaks, though bullying and threatening, dare not come out. The evil to be feared is, that they may influence some of the interior Kayans, to view us as enemies, and this evil will arise from the weakness of the Government in not supporting us.

I will not write more—I write with pain to myself— but you, dear friend, are often and often in my thoughts. I long to hear that you are a Master. My love to Hannah and the chicks, and say all that is kind to Mr. Drummond, Lovaine, Wm. Adam, Sir James, &c., &c. Send me the Sidney Herbert correspondence—Vale.

Your affectionate friend,

J. BROOKE.

---

* Mr. Woods, the subject of the Butterworth correspondence, *ante* page 72.

The following is a copy of the extract from the "Straits Times" newspaper, containing, with an introductory preface, Mr. Hume's letter. It appeared to the Editor proper at once to bring the subject to Lord Aberdeen's notice, and the correspondence that ensued upon it, will be found to follow :—

COPY OF EXTRACT FROM "STRAITS TIMES" NEWSPAPER.

"The fact has gone forth.—The inquiry which was so much needed by the lovers of truth, and which was not a whit the less dreaded by those, whose deeds were to be the subject of investigation; that inquiry which has been so loudly and untiringly demanded by Mr. Hume, in Parliament, has at length been granted. The Borneo question is to be brought before the crown, the public, and the legislature, in a way that is likely to satisfy every inquirer after truth. On the night of March 15th, Lord John Russell, in answer to a question put by Mr. Hume, in the House of Commons, replied in an off-hand manner, that there would be ' no inquiry.' Her Majesty's ministers were, however, of a different opinion. A cabinet council was convened for the purpose, and it was resolved that an inquiry into Sir J. Brooke's conduct, should take place by Royal Commission. Hearing of this intention of

Government, Sir J. Brooke applied to his friends, Lord John Russell and Lord Palmerston, on the subject, who referred him to the Earl of Aberdeen; but as Sir J. Brooke has long been aware of the opinion of the Prime Minister, as to the necessity of inquiry, he decamped forthwith, in order to prepare for the coming ordeal. This accounts for the rajah's sudden appearance by the last mail steamer. Sir J. Brooke is no longer Governor of Labuan, nor any longer " His Excellency." The nature and value of the credentials, with which he again appears among us, will be best known by the *official* correspondence we give below. Her Majesty's Commission will be directed to the Earl of Dalhousie, the Governor-General; and it is proposed, we hear, that the inquiry shall take place in the most public manner possible.

" The following letter to our address from Mr. Hume, intimates that gentleman's concurrence in the measure adopted by the Cabinet.

" ' TO THE EDITOR OF THE " STRAITS TIMES."

' London, April 8, 1853.

" ' DEAR SIR,

" ' THE interest you take in the affairs of Borneo, and in my efforts to obtain an inquiry into the sacrifice of human life on the coast, and in the rivers in Borneo, and especially into the great loss of life on the 31st

July, 1849, induces me to communicate to you the present state of the question.

" ' I was desirous that an inquiry should take place into Sir J. Brooke's conduct before he left England; and I had a notice on the books of the House, that I would move again for an inquiry.*

" ' The Earl of Aberdeen, the Prime Minister, having informed me, that he had determined that an inquiry should take place at Singapore by Royal Commission, under direction of the Earl of Dalhousie, in the same manner as the inquiry into the conduct of Lord Torrington, in Ceylon, in 1851, I have concurred in the proposed proceedings, and shall withdraw the notice that stands before the House of Commons, and hereby leave the whole in the hands of the Government.

" ' My high opinion of the Earl of Aberdeen satisfies me that a full and fair inquiry will take place, and that justice will be done on this most important question.

" ' I am, &c.,

" ' J. HUME.' "

---

* The following notice is that alluded to by Mr. Hume :—

Mr. Hume.—That it is the opinion of this House that an immediate inquiry should be instituted into the grave charges now upon the table of the House, against Sir J. Brooke, and that it is the imperative duty of Her Majesty's Government, to make the said inquiry full, searching, and effectual for the good of the public service and the maintenance of national honour.—(After Easter.

Hatcham Lodge, New Cross,
August 31, 1853.

MY LORD,

As a friend of Sir J. Brooke, I have the honour
to enclose the copy of an extract from a Singapore
newspaper, purporting to transcribe a letter from Mr.
Joseph Hume, which the editor does not scruple to
speak of as an " official correspondence."   That editor
being the person denounced by Sir J. Brooke, as a
libeller, in a communication addressed to the authorities
in Singapore, which has been printed by order of the
House of Commons.

If Mr. Hume had authority from your Lordship, to
make the statements, he has done in that letter, with
every respect to your Lordship, you will pardon my
saying, that they are at variance with what was understood by the friends of Sir J. Brooke, as the basis on
which he consented to receive the commission ; but as
Mr. Hume is in error in speaking of an inquiry into
the conduct of Lord Torrington, at Ceylon—there
having been no such inquiry there, as he of all persons
must well have known—his own motion to that effect
having been expressly negatived—perhaps he is equally
in error in speaking of a communication from your
Lordship, that there was to be an inquiry into the conduct of Sir James Brooke.   However this may be, my
Lord, my duty to a valued and absent friend impels

me to bring to your Lordship's notice, the use Mr. Hume is making, of what he at least is anxious to have considered, as the confidence Her Majesty's Government have been pleased to extend to him in this matter.

I have, &c.,

JOHN C. TEMPLER.

To the Right Hon. Earl of Aberdeen,
&c. &c. &c.

————

Downing Street, September 3, 1853.

SIR,

LORD ABERDEEN desires me to acknowledge the receipt of your letter of the 31st ult., enclosing copy of an extract from a Singapore paper, purporting to transcribe a letter from Mr. Joseph Hume : and his Lordship directs me to enclose for your information, the accompanying paper, printed by order of the House of Commons, in explanation of the course pursued by Her Majesty's Government in the matter to which your letter relates.

I remain, &c.,

CLINTON G. DAWKINS.

John C. Templer, Esq.

————

Hatcham Lodge, New Cross.
September 9th, 1853.

MY LORD,

I HAVE the honour to acknowledge the receipt of Mr. Dawkins' letter, enclosing, by your Lordship's

L 3

direction, a copy of the instructions to the Governor General of India, " to issue a commission to inquire how far the position Sir J. Brooke holds in Sarawak is advantageous to the commercial interests of Great Britain." Those instructions, however, I had before seen, and as a duty to my absent friend, had transmitted to Lord Clarendon, a protest against them, which is now in his Lordship's hands. I trust, therefore, my Lord, you will allow me to observe, that those instructions are not in point with reference to my former letter; nor do they in any way acquit Mr. Hume of the misstatements he has made; and with every respect to your Lordship, to repeat :—1st. That at the time Sir J. Brooke left this country, it was distinctly understood by him that the inquiry was not to be into his conduct, or to be carried on in any way in a manner derogatory to him. For, that I had his own statement, immediately after his interview with your Lordship. 2ndly. That there never was any inquiry in Ceylon, into the conduct of Lord Torrington. Mr. Hume was a member of the Ceylon Committee which authorized the inquiry in Ceylon, having for its object the ascertaining whether a certain proclamation alleged to have been issued by Captain Watson, was issued and signed by him—Captain Watson asserting that his signature was a forgery. It is this inquiry which is mentioned in the instructions, and to which, perhaps,

Mr. Hume refers. How he could confound and speak of it as a commission to inquire, in Ceylon, into Lord Torrington's conduct, when Mr. Hume's own motion with that object was expressly negatived by the House, except to serve some purpose of his own, it is difficult to imagine. He must have known the distinction; and if regret at the part he took in those proceedings could imprint a deeper remembrance, ought not to have forgotten; for I believe Lord Torrington carries with him into private life, the sympathy of the great majority of his countrymen, at the manner the attack on him was conducted.

If, therefore, my Lord, Mr. Hume is allowed to make these assertions as it were upon authority, and to accredit a local newspaper as a Government organ, it is more than ever important, and I say it with every feeling of respect, that their direct contradiction should be brought frankly and fearlessly to the notice of your Lordship.

I have, &c.,

J. C. TEMPLER.

To the Right Hon. Earl of Aberdeen.
&c.　　&c.　　&c.

No. 182.

JOHN C. TEMPLER, ESQ.

Sarawak, June 28, 1853.

MY DEAREST FRIEND,

BROOKE wrote by the last account, that I had
been attacked with small-pox, in a mild form. It
proved not to be so—the scourge came upon me with
a terrible severity; we had no medical man, and I
placed myself in the hands of a gentleman of Arab
descent, acquainted with the native treatment of the
disease—three of my old followers devoted themselves
night and day to my case, and my cousin, Arthur
Crookshank, has tended me with an affectionate care,
to which I owe my life.

For fifteen days I lay raging with fever, or shiver-
ing with the cold water, which they threw over me
in my bed—my mind wandering, and without sleep,
lingering between life and death. My constitution
triumphed over disease, and after a prolonged sleep,
brought on by a dose of opium, given me by Crookshank, I woke sensible to the loathsome state to which
I was reduced; literally from head to foot I was
seamed with this frightful disorder; and feeble as an
infant, I strove to reconcile myself to the will of God,
who had afflicted me.

Since then I have been improving, and am now

clear of the disgusting part of the disease, though I fear, my friends must learn to know me under a different face to any I have yet worn towards them.

I have now many alleviations, peace of mind and ease of body. Twice a-day I bathe in water deliciously fragrant with flowers; and with a good appetite, I am regaining strength, though slowly, and able to sit up for an hour or two daily. Such has been my past history of the month—little to tell of, but much to go through.

How I rejoiced in the intelligence that you had obtained the mastership—on every account it is most desirable.

Now to business. I quite concur in what —— —— says—nothing can be more noble or more friendly than his letters, and I have no doubt that they will carry due weight with his own party.

Lord ——'s statements to Mr. Drummond are the most extraordinary in the world, and I should not care in the least for the inquiry, were it not for the marked spirit of the Government.

We will wait then patiently, and see what comes of it, and with Lord Dalhousie's selection of two or three good men from India, I still believe it will be shown that the Government is the responsible party for everything that has been done, excepting the good, which has resulted from my efforts. When I witness the

security which reigns, and the prosperity and happiness
of all classes here, the advance of the other rivers on
the coast in the same direction, I cannot believe, after
all that has passed, that this can lightly be destroyed,
by the prejudices of any set of men.

I write no more of this, for I am weak, and only
say how happy I was at your opinion as to the result
of the writ of error, and should it go to the Lords, I
have still no doubt of the result.

I do not answer Hannah's letter, though I too, could
talk of cows and calves, and milk and butter. I con-
gratulate her most sincerely on her new dignities. I
shall always for the future address her as *Mrs. Master
Templer ! ! !*

Tell her, too, not to be horrified at my ugliness, for
though I am fifty years of age, and did not boast of
being handsome before, yet I know that a poor, scarred
face is distasteful to the female sex. I cannot help
telling you, though it may look something like boast-
ing, of the many simple, yet touching tokens of kindly
feeling, which have been evinced by the inhabitants of
this place, since my illness. Many of the Mahomedan
houses have nightly had prayers, and many have been
the vows that, if God granted me life, they would pray
with feasting.

The Klings, our despised people of the Malabar

coast, have distributed alms to the poor, as an offering for my safety; and the Chinese, after their fashion, have made votive offerings for the same purpose.

How I turn from the suspicions and abuse of some of my own countrymen, to the simple attachment of those who live about me!

The Dyaks are again quiet, and there is no doubt, that, with the mass of them living towards the sea, a great change is taking place in their habits, and that a propensity for trade, is gradually gaining ground over the habit of piracy, as that occupation becomes more difficult and more dangerous.

Directly I grow strong enough, I shall go on to Borneo, to meet and arrange matters with the new sultan, and see what can be done for his good, and more for the good of the people.

Brooke left me last night, to go up a mountain called Paningow, where we are about to build a small sanitarium as my residence; the climate there will be some six or eight degrees cooler than down below, and the scene is one of the most charming in the world. I could tell you a great deal more, being in a babbling humour, but I am somewhat tired, and my time is short.

I have written this long letter, in the hope that you will show it, or parts of it, to my family, and some of my intimate friends—my uncle, my sisters, Dr. Rigby (36, Berkeley-square), the Archdeacon of Lindisfarne (my old friend, Richard Coxe, the late vicar of Newcastle), and others nearer home to you.

My kindest love to Hannah and to the children, and my best regards to Sir James, and all the party at the hospital, not forgetting William Adam.

Farewell, my dear Jack, and to prove to you that I have some strength left, I put my own signature to Charlie Grant's writing.

Your affectionate friend,
J. Brooke.

The following are the Government Instructions before referred to, with the correspondence which ensued upon them :—

COPY of the INSTRUCTIONS that have been sent to the GOVERNOR-GENERAL of INDIA, directing him to issue a COMMISSION to inquire how far the Position which Sir JAMES BROOKE holds in SARAWAK is advantageous to the Commercial Interests of GREAT BRITAIN.

Letter from Sir CHARLES WOOD, *President at the India Board, to the Chairman and Deputy Chairman East India Company.*

India Board, June 28, 1853.

GENTLEMEN,

I HAVE the honour to transmit to you a copy of a letter, dated the 21st instant, which I have received from the Secretary of State for Foreign Affairs, informing me that it is deemed expedient that an inquiry should take place with respect to certain matters connected with the position held by Sir James Brooke, the British Consul-General and Commissioner in Borneo, and that it should be convenient to Her Majesty's Government that this inquiry should be conducted under the authority of the Governor-General of India in Council.

As the interests of India are, in a great degree, connected with the trade of the Eastern Archipelago, and as persons fully competent to discharge the important duty of this inquiry may be more readily selected in India by the Governor-General than in this country, it appears to me that this investigation should be undertaken in the manner proposed by the Earl of Clarendon; and I request that you will move the Court of Directors of the East India Company to cause the draft of an instruction to the Supreme Government in India to be prepared accordingly.

When the answer of the Court has been received, the several documents mentioned as enclosures to Lord Clarendon's letter will be forwarded to the East India House.

I have, &c.,

(Signed)　　CHARLES WOOD.

Letter from Lord CLARENDON, *at the Foreign Office, to* Sir CHARLES WOOD, *India Board.*

Foreign Office, June 21, 1853.

SIR,

THE attention of Her Majesty's Government having been drawn to certain anomalies in the position at present held by Sir James Brooke, Her Majesty's Consul-General and Commissioner in Borneo, and to certain inconveniences thence arising, I have to inform you that it is deemed expedient that an inquiry should take place with respect to these matters, and that it would be convenient to Her Majesty's Government that this inquiry should be conducted under the authority and by the direction of the Governor-General of India in Council.

In addition to the office above adverted to, of Her Majesty's Consul-General and Commissioner, which constitute Sir James Brooke guardian and protector of British trade generally throughout the district to which his commission extends, Sir James Brooke, by virtue of certain possessions held by him originally under the Sultan of Borneo, but now, as he states, independently, by the free will of the people, claims to be considered as one of the independent rajahs of that country, and is stated to be engaged in trade on his own account in the produce of those possessions.

Her Majesty's Government are of opinion that the apparent conflict of the multifarious duties which attach to these positions afford a valid and just ground for the proposed inquiry. This inquiry will at the same time enable Her Majesty's Government to judge whether the conduct pursued by Sir James Brooke, since his appointment, and the relations which he holds with the native chiefs, have been such as are becoming a servant of the British Crown, and conducive generally to British interests. It will also give to Sir James Brooke a fit opportunity of meeting the various charges which at different times have been brought against him.

In pursuance of the object which Her Majesty's

Government have thus in view, I have to request that
the Court of Directors may be moved to take the subject into their consideration; and I have to express the
wish of Her Majesty's Government that the Court will
send instructions to the Governor-General of India to
select two or more prudent and impartial persons to
act as Commissioners for the purposes of this inquiry;
and, if he should see fit, to give to those Commissioners
the assistance of a legal adviser and of the necessary
interpreters; and the Governor-General should furnish
them with instructions for their proceedings, based on
the contents of the present letter.

It is the intention of Her Majesty's Government
that the Commissioners should, in the first instance,
proceed to Singapore, on account of the facility which
that possession, as centre of the trade with the Eastern
Archipelago, would afford for the collection of evidence
bearing on British commercial interests. As it will,
however, be necessary that power and authority should
be given to the Commissioners for this purpose, to
compel the attendance of witnesses within the jurisdiction of the East India Company at Singapore, and to
examine such witnesses on oath, I have to suggest that
the Indian Legislature should pass an Act giving the
necessary power to the Commissioners, the terms of
which should conform as nearly as possible to the terms
of an Act passed by the Governor of Ceylon in respect

to a late inquiry in that island, a copy of which I here-with enclose.

The period for opening the inquiry having been fixed, the Commissioners will give notice thereof to the authorities at Singapore and to Sir James Brooke, and will invite the latter to attend, and will afford him every facility for so doing; and for this purpose the Admiral commanding on the station will receive instructions to place at the disposal of the Commission such naval means of transport as they may require, either for themselves or for the conveyance of persons who may have to attend the inquiry as witnesses, or otherwise.

The first question to which the Commissioners will have to direct their inquiries is, whether the position of Sir James Brooke at Sarawak, either as holding that possession of the Sultan of Borneo, or, as he now alleges, as an independent rajah, holding it by the free choice of the people, be compatible with his duties as British consul-general and commissioner for trade, and with his character of a British subject.

With reference to this portion of the inquiry, it is to be observed, that by no act of Her Majesty's Government has countenance ever been given to Sir James Brooke's assumption of independence, and that his possession of Sarawak has never been considered otherwise by them than as a private grant bestowed by a foreign sovereign upon a British subject.

In the next place, the Commissioners will have to inquire whether the interests of Sir James Brooke, as a holder of territory, and as a trader in the produce of that territory, are compatible with his duties as consul and commissioner for trade, to promote and foster the general trade of other British subjects.

Thirdly, it will be the duty of the Commissioners to inquire into the accusations brought against Sir James Brooke by British subjects, whether in their private capacity, or, as in the instance of the Eastern Archipelago Company, in a corporate capacity, of having sought to injure their interests, with a view to the promotion of his own.

Lastly, the Commissioners will have to inquire into the relations of Sir James Brooke with and towards the native tribes on the north-west coast of Borneo, with a view to ascertain whether it is necessary that he should be intrusted with a discretion to determine which of those tribes are piratical, or, taking into view the recent operations on the coast, of calling for the aid of Her Majesty's naval forces for the punishment of such tribes.

As in the course of the inquiry it may be expedient to move the Commissioners to some localities off the

coast of Borneo, or to the island of Labuan, in order
to enable them more efficiently to discharge the duty
intrusted to them, and as it will in such case be
necessary to confer upon them power and authority to
exercise their functions at those localities, I have
further to request that the Governor-General be in-
structed, as soon as he shall have made his selection
of the Commissioners, to communicate their names and
designations to the Court of Directors, in order that
those names and designations may be inserted in an
Order in Council, to be submitted to Her Majesty,
giving power and authority to the Commissioners
within the territories under the jurisdiction of the
Sultan of Borneo, to compel the attendance of witnesses, being British subjects, and to examine them on
oath, will be issued under the powers vested in Her
Majesty by the Act of the 6 & 7 Vict., c. 94, intituled
"An Act to remove Doubts as to the Exercise of
Power and Jurisdiction by Her Majesty within divers
Countries out of Her Majesty's Dominions," &c., and
by the additional article to the treaty concluded on
the 7th May, 1847, between Her Majesty and the
Sultan of Borneo, granting jurisdiction in certain cases
over British subjects within his dominions.

Copies of the Act of Parliament, and of the treaty
referred to, are herewith enclosed.

As regards the power to be conferred on the Com-

missioners within the jurisdiction of the island of
Labuan, I have to request that the Governor-General
be informed that the Lieutenant-Governor of that
island will be directed to issue an ordonnance similar
to that already adverted to which was issued by the
Governor of Ceylon.

As soon as the Commissioners shall consider that
they are in possession of all the information on the
several points to which their attention will be directed
by the Governor-General, they will make a full report
upon the matters submitted to them, and close the
commission.

As the expense of this inquiry will have to be borne
by the public, care must be taken to exercise the
strictest economy in carrying out the wishes of Her
Majesty's Government.

I enclose, for the information of the Commissioners,
one volume of papers, containing, first, a confidentially
printed copy of the correspondence which passed previously to the appointment of Sir James Brooke, and
secondly, copies of the several papers and documents
relating to this matter which have at various times
been presented to Parliament.

I further enclose copies in manuscript of letters
from Sir James Brooke, from which you will see that
he is desirous by every means in his power to further
the objects of the inquiry, together with copies of

certain documents which Sir James Brooke, in his letter of the 2nd of April, states that he wishes to be in possession of the Commissioners, and which are not included in the other printed papers herewith transmitted.

I likewise enclose a printed copy of a letter from Mr. Hume, together with three volumes of papers annexed to it, containing his charges against Sir James Brooke, and the points to which he considers that the inquiry should be directed.

I have, &c.,

(Signed)   CLARENDON.

Hatcham Lodge, New Cross, Deptford,
August 1, 1853.

MY LORD,

I PERFORM but a simple duty to an absent friend in protesting, at least until he has seen them, against the tenor of certain instructions, that have been issued for an inquiry in the case of Sir J. Brooke. I do so, I need scarcely assure your Lordship, with extreme reluctance, and because from my intimate knowledge of his proceedings both in Borneo and at home, I feel I can demonstrate to your Lordship the incorrectness of certain statements of facts which are assumed in your Lordship's letter to Sir Charles Wood as the basis of the inquiry, and as to which Her Majesty's Government have been so clearly misinformed, that any report founded on them, could scarcely fail to inflict an injustice on Sir J. Brooke, as well as an injury to the national interests involved. To follow the order in which they occur:—

1st. With reference to the first head of the inquiry, your Lordship states as a fact, " That by no act of Her Majesty's Government has countenance ever been given to Sir James Brooke's assumption of independence, and that his possession of Sarawak has never been considered otherwise by them, than as a private grant bestowed by a foreign sovereign on a British subject."   Upon this I would call your Lordship's attention to the following facts as connected by their dates,—

On the 1st August, 1841, the sultan granted the country and government of Sarawak to Sir James, then Mr. Brooke, thereby confirming a prior cession by the Rajah Muda Hassim.   On the 14th September, 1843, a translation of this grant was forwarded to Sir Robert Peel by Mr. Brooke's agent.

On the 14th September, 1844, Lieut.-Colonel Butterworth, Governor of Singapore, wrote to the Governor-General of India, for instructions how to act with reference to Sir J. Brooke's position in Sarawak, and refers to a fact noticed in the log of the " Phlege-thon," dated the 2nd day of September, regarding the appointment of the Governor of Linga, by the Rajah Budrudeen *and* Mr. Brooke, as corroborating the supposition that the English were supporting the latter.

On the 7th January, 1845, this letter was forwarded by the India Board to Viscount Canning.

In the year 1846, Captain Keppel's narrative containing Mr. Brooke's journals, was published, which stated that on the 24th September, 1841, Mr. Brooke was declared Rajah and Governor of Sarawak; that on the 5th November, in the same year, a court of justice was opened by him; that on the 10th January, 1842, he promulgated a simple code of laws for the people of Sarawak; and from the period of this publication, Sir J. Brooke has been commonly called in this country by the name of the English Rajah, or Rajah Brooke.

In November, 1844, Mr. Brooke was appointed agent for the British Government in Borneo.

In the year 1847, he received the appointment of Her Majesty's Commissioner and Consul-General to the sultan and independent chiefs of Borneo.

In October, 1847, Mr. Brooke returned to England, was in constant communication with the departments of Government, and left England in February, 1848, having received the further appointment of Governor of the Island of Labuan. He was thus administering the government of Sarawak within the knowledge of

Her Majesty's Government at the time he was appointed to this governorship.

Early in the year 1848, Captain Mundy's Narrative was published, which details the punishment of the sultan for the murder of his relatives.

On the 14th March, 1849, Sir J. Brooke communicated to Lord Palmerston that "he had hoisted a Sarawak flag as a distinguishing mark of country," and requests the sanction of Government to its use, on the ground that it would afford a recognised permanency to the country. On the 20th June, 1849, Lord Palmerston replied that "Her Majesty's Government approved of Sir James Brooke's proceedings on that occasion." It is therefore very clear that Sir J. Brooke has always represented himself as governor of Sarawak, first as tributary to, and afterwards as independent of, the sultan; and never in any manner as the holder of territory in the nature of a private grant, or as entitled to any property in Borneo, except in the right of the state of Sarawak. With respect to Sarawak, he has always acted as a ruler, independent of Her Majesty's Government. When, therefore, Her Majesty's Government, knowing this, and I may say in consequence of this, selected Sir J. Brooke as the person best fitted to extend British interests in those seas, conferred the above appointments, continued him in them, and at length approved of the use of a Sarawak flag as a distinguishing mark of country, I must, as I before stated, as a friend of Sir J. Brooke, who is cognizant of these facts, protest against the unqualified assertion which forms the basis of the first query, viz. :—

"That by no act of Her Majesty's Government has countenance ever been given to Sir J. Brooke's assumption of independence, and that his possession of Sarawak has never been considered otherwise by them, than as a private grant bestowed by a foreign sovereign on a British subject."

This assertion, connected as it is with the first question, entirely conceals from the Commissioners that up to a very recent period, Her Majesty's Government had no idea of those inconveniences which are spoken of as facts, in the commencement of your Lordship's letter; and certainly in 1851, the Right Honourable Mr. Gladstone had not come to that conclusion. In the debate of the 10th of July of that year, after stating that "in the personal feeling of hostility to the character of Sir J. Brooke he did not share, that he believed him in his heart and intentions, however liable he might be to errors of judgment, to be a man of philanthropy truly Christian," he goes on to say, " I cannot think there is any reason whatever, whether in respect of the general position of Sir James Brooke or in respect of the combination of offices in his person, however liable to criticism his position may be, I cannot think an address to the Crown upon the subject would be expedient, either upon general principles, or altogether just to Sir J. Brooke." I need scarcely remark to your Lordship that a misconception on this point in the minds of the Commissioners, prejudges this essential portion of the inquiry.

2ndly. Under the second head of inquiry, your Lordship speaks of Sir J. Brooke as a holder of territory and a *trader* in the produce of that territory, while in the preamble your Lordship speaks of such trading as merely stated by others. I need not remind your Lordship that Sir J. Brooke alleges that such trading is precisely analogous to that of Her Majesty in the mineral productions of Cornwall, or in the Oaks of the New Forest. This distinction is important, as directly arising out of his position as rajah, or governor of the country; and if it be understood by the Commissioners as a statement of fact, it could not fail to create a serious misapprehension on a very disputed point in the contention.

3rdly. Under the third head, as to the accusations of the Eastern Archipelago Company, I conclude that your Lordship is aware that Sir J. Brooke, with the knowledge of Her Majesty's late Government, took proceedings by *scire facias* against that company, to cancel their charter, and for that purpose presented a petition to Her Majesty's Attorney-General, in which Sir J. Brooke's interest in cancelling the charter was distinctly stated ; that judgment of the Court of Queen's Bench has been given in that action against the company, for breaches of condition, under circumstances on the part of five directors, who subscribed a false certificate of capital, which Lord Campbell, in one part of his judgment, described as a " gross fraud," and in another " as gross misconduct established by the verdict of a jury,"* —that the company have brought error on that judgment not impugning the facts or the finding of the jury, but merely that under their charter the *scire facias* was not the proper legal remedy. The judgment of the Court of Error yet remains to be given, but of course as this injury is the deepest a corporate company is capable of receiving, and as Sir J. Brooke would scarcely have incurred the expense and trouble of the prosecution, except with a view of promoting his own interests, though not perhaps in the sense imputed in the instructions, it follows that, unless the accusations of the Eastern Archipelago Company be confined as to time and place, but one answer can be given to this part of the third query, and that also upon facts which have exclusively taken place in this country, where only an inquiry as to them can be of any avail.

4thly. The last query contains no statement of fact, but I respectfully submit to your Lordship, whether in

* See the result of the writ of error, *ante* p. 140, Editor's note.

common with the whole tenor and language of the
dispatch, it is not calculated to inflict a grievous injury
upon a government like that of Sir J. Brooke's at
Sarawak, which necessarily rests much upon opinion,
and also to awaken deeper feelings than those of irri-
tation in a mind like his. As instances, I point to the
passage, as to intrusting him with a discretion to determine what tribes are piratical, as indicating at the best
in prospect but a very limited confidence, when he
would require a fair and generous support. As a
further instance, that the Serebas and Sakarran tribes
are not even mentioned by name. Whether these tribes
were or were not piratical, was the whole of the original
question ; by it, the clamour was got up, and by it alone,
Sir J. Brooke's enemies were enabled to mix up a
number of minor charges, with that of a deadly crime.
On these instructions the grave accusation, which, had
there been the slightest faith left in it, should have led
the van of the attack, is virtually abandoned. And as
a further instance, that while the commission is to hold
its head-quarters at Singapore, the place from whence
the enemies of Sir J. Brooke have been in direct communication with Mr. Hume, Sarawak, the seat of Sir
J. Brooke's government, and where his policy and its
fruits, may surely be seen and judged, is not only not
mentioned by name, but it is doubtful from the expression used, " localities off the coast of Borneo," whether

the Commissioners are empowered, however essential they might consider it, to go to that place at all.

I cannot believe, my Lord, that these can be intentional defects in a document, which must affect for good or evil a large national interest; for if they were, they indicate that Sir J. Brooke's adversaries could only hope for a decision against him, by presenting their case, upon statements which would prevent his entering into evidence, to show their fallacy; and then, my Lord, I may be permitted to express my conviction that Sir J. Brooke and his friends will never be satisfied without that further inquiry which in 1851 Lord Palmerston did not think it necessary to pursue. In the debate of the 10th July of that year, his Lordship said, " Well, then, I say the whole accusations fall to the ground; there is really nothing to inquire into, unless it be an inquiry (which I do not wish to pursue) into what could have been the source whence the various and persevering, and malignant persecutions proceeded. I do not apply that word to any course which has been taken in this House, but I must denounce these charges as malignant, and persevering persecutions of an innocent man. Sir, I am convinced that this House will, by an overwhelming majority, negative the motion of my honourable friend, and that by so doing they will proclaim to the world, that Sir J. Broooke retires from this investigation with an untarnished character,

and with unblemished honour; and I am persuaded
that he will continue to enjoy the esteem of his countrymen, as a man who, by braving difficulties, by facing
dangers in distant climates, and in previously unknown
lands, has done much to promote the commercial interests of his country, and to diffuse the light of civilization
in regions which had before been in the darkness of
barbarism." Such an inquiry would then become not
only necessary but indispensable to attain the ends of
justice. The witnesses to be examined, and the
evidence to be adduced, are in this country. The
character of William Henry Miles,* one of Mr.
Hume's earliest witnesses, by evidence recently arrived
here, can be shown: and the inquiry would necessarily be incomplete, which would fail to expose the
manufacture of that man's testimony. Mr. Hume
and Mr. Wise are both here, and I feel confident that
if it be extended to this country, with full power of
examination as conferred in the recent election commis-
sions, Sir J. Brooke will be able to demonstrate to the
public the machinations by which this persecution was
commenced, and the deep personal enmity by which it
has been continued.

In conclusion, my Lord, I cannot, although (and with
pride I say it) I know Sir J. Brooke's sentiments and
position as well as any man—I know his noble love of

* This man is since dead.

truth, his keen sense of injustice, his self-respect and self-dependence,—I cannot, I say, foresee how he will receive these instructions; he may be willing to consider them reconcilable with the purport of Lord Wodehouse's despatch, and with the more recent declaration of Lord John Russell in the House, and accept them as in accordance with the spirit, in which he understood the commission was to issue before he left this country; or he may, looking at the high interests of his adopted people, whose welfare and happiness he seems by Providence chosen to protect, consider that they depart so widely from that understanding, as to justify him in refusing to meet a commission, which is to base its inquiries upon assumptions which strike at the very root of his native power; and I may be further excused in stating, that if the instructions were framed to effect the latter object, and to produce the antagonism which can scarcely fail to be fatal eventually, to every British interest, they appear to me to be likely to attain their object. To avert so serious an evil, and to guard, as far as a humble individual can, the honour of my friend, must be my apology for intruding this protest on your Lordship.

I have, &c.

(Signed)   JOHN C. TEMPLER.

To the Right Hon. the Earl of Clarendon, &c.

Foreign Office, September 9, 1853.

SIR,

I AM directed by the Earl of Clarendon to acknowledge the receipt of your letter of the 1st ultimo, protesting against the tenor of the instructions, which have been issued by Her Majesty's Government for a commission of inquiry into certain matters, affecting the position of Sir James Brooke, Her Majesty's Commissioner and Consul-General in Borneo.

In reply, I am directed to observe, that you are in error with respect to many of the statements contained in your letter, and that if your objections were valid, the inquiry which Her Majesty's Government have considered necessary, could not take place.

I am further to remark that it is unlikely that Sir James Brooke would refuse to appear before the Commissioners, who will be appointed to conduct this inquiry, as he himself has expressed his anxious wish for an inquiry respecting every transaction in which he has been engaged, and has offered to give every facility for conducting it.

I have, &c,

(Signed)   H. M. ADDINGTON.

John C. Templer, Esq.

Hatcham Lodge, New Cross,
September 12, 1853.

My Lord,

I have the honour to acknowledge the receipt
of Mr. Addington's letter of the 9th instant, in which
he is directed by your Lordship to observe, that I am
in error with respect to many of the statements contained in my letter of protest. With great deference
to your Lordship I may be permitted to reply, that as
no particular statement out of the many alleged to be
erroneous, is mentioned, I might content myself with as
general an assertion, that they are each and every of
them correct, those of fact strictly so, and those that
allege opinions, as far as my knowledge and belief
enable me to form them. I will, however, do more
than this, and as far as can be, without prolixity, maintain them by saying, that the facts and dates which
support the objection to the first head of the inquiry,
are, either shown by public documents printed by
order of the House of Commons, or relate to circumstances which have taken place within my own knowledge. That the objections which bear on the second
head of the inquiry, are patent on the face of the instructions themselves; while to the statements which
relate to the third head, as to the proceedings and position of the Eastern Archipelago Company, I can depose

with direct certainty. Those proceedings were all taken within my own knowledge. I was an eye-witness of the trial, and can speak personally, if need were, to the accuracy of every statement in the protest, as to the procedure and present position of that unparalleled case. The fourth head then, my Lord, is the only one to which I conceive your Lordship's assertion of erroneous statement in the protest, can attach. In dealing with that head, I advanced an opinion as to the general tenor of the instructions, and cited three instances that appeared to me decisive of the adverse spirit in which they had been conceived. On this subject I should rejoice, my Lord, to find that my opinion was erroneous, that the passages I referred to as indicative of that spirit, have no such construction; that Her Majesty's ministers, upon a return of the commission in Sir J. Brooke's favour, are prepared to accord his policy a fair and generous support; that the question of the Serebas and Sakarran piracy is by them *bonâ fide* intended to be raised by the inquiry; and that Sarawak as well as Singapore, is to be a place where the commission is to hold its sittings. If these things be according to the tenor of the instructions, I am the first, my Lord, to confess that I was in error with respect to them. I also trust, my Lord, you will allow me further to dissent from the conclusion of your Lordship, " that if my objections were valid, the inquiry which Her Majesty's Government had considered necessary, could not take place." My protest was addressed against a particular inquiry—against an inquiry based on statements manifestly erroneous—on statements which could not stand the touchstone of truth; but by no means against the inquiry which Her Majesty's Government had informed Sir J. Brooke they were about to issue; and certainly not against that full, fair, and searching one, that is now rendered so imperatively necessary; an inquiry that will show Sir James Brooke on the one side, and his enemies on the other; an inquiry that by its results will raise the question, whether some constitutional check cannot, and ought not, to be put on the license which now, apparently, enjoys an immunity of action, upon the character and fortunes of any public servant, and thus from individual injury educe a general good.

With regard to the concluding paragraph of Mr. Addington's letter, I trust, my Lord, you will forgive me if I speak plainly to your Lordship. Whether Sir J. Brooke will refuse to appear, remains to be seen. To deal frankly with your Lordship, were I in his place, unless the erroneous statements in the instructions were amended, by allowing Sir J. Brooke to dispute the fact, stated as the basis of the first head of the inquiry, after all that has occurred, I would not appear; and I should be quite content to place my reputation and character upon the verdict of my countrymen upon that course against that of Mr. Hume and his associates. Whatever may be alleged to the contrary, Sir J. Brooke is independent in Sarawak, and that independence has been virtually acknowledged by Her Majesty's Government, and independent there, he will remain, unless Great Britain should make war upon Sarawak, as some return for the services her ruler has, according to more than one public acknowledgment, conferred upon his native country. I have now a letter before me, which speaks of the touching tokens of attachment which his recent illness has called out from the people of his adoption. The Mahomedans nightly had prayers, and vowed, if God would spare his life, they would pray with feasting. The Klings distributed alms, as an offering for his safety, and the Chinese, after their fashion, made votive gifts for the same purpose.* How one turns, my Lord, from the suspicions of some of his countrymen, and the abuse of Mr. Hume, to these simple instances of attachment. I will only, therefore, say, that it should not be disguised from your Lordship, that, with every wish on the part of Sir J. Brooke and his friends to meet a fair, full, and searching inquiry, and to give every facility for conducting it ; it is on the condition, and that condition only, that it be fair, full, and searching ; and that, however triumphant to Sir J. Brooke the result may, and indeed as I know cannot fail to be ; still, in the opinion of his friends, a

* See *ante*, No. 182.

grievous personal injury has been already inflicted, by conceding it to Mr. Hume; and it will need all the magnanimity and forbearance of the noble English character against whom it has been directed, to avert the national evils, that, in other hands, might readily have been worked by it.

I have, &c.,
JOHN C. TEMPLER.

Earl of Clarendon.

———

Foreign Office, September 19, 1853.

SIR,

I AM directed by the Earl of Clarendon, to acknowledge the receipt of your letter of the 14th inst., reiterating the statements and objections advanced by you in your previous letter of the 1st ult., with regard to the instructions issued by Her Majesty's Government for a commission of inquiry into the position of Sir J. Brooke, Her Majesty's Commissioner and Consul-General in Borneo; and I am to observe to you, in reply, that as the Earl of Clarendon does not apprehend that any useful object would be attained by continuing this correspondence, his Lordship must decline to enter into a discussion with reference to the contents of your letter.

I am, Sir,
H. M. ADDINGTON.

John C. Templer, Esq.

CHAPTER VII.

From July 6, 1853, to September 28, 1853.

No. 183.

The Rev. Archdeacon Coxe.

Sarawak, July 6, 1853.

My dear Archdeacon, and very dear Richard,

If my own fortunes be depressed, and I have been afflicted with a cruel disorder which has brought me near to death's door, I have still reason to rejoice at the success of my friends.

Your appointment to the archdeaconry gladdened my heart, more than I was able to express to you, whilst I was in England; and was followed by the agreeable intelligence, that my friend Templer had obtained a mastership in the Exchequer.

I do most sincerely rejoice, dear Richard, in your success, and in his : and with the one as well as the other, I prophecy that the first step is but the prelude to a higher rise. Whether it be so or not, you have leisure and competence, and the capacity for that enjoyment of life which is bestowed upon us as a blessing.

Let me hear, then, no more of headaches and ill-health; and let the breeze on the mountain, and your happy fireside, eradicate from your constitution the impurities of the great commercial city of Newcastle.

Of myself, I must give you somewhat of a history. A few days before I left England, to my great surprise, I learned, through a private channel, that the present ministry had not only decided on granting a commission of inquiry into the affairs of Borneo, without a further appeal to Parliament, but that they had been in communication with Mr. Hume on the subject; whilst they had studiously concealed it from me, intending to carry it into execution, without my knowledge.

I saw Lord —— and Lord —— on the subject, who, to their credit be it said, appeared ashamed of the transaction; but from what passed, and from what has since occurred, I am quite convinced that the English protection and assistance will hereafter be withdrawn or evaded.

The Government is embarrassed, however, as to the mode of carrying their intention into execution.

The approval of the two former Governments (the

component parts of which this ministry is composed) is so full and warm, of the various measures pursued during past years, that they can hardly cast these decisions aside with impunity.

The majorities in Parliament confirming the views of the ministry, are likewise a stumbling block. And they are equally afraid of involving the reputation or conduct of their naval officers of high rank, by doing which, they would lead to a far more serious inquiry, which could only be carried on by an enormous outlay of money, and by a loss of many of their parliamentary supporters.

Under these circumstances the commission must be circumscribed to investigate my position and acts alone, and will be a mere nullity; or, should it go further, it will be found that the measures stated to be mine, emanated with the Government; and that by far the larger share of the responsibility of their execution, rests with the officers of the Queen's service.

For the commission I care nothing. I know that we have done right. I know that those people were pirates, and that the ordinary dictates of humanity required their suppression; I would take the whole responsibility on myself. I do not shrink from a single act, for I know they are to be justified before God and before upright men; but I was indignant and shocked at the concealment which aimed a petty government

intrigue against an individual, and sought to conceal it
from him, until he was separated from his friends and
advisers.

However, dear Richard, it is our duty to obey the
Government which rules our country for the time being;
and I wait the commission, therefore, with something
of curiosity, but nothing of fear. More than this I
know not on the subject.

I came out, as you are aware, early in April. I was
not well when we got to the Red Sea. I said I would
enjoy repose; but it was only repose of body, for my
mind preyed upon itself. I dwelt upon the persecution
of five years—upon the wrongs which have been done
me, and upon the crowning act, perpetrated by those,
from whom I should have found support.

I arrived in Singapore, and after a fortnight's stay
there, embarked for Sarawak. It was within sight of
the mountains of my own land, that I was attacked by
a frightful smallpox. I wrote an account of my illness
to Templer, which I asked him to show you, so I need
only add here, that I am convalescent, very comfortable, with a good appetite, and just able to crawl, with
a little support, from one room to another.

I shall be a good deal disfigured; but my friends
will not esteem me the less, for being a little uglier
late in life.

I now look upon the commission with perfect complacency; I everywhere witness the marks of peace and advancement; even in the piratical settlements themselves, so great a change has taken place, that I am sanguine that, in two or three years more, we shall no longer require force to check the depredations of these tribes, upon their innocent and peaceful neighbours. My paper is exhausted; but from the length of my letter, you may judge how free I am from official business, or political controversy.

I hope (the commission over) to have little to do with them in future. Let John Longe * know something about me, if you have time. And, although the yearly Valpesian dinner will be over before this reaches you, yet this, with the proceedings of the commission, will supply something. to tell of your poor president at the next meeting.

My kind love to Mrs. Coxe, and your family circle, and dear, dear Archdeacon Richard,

Believe me, your affectionate friend,

J. BROOKE.

P.S. I write by the hand of Grant, because my eyes are weak, and I do not like to try them.

* John Longe, Esq., Spixworth Park, Norwich.

No. 184.

JOHN C. TEMPLER, ESQ.

Sarawak, July 22, 1853.

MY DEAR JACK,

I HAVE been progressing favourably since I last wrote, and, though of course still weak, have little to complain of. I can walk a little, ride at a foot's pace a little, and write a little, though not comfortably, as from the severity of the disorder the nails on my hands are all coming off; however, I have reason to be thankful, and I trust I shall be a happier man, and perhaps even a healthier, in the time to come.

By the last mail which we have received here, there was no letter from you, but Mr. M'Dougall made mention of you, which assured me you were not ill.

There is now a mail waiting in Singapore, which has not been sent to us, and which now I shall not receive for six weeks to come. The admiral is on his way to China, viâ Labuan, where he is to stay a few hours to qualify himself to report whether it is worthy of retention. In my opinion, Labuan ought to be abandoned, because the Government of England have not made, and will not make, the necessary exertions to develope its capabilities and to ensure its success. Retrenchment seems to be the panacea for all evils, and all failures alike, and begets the very evil which we seek to avoid.

I enclose you an extract of the admiral's public despatch to me; it is unique as a specimen of policy in the Government of a large country. These orders from the Admiralty are in direct violation of our treaties with Holland, and with Bruné. Such a course of action with pirates has never been pursued before, by any civilized nation, and is manifestly calculated to destroy our commerce, wherever it may be practically acted upon. Let either the Lanoon or Chinese pirates know, that we shall not molest them, unless they commit depredations on the English flag, and they would sweep away a million of commerce in these seas, which was bound to English markets in native bottoms.

I have every reason to be satisfied with the condition of Serebas and Sakarran. The disaster which led to Lee's death, only proved the weakness of the piratical party and the strength of our adherents amongst the same people.

The only question at issue between us, is, whether they shall put to sea in their war-prahus for piratical purposes. Rentap, who was engaged with Brereton, retired, having little to boast of; for though the loss on either side was very inconsiderable, it fell more severely on his, than on our party. Gasim, whom you have heard of, without European aid or encouragement, and without Malay support, raised his standard and was joined by three-fourths of the entire tribe, and marching against Rentap, captured his village and brought down not only his large war prahu, but also all his property.   Rentap fled with a few followers.   This prahu is famous in Dyak annals, as having captured a boat, in which were some six or eight of the royal family of Pontianak; a Dutch gun-boat was present, but could give no support to her luckless consort; the crew of which were decapitated, before they could reach the scene of action.   The guns belonging to the Malay prahu, and the rich krisses, ornamented with gold, belonging to these unfortunate princes, were amongst the property taken from Rentap.

Were we now to abandon our forts, and sneak out of the policy which has heretofore been pursued, the piratical party would again gain the ascendancy, and their fleets would ravage the coast as they did before my advent; but by holding firmly, we are correcting their evil propensities, and the mass of the population which always leans to the side of power, are inclined to support us.

I hope in another week to be strong enough to proceed to Labuan and Brunè.

I want to know what the rajahs are about, and to settle our relations with them, for it is really no use to allow all these fine rivers to continue without a government and with resources undeveloped; it is the only chance the Borneon rajahs have, of recovering a shadow of power and a suitable maintenance. Were I to leave matters to take their course, the very name of government would cease to exist in Bruné, and these foolish fellows, in their own pettish jealousies, do the: best to ruin themselves, as well as their opponen.·, and to render affairs irretrievable.

I think I have now exhausted my budget of political news.

I have built a house on the Paninjow Mountain, where I shall reside on my return from Bruné, and where I expect to find it several degrees cooler than our locality below; it is about twelve hundred feet high, and the view, almost as fine as it is possible to conceive. At present we are suffering from very hot weather, which is rare with us. Everything is quite quiet and prosperous. We have five schooners and brigs loading in the river, and great improvements have taken place under Brooke's rule during my residence in England.

Give my best love to Hannah and the chicks, and regards to the Bridport and Greenwich party. I shall write to Hannah upon our domestic arrangements, when I have more strength and know a little more about them.

Farewell, my dear Jack, do not fail to give my kind regards to Drummond when you tell him my news. I

admire him more and more, when I reflect on what he
has done and contrast him with other politicians.

Ever, &c.,

J. BROOKE.

No. 185.

JOHN C. TEMPLER, ESQ.

Brig " Weraff," off Tanjong, Barram,
September 12, 1853.

MY DEAR JACK,

So soon as I could muster my scattered strength,
I set sail from Sarawak to Labuan, and after staying
there a few days, passed over to Bruné. Pangeran
Mumein had been advanced to the nominal sovereignty,
and ——, to all intents and purposes, was his prime
minister—on either side was Pangeran —— and the
party of the late Muda Hassim, and Pangeran ——,
and the family of the late sultan. I went frankly to
work, expressed how sincerely rejoiced I was, at the
accession of so good a man as the present sultan—
offered to support him in every way, and pointed out,
that any civil commotion between the above-named
factions, must lead to the dissolution of their government and sovereignty. The clouds cleared off, and it
soon appeared, that for three years, my enemies had

N 2

been hard at work to undermine my influence, but
without effect, excepting the statement, that I was hostile to Mumein, and would never acknowledge his title
to the throne.   I heard all their defamation of my
character—their exaggeration of the pending commission—their efforts to procure evidence—their assertion
that I was disgraced and beaten at every point, &c.,
—all this I heard ; but —— gave me two letters, one
addressed to the sultan, and one to himself, by Mr.
Napier,* and delivered by Mr. Motley ; these letters
are *apparently guarded*, but very damning to the cause
they are intended to sustain.   They both intimate, that
the Queen of England has resolved upon an inquiry.
" The Queen wishes to know whether the Serebas have
enemies, and whether they attack (or disturb) *every*
English vessel passing along the coast."   The Queen
wishes further to know this and that—setting forth in
the *Queen's name*, and making it seem that the writer
was authorized to convey the Queen's wishes to her
royal cousin, when in fact and in truth Mr. Napier could
know nothing of the subject of the commission, excepting what he had heard from common report.   *   *
*   *   *   In short, my dear Jack, I told all
the rajahs the whole affair of this commission.   I gave
them much wholesome and good advice about the conduct of their government : and I was fully and firmly

* The late Lieutenant-Governor.

reinstated as their friend and adviser. Without the least
difficulty, the sultan ratified the former sultan's grant of
Sarawak; and we arranged the future government of
the other rivers from Sarawak to ——, which are to be
in my hands on the payment of a yearly revenue of
—— and half the surplus revenue whenever derived.
The —— is my fast friend; and one and all scout the
idea of the commission, and are not moved in the
slightest degree by all that has passed. Mr. Hume
no doubt will say, that I procured the ratification of
this grant of Sarawak by force, for I was living in
the sultan's palace, and my vessel (a merchant brig)
not even off the city! The rest of the story is
soon told. I returned to Labuan for a few days—
sailed for Sarawak—off this point of Barram fell in
with a barque aground, (belonging to the Eastern
Archipelago Company) I returned for assistance, and
we are now passing the same point; the " Royalist," a
vessel of war employed in a survey, being at hand.
The breeze is fair, and in a week at farthest, I hope to
be at home. after an absence of two months, to receive
the accumulated intelligence from you, and from the
commission, if it be ready. The commission now may
come whenever it pleases, and the sooner the better.
I need only add, that my health has greatly improved,
and that I am better than I have been for some time
before. I am not *hideous now* – only simply ugly, and

I certainly improve by the smoothing of the skin. Vale.

17th. Off Sirik.—I wish you would send me your new address very plainly written.

Sarawak, 23rd September.—Safely arrived at home, finding all well. There is intelligence (in some measure to be relied upon) that Buah Riah, the refractory chief of Serebas, and Kum Nipa, a Kayan chief of the Rejang, have agreed to cut off our fort by treachery. The former part of this report I believe, the latter is doubtful; but it is certain, that when Buah Riah passed our forts, and committed the brutal murders I informed you of, he intrigued with Kum Nipa, and his statements may have rendered the latter suspicious. Forewarned forearmed! They *will not take* our fort, whether by treachery or by force; and if the Kayans like to break their heads against it, the fault is not mine, for I have only recently made the most friendly advances to Kum Nipa, and sent him my Governor's uniform as a present. In the mean time I shall make every effort to conciliate the Malay community of Serebas, so that they may check, and in time govern the Dyaks. Sakarran is safe. Linga is flourishing. Charlie Grant rules at Lundu, but I intend to remove him to Sadung, where I form a government, as soon as I can.

*   *   *   *   *

In Sarawak our progress is most satisfactory, and even our revenue is not deficient for our present want. I am going to allow the Chinese to farm land, and this will lead to the cultivation of pepper and gambier. But the most important measure about to be carried out, is the taking the Dyaks from the Datus into my own hands—of course giving them an equivalent sum from the revenue, in money. This has long been an object near my heart, and the time has now arrived, when I can carry it out with safety and with advantage to all parties. This will bring twenty-five thousand Dyaks under the direct rule of the English, and we shall. see them advance as I wish. Brooke has been up at my mountain residence at Paninjow, where he reports, it is cold enough for a fire and blankets. When I get over the business I have to do, and provided I can keep the peace with honour, I shall retire there. On Saturday next I meet *the country*, to explain the present position of the Government in relation to Bruné, to England, and to Serebas.

This is our intelligence, and I now turn to your letters :—

1st. Having assented to the commission, forbearance is our proper course. Delay, however, is a serious evil and a just cause of complaint. It is an injury done to thousands besides myself, and completely paralyzes our local government. The copies of Keppel's orders are very satisfactory, but you have forgotten to authenticate them, and I should like a line from Keppel, addressed to me, stating that the copies forwarded to you, are the *only orders* he issued relating to Mr. Burns leaving Bintulu, and that there were no secret instructions to remove him. Will you likewise look over all the Parliamentary papers, and send me whatever may appear useful.

2ndly. The sooner the commission comes the better. The government of Bruné never has, and never will (excepting by force), acknowledge the exclusive tenor of that deed; and it will insist upon a *bonâ fide* execution of the work, or set the Company aside altogether, as they retain the right of way in their own hands.

3rdly. I am *a fate* to the Serebas; and having now brought half of that community over to my way of thinking, it would indeed be wicked to allow the murder of many hundreds of people, when my efforts can save them, merely because the English Government looks black.   *   *   *   *

Mr. Wise, I am informed, has resigned all his valuable privileges and *prizes* guaranteed by the deed of settlement. The Parliamentary paper referred to by the Company, is the affirmation of the original grant, but not defining its meaning in any manner. As I have said before, the Bruné government read that document as I do, and stated officially to the Lieu-

tenant-Governor of Labuan, that they did so, during
my absence. I am glad you have determined upon
publishing the correspondence, and I hope it will
include the letters to my mother, because a man
cannot be suspected of playing a part there. We
have many friends in common, but there are others I
should like to distribute the work to, and if the number
we have be insufficient, purchase a dozen or more for
me. Besides, I should like one copy nicely bound for
my library, and six other copies for distribution in
Singapore, forwarded overland. The latter may come
out at once—the bound copy follow. You should
state in your preface, that some omissions were unavoidable, but that any honest man was welcome to look at
the original letters. As you say, it will indeed be a
record.

Thank you for all this, dear Jack, but do not let me
interfere with your distribution of copies. Would it
be proper for you, as my friend, to inform the Government that powers should be sent to the Commissioners
to pay all expenses; and further, that I have no means
of moving from place to place, unless a steamer, a
vessel of war, or a hired merchant-ship, with suitable
accommodation, be placed at my disposal? I will not
add anything further to this voluminous letter, excepting
my ardent wishes that you may be all well, and as
happy as the world can make you. I enjoy myself

amazingly. I shall write Lord —— by this mail, and to Mr. Drummond likewise. My kindest regards and loves to your family circle and to our old friends, and ever

Yours affectionately,

J. BROOKE.

No. 186.

JOHN C. TEMPLER, ESQ.

September 27, 1853.

MY DEAR JACK,

I HAD just finished my long letter, when yours of the 8th of August, containing the Instructions, and other papers, arrived. Your paper is all that it could be; but should you not have sent it in, there is a mistake. The flag was a commercial flag, meant to be applied as a commercial distinction, in all the other rivers of the coast, as well as Sarawak: but who ever heard of a flag being allowed for any purpose to be displayed over a private grant of land; or, in other words, *a private property!* If Sarawak be a private property, I am rich, indeed! How many slaves I have! how many serfs! But it is nonsense.

I shall meet the commission, with the full view and intention of making the inquiry searching and complete; but it must be just, and, to make it just, I must except to the Instructions. I particularly insist upon having the charges defined before the Commission begins, and having my accusers face to face. You will see that, having access to the public correspondence, my information is more complete as to what the former Government actually did; and the proof of their tacit acknowledgment of my public position is fully shown.

*   *   *   *   *

I met all the people collected (as I told you) on Saturday. I read them the documents from Bruné; told them of the commission, the objects of the inquiry, &c.; and we had a good deal of discussion on the subject. The Datu Patingi said, the white men in England must be fools, and were giving themselves a great deal of trouble about nothing. They all agreed that they were a free people; and old Datu Tumangong declared they would fight any one who doubted it. I have written to Mr. Cameron for several papers which I wish. I send you likewise an extract of a note from Lord ——, which may be useful, and the correspondence about the Sarawak flag, whence it appears that you are right after all, as it is very strong indeed.

*   *   *   *   *

No. 187.

JOHN C. TEMPLER, ESQ.

Sarawak, September 28, 1853.

MY DEAR JACK,

I WRITE a very few lines *viâ* Marseilles, to say that all is right and well here, and in Bruné, and that you will receive a large packet *viâ* Southampton.

Directly I get rid of this mail, I shall turn my attention, as far as I can, to the detail of the commission. I shall, on being invited, proceed to Singapore, arrange what expenses the commission is to incur, and how it is to be discharged; the question of interpreters: for, as the evidence will be in many dialects, unknown excepting in this place, some interpreters must be paid, and paid liberally. Then comes the protest—then the first charge—and I hold it as a maxim, that any accusation brought against me by individuals, must be on matters relative to themselves—whilst Mr. Hume or the Government, one or both, are to support the charges of a public nature.

*   *   *   *   *

Vale. Love to all. I trust dear Dora felt no ill-effects from her fall.

Ever your friend,

J. BROOKE.

Thus concludes this eventful history to the present time—and what Englishman can read the story, and not feel proud that Sir James Brooke is his countryman. With what noble energy and resolution, did he oppose himself to the clamour which was raised against him, upon the ostensible ground, that the Serebas and Sakarrans were not pirates—meeting statement with statement—argument with argument—until the point was abandoned by his adversaries, and (assuming him to have seen and approved the Government instructions *) at last even by Mr. Hume himself.——The prosecution of such a Company—as the Eastern Archipelago Company through the acts of its Directors was proved in a court of justice† to have been—was due alone to his hardy and resolute love of truth and justice—" Right was in the scale against wrong—and Old England was Old England still."————Who can read his letters‡ to Mr. Wise, without being touched with the unselfish spirit of consideration towards an erring servant, which breathes through every line, explaining and refuting at a glance, his so-called " mercantile speculations ? " —Who but must reverence the strong sense of public duty, which, at every personal sacrifice, induced him to vindicate,§ against the authorities at Singapore, the first principle, that truthfulness and character are the qualifications for office ?

* See *ante*, p. 233.   † See *ante*, p. 175.
‡ See vol. ii. p. 185.   § See *ante*, p. 72.

His endeavour* to trace home the libels of the
" Straits Times," which led to the inquiry on Dr.
Miller, was the only course open to an honourable and
upright mind, determined to sift and meet every accusation against him.———His judgment in the case of
the Lieut.-governor of Labuan was approved after a
long and careful consideration, and confirmed by a strong
judgment of the department of the Government to which
it was referred. †——— In his construction of the
sultan's‡ grant of the right to work coal, on the mainland
of Borneo (the subject of a long and adverse correspondence with the Colonial Office), he is supported by high,
perhaps the highest, legal opinions at the bar, taken
after that correspondence had closed—and lastly, was
he not justified in resisting an inquiry, which, when quite
willing to submit to it, he was again and again assured
by the House of Commons, and the voice of his countrymen, was unreasonably called for, that no grounds had
been shown for it, and that it was manifestly intended,
by those who demanded it, as a mark only of censure
and disgrace? These have been and are the salient points
of the clamour, mixed up with an affected consideration
for the rights of the inhabitants of Borneo—inhabitants
who along a coast line of five hundred miles, hail
him as their deliverer from a system of piracy, rapine,

* See *ante*, p. 25.

† See Parliamentary Papers, entitled Mr. William Napier,
8th August, 1851, p. 73.   ‡ See *ante*, p. 114.

and bloodshed, and bless him as the instrument of
that security and good government they had never
known before. Such is the view of Sir James Brooke's
friends—such the opinions of men, who have known
him long and intimately, and bear witness to the
purity and goodness of his life and manners—of men,
who feel that devotion towards him which true great-
ness alone can inspire : and if their homage be not unworthy, their testimony no light one, where is this commission of inquiry ?   Are the Directors of the Eastern
Archipelago Company in a position to prosecute ?
The judgments from the Bench are an answer there.
Is Mr. Hume to be the accuser ?   He must himself
submit to a cross-examination.   Is it then to be intrusted to the hands of Mr. Napier, and Mr. Woods,
at Singapore ; or is the Government itself to back the
indictment, to satisfy the doubts of Mr. Sidney Herbert ?
However this may be, the inquiry will soon have
passed away, and with it all the heat and animosity
to which it has given rise -- not soon, however,
will pass away the fame of that man, who first
conceived* the idea of opening the vast island of
Borneo to the enterprise of his countrymen, and who
executed his resolution amid numberless privations
and trials, with a moderation, ability, and justice,
which has conferred happiness on thousands of his

* See Vol. i. pp. 2 to 33.

fellow-men, and, if his measures and policy be carried out after him, will continue to confer it on thousands yet to come. Posterity will doubtless wonder at the treatment he received at the hands of some of his countrymen, for while our literature remains, these his letters will remain, and teach the moral, that, however beset with difficulties and dangers, high and worthy ends may be accomplished, and a great reputation achieved, without submitting to one false expedient, or sinking one principle of truth and honour.

For himself, the Editor may be permitted to say, that the first pleasure with which he received and read the letters, has been again and again revived in the execution of the work; and what he wished is done—to show a genuine English character in his own native colours, and to leave it with confidence to the judgment of his country.

> " This let the world, that knows not how to spare,
>   Yet rarely blames unjustly, now declare."

APPENDIX No. 1.

——

AN EXPLANATION and EXPOSURE of the CHARGES made against SIR JAMES BROOKE, with reference to the CAPTURE and EXECUTION of CRIMINALS in SARAWAK.

AN attempt has been made to place a forced construction on the passages in Sir James Brooke's Journal, which relate to the deaths of the Pangaran Budrudeen with two of his followers, and of the two Dyak Chiefs, Pa-Rimban and Pa-Tummo; and a charge has been publicly made against Sir James Brooke, that, "*they were executed by him without trial, and on his own mere motion.*" The following statement of facts, filling up the brief outline of the Journal, will refute these unfounded charges, and place the real merits of the case before the public.

On the 24th of September, 1841, Sir James Brooke was declared Rajah of Sarawak. On the 3rd of November he wrote as follows, " I have a country, but

See " Examiner," of June 14th and 28th, 1851.

oh! how beset with difficulties, how ravaged by war, torn by dissensions, and ruined by duplicity, weakness, and intrigue."

On the 5th November a Court of Justice was opened on a simple plan for the substantial redress of wrongs. On the 10th January 1842, a brief code of laws or regulations was published, the first article of which was as follows :—

" That murder, robbery, aud other heinous crimes will be punished according to the Ondong Ondong (the native laws then in force), and no person committing such offences will escape, if after *fair trial* he be proved guilty."   And concludes thus :—

" 8th.—The Governor issues these commands, and will enforce obedience to them, and whilst he gives all protection and assistance to the persons who act rightly, he will not fail to punish those who seek to disturb the public peace or commit crimes, and he warns all such persons to seek their safety, and find some other country, where they may be permitted to break the laws of God and man."

The entire Journal will prove that great firmness was necessary to establish a government, and to administer justice. " It was enough (remarked Sir James Brooke) that a follower of the rajah was concerned to hush up all wrongs ;" and he adds, that, " equal justice is the groundwork of society, and unless it can be administered, there can be no hope of ultimate improvement. The country may have bad laws, but such laws as it has, must be enforced gently and mildly as may be towards the superiors, but strictly towards the guilty, and all crimes coming under my cognizance must meet with their punishment." Keppel, vol. i. p. 277.

These extracts from Captain Keppel's work are preliminary to the two cases; the first, that of the Pangeran Budrudeen and his two followers, and the second, that of the two Dyak chiefs, Pa-Rimban and Pa-Tummo, and a most cursory reference to that work will further show,—

That the country was disorganized and distracted, and that a firm and equal administration of justice was necessary, though difficult and dangerous.

That the native laws were in operation against " murder, robbery, and other heinous crimes," and

That a court of justice had been opened, that witnesses were heard, and that the native rajahs assisted Sir James Brooke in administering justice. Keppel, vol. i. p. 257.

These principles are plainly set forth in the Journal, and it is rather a violent assumption to infer, from the incidental mention of judicial cases subsequently made in the Journal, that they were departed from.

The first case, that of the Pangeran Budrudeen, is mentioned in Captain Keppel's work; but the chase, capture, and execution of the criminals, as they stood in the original Journal, were suppressed in the manner hereafter mentioned, and were subsequently published in full in the work of Captain Mundy On the 28th April, 1842, or six months after his taking charge of

the government, Sir James Brooke wrote as follows:—
"The other cause of uneasiness is the attack of a Chinese
boat at the mouth of the river.   The boat that attacked
her is a small one, with eight or ten men, which came
out of Sadong, and had been lying here (Sarawak) for
a week or more.   She is commanded by a Pangeran
named Budrudeen, has some Illanuns on board, and is
bound on a piratical cruise.   As she descended the river,
she met with the small China boat likewise, from
Sambas, with eight men, which she treacherously
assailed, desperately wounding one man and severely
another—but the China boat's consort heaving in sight,
the pirate pulled away.   I must redress this if in my
power."   Sir James Brooke adds, that he thought one
of these Chinese "*must die*" (as in fact he did shortly
afterwards), and that the other was " very severely, and
perhaps, without medical attendance, mortally hurt."
This was the crime committed, and thus far, but no
farther, we read in Captain Keppel's work.

Captain Mundy's work gives an account of the subsequent events relating to this heinous crime.   " At Siru
the pirates were found on the 5th of May, when the Ma-
gindano Illanun lashed himself to desperation, flourishing
his spear in one hand, and the other on the handle of
his sword, he defied those collected about him ; he
danced his war dance on the sand—his face became
deadly pale—his wild eyes glared—he was ready to
amok—to die—but not to die alone."

" To catch him was impossible."   He was killed

openly, and madly defying authority, and ready to run a muck had an attempt been made to seize him. If there is to be any government, it will probably be conceded that a criminal cannot be allowed to escape, because he is desperate enough to resist to the last extremity. To catch him was impossible, and it was better to prevent a muck, than to wait till the lives of the innocent were sacrificed to the fury of a desperado.

The same course would have been pursued, whether in Java or Singapore, and those who know *what a Malay muck is*, can best appreciate the necessity of preventing it. The Pangeran Budrudeen, and his brother-in-law, were at the same time made prisoners under a "guarantee" that they should be taken to Sarawak, they, no doubt, hoping that their influence there would be sufficient to procure their release—for it must be remembered, that the Pangeran Budrudeen was noble by birth, a distant connexion of the Royal Family, and with many influential relatives. To execute such a criminal, for being guilty of *ordinary murder* and piracy, was almost unprecedented. Sir James Brooke's Journal best explains this, when he writes that—"To a people, who, if they know what justice is, have never obeyed its dictates, its impartial administration in the mildest manner, is a high offence; and *amongst the* Mundy, vol. i. p. 311. *Pangerans, each desires to claim an exemption for himself and his followers,* and takes little concern about the rest. At all hazards, however, I am resolved to enforce justice, and to protect property, and, whatever the results may be, to leave them in God's hands." Whatever their expectation may have been, the condition was fulfilled, and to Sarawak they were taken. And on the 8th of May Sir James Brooke mentions—" that Muda Hassim, having been informed of the circumstances, consented to the execution of the pirates," in other words, that Muda Hassim was willing that the law should take its course, even against these noble persons, should they, after trial, be found guilty. They arrived at Sarawak at nine o'clock on the morning of the 9th of May, and they were tried by the Rajah Muda Hassim himself, at eleven o'clock, and found guilty upon the clearest evidence, and at about one o'clock they were executed. Sir James Brooke did not sit upon their trial, having taken so active a part in their pursuit and capture (for it may be mentioned that he had been absent from Sarawak eight days and eight nights in chase of them).

They were judged by their native prince, and the blood connexion of one of them; their relatives were present at the trial, and consented to their death. The evidence against them was conclusive: the Chinese in the boat attacked, knew them; several of their own boat's crew admitted the fact, and the Pangeran Budrudeen himself never attempted to deny it; his last words being—" What! am I to be put to death for only killing the Chinese?" Had they been able to urge any reasonable plea in self-defence, or even to raise the slightest doubt of their guilt, Muda Hassim, whose feelings were

Mundy, vol. i. pp. 311 and 312.

enlisted to spare them, would never have condemned them, nor would their relatives have consented to their execution. On the morning of the 9th of May, Sir James Brooke conferred with Muda Hassim, who declined Sir James Brooke's suggestion, that " the example of the Pangeran would suffice for the ends of justice," and was resolute that justice should take its course on *both* the criminals. The trial is not mentioned in the Journal, for there really could be no reason for mentioning it, and the incidental omission furnishes no ground for the forced assumption, that it did not take place. " That they deserved death," writes Sir James, " none can doubt ;" and no candid person can doubt their guilt, or the stern necessity of establishing the administration of justice over the rich and great, as well as over the poor and lowly.

Can it in common fairness be said, that the Pangeran Budrudeen and his followers were executed by Sir James Brooke, " without trial, and on his own mere motion?"

The second case, that of the two Dyak chiefs, Pa-Rimban and Pa-Tummo, was as follows. Sir James Brooke's government had positively forbidden the Dyak tribes within the territory of Sarawak, to war one upon the other. This new law was publicly promulgated according to the Dyak customs, and was absolutely necessary to establish security, and to end the barbarous custom of taking heads, to which the Dyaks were addicted. There was some danger in promulgating such a law, but there can hardly be a question either of its propriety or humanity. Pa-Rimban and Pa-Tummo were the head men (or Orang Kayas) of Singé, a Sarawak tribe of Dyaks; their appointment was made by the Datus, the local Malay rulers of Sarawak, by whom they were removable at pleasure, and in every respect they were as much subjects of the Sarawak government as the Lords-Lieutenant of Counties are subjects of England.

Both these chiefs had direct notice of the recent law, and not only disobeyed it, but committed a heinous crime against Dyak customs, by treacherously murdering some of the Sigo tribe, living within the territory of Sarawak, with whom the Singé were at peace. Upon this Sir James Brooke went up to the tribe (a day's journey from Sarawak), and called together a number of their chiefs, who "all" disapproved of this murder most highly, asserting that the Sigos were "their younger brothers;" and upon being asked if they were willing to force Pa-Rimban to purchase peace, they replied that they were willing to do so.

This occurred in June, 1842, and Pa-Rimban insisting that they had not attacked the Sigo, but that the heads belonged to the Simpoke tribe (not a Sarawak tribe), with whom he alleged they were at war; and there being a difficulty at that time of getting clear proof of the fact, the case against them was suspended for the time; new chiefs, or Orang-Kayas, were appointed in their places; and in Captain Keppel's book, the ac-

count of Pa-Rimban and Pa-Tummo abruptly closes
here, and nothing further is heard of them. The sequel,
however, is contained in Captain Mundy's book, and
shows that Sir James Brooke was called away to Borneo,
and did not return to Sarawak until September, 1842;
and finding on his return that these chiefs, Pa-Rimban
and Pa-Tummo, had been the cause of fresh disturbances
in his absence, and that they openly refused obedience,
defied his authority, and declined holding an interview
even with the Datus; that they asserted, moreover, that
they had killed the Sampro (another tribe of Sarawak
Dyaks), and other Dyaks, because they were enemies,
and that they would kill more of them,"—Sir James
Brooke proceeded to take the measures against them
which are there detailed.

Pa-Rimban and Pa-Tummo were made prisoners, and
Sir James Brooke told them *he* would not kill them,
but take them to the rajah (that is to the Rajah Muda
Hassim), and they would then know what were the
rajah's orders; this condition was observed, they were
brought to the rajah, they were tried in public by him
and his brothers. The charge against them was—that
they had killed "their younger brothers," the Dyaks of
Sigo, a Sarawak tribe—that they had been, according to
the mildest form of Dyak custom, called upon to purchase peace; instead of doing which, in open defiance of
a recent law (which every lover of humanity must approve), they had added to their crime by killing some
Sampro and other Sarawak Dyaks, and " threatened to

kill more of them." For this they were tried by Muda Hassim, their native prince, the uncle of the sultan, one of the four great hereditary nobles of Bruné, himself a claimant to the throne, which his father had possessed, and who was not " an *ex*-governor," but standing in the position of a lord paramount, and possessing the power of life and death throughout the Borneo territories. Sir James Brooke, in 1841, wrote, that without the undoubted and spontaneous support of this prince, he was by no means eager to undertake the government; and this support he received from Muda Hassim, in serious judicial cases, before his own power was established.

See " Examiner" of June 28th, 1851.

Letter to James Gardinar, Esq. p. 29.

Sir James Brooke left the trial of Pa-Rimban and Pa-Tummo to their native princes, because, as in the case of the Pangeran Budrudeen, he had been an active party in their capture. No doubt he felt reluctance at the idea of their execution, but he would not interfere with it, as he entirely concurred in its justice, and he was assured of the necessity of the step, for the safety of many other lives. Had mercy been extended to them, the suppression of that barbarous custom of head-hunting could not have been effected; the Sigo and other tribes must have been allowed the right of retaliation, and the country would have been distracted once more with the feuds of the Dyak tribes, and all the insecurity and bloodshed which resulted from them.

Mundy, vol. i. p. 330.

As in the former case, the circumstance of their trial is not mentioned in the Journal, simply because it was a matter of course, and in a narrative in which the prin-

cipal events themselves are so cursorily and unconnect-
edly entered, it is a forced and uncandid assumption.
that the omission to mention it should be taken as a
proof that it did not take place.

"Sept. 7th.—At six o'clock in the evening, as the
sun set, Pa-Rimban and Pa-Tummo closed their earthly
career. They were taken out to the rear of my house,
and dispatched by the knives of the rajah's followers."

Such is the entry in the Journal; or, in other words,
they were executed in the usual manner, with the krais
or knife, by the rajah's followers, IN THE JUNGLE behind the Rajah Muda Hassim's house (for his house and
Sir James Brooke's stood together). The result, then,
of the whole case is, that they were charged with the
crime of murder, were tried by their native princes,
were condemned upon the most conclusive evidence, and
were executed according to the custom of their country.
Sir James Brooke remarks, " that the necessity was a
stern one, and their death merited."

It must be remembered that Sir James Brooke himself
gave both these cases to the world; that they were
published as parts of a rough journal, the entries in
which were often noted down in great haste, and amidst
numberless distractions; and that they were read without producing a suspicion on the minds of the numerous
critics who reviewed Captain Mundy's work.

It has now been shown, that a false construction has
been forced upon the passages which narrate the events
above detailed, and to complete the case, it only re-

mains to exhibit *how*, and by *whom* this has been done.

Sir James Brooke gave his Journal to Captain Keppel for publication; and the narrative of the cases of the Pangeran Budrudeen and his two followers, and of Pa-Rimban and Pa-Tummo, was, at first, printed exactly as they stood in the original manuscript. A Mr. Wise was Sir James Brooke's agent at this time, and having just returned from Sarawak, he objected to the publication of the first volume in the form in which it had been printed, and represented to Sir James Brooke's relatives and friends the injury it would do him in its then shape, on account of the free expression of Sir James Brooke's *political opinions*. This was the only reason he assigned to them, and, after much solicitation, he succeeded in inducing Captain Keppel to suppress the first volume as it was originally printed. Mr. Wise then managed to get the arrangement of the work into his own hands, and brought it out in its present form; *having suppressed* the conclusion of the narratives in question without his saying a single syllable of the objection, he afterwards thought fit to make. either to Sir James Brooke or to his friends.

This will appear clearly from the following extract from a letter dated 24th September, 1845, written by Mr. Wise to Sir James Brooke on the subject, in which, after complaining of the interference of a gentleman whose influence with Sir James Brooke he was anxious to undermine, he continues :—" Poor Keppel

has been led into a sad scrape with his book, I most
fortunately discovered the mess in time (I hope), it will
nevertheless cost something considerable. Volume I.
of Keppel's work must be suppressed; I will look after
the second edition, and I hope to see you prosper yet,
in spite either of yourself or the party I allude to.
Nothing could be handsomer than Keppel's conduct
throughout this very untoward affair; his readiness to
meet my views was in perfect keeping with the devotion
he has ever shown to your interests. The opinions of
Mr. Savage, and of another confidential adviser, I
transmit, to confirm my statement of the dangers so
recently averted."

Mr. Wise,
doubtless,
has retained
copies of
these letters
but their
substance
can be
gathered
from Sir J.
B.'s reply.

This was the language used by an agent to his employer, whom, according to his more recent revelations,
he had discovered, from this very journal, to be a
murderer. Sir James Brooke replied to this letter on
the 4th December, 1845, in the following terms:—

" I often laughingly said to Bethune, that I thought
my Journal in its rude, disjointed state, would puzzle any
son of literature, and I had great doubts whether anybody but myself, could lick it into shape. Keppel,
however, thought otherwise, and intended to take the
best literary opinion on the advisability of making it
public, and so I gave it to him to do as he pleased with
it. I am sorry your opinion is so strongly against the
publication, and as you do not say anything of the
literary defects, I conclude the extracts are injudiciously
made. Most of the Journal is quite unfit for the

public, and must be devoid of interest; but other considerable portions relating to the geography of the country, the different governments, and the habits and manners of an unknown aboriginal race, would in my opinion be acceptable to intelligent readers. As a general rule, therefore, I may say, that if the substantial parts of my Journal have been extracted for publication, all is right; but if my private views, feelings, and opinions have been selected, *it must be bad*, for it may look like *a puff;* Keppel will acquire the credit of being an interested party; and I shall be made *a hero and a fool.* I would not for the world that Keppel should be hurt or vexed, because, independently of my esteem for him, his intention was good. One thing, however, is certain, that the suppression of the work can do us no harm, and the suppression of portions that might injure our cause must do good. At a distance of some thousand miles this is all I can say, and even this will be of little consequence, and whatever is done will be done before my opinion arrives. *I consider your view of the matter somewhat too serious,* for I believe the worst penalty would be, to become a nine days' laughing stock. *Books do not ruin characters or break heads,* and it is quite impossible before a work is published, to judge what impression it may make out of doors. *I am very indifferent on the subject,* but I have told you the best course in my opinion, and shall therefore not be sorry if the work is burked, or altered, so as to bring me forward as little as possible. The friendly critics have my thanks, for I am not of the irritable tribe, and have none of the pride of authorship."

This letter speaks for itself, but it was in the course of arranging the first volume for publication that the manuscript journals, with other papers relating to the work, came into Mr. Wise's hands; and amongst them, the copies of a private correspondence, addressed by Sir James Brooke to the very friend Mr. Wise complained of. This correspondence had been lent to Captain Keppel to assist him in bringing out the Journal, for the single purpose of verifying dates, and places, and by an inadvertence on Captain Keppel's part, was passed with the other papers into Mr. Wise's hands; this correspondence Mr. Wise read, and claimed to retain; but on its being peremptorily demanded, he returned it immediately; not until, however, he had secretly copied it, which he never disclosed to any one: nor did it come out until nearly five years afterwards, when extracts from these very letters were furnished by him to Mr. Hume, and were read by Mr. Hume in the House of Commons. He claimed to retain it, on the ground that he found in it expressions which were injurious to him, as inconsistent with what Sir James Brooke had written to him, Mr. Wise; and he accordingly wrote Sir James Brooke on the subject, complaining that the correspondence had been handed about.

Sir James Brooke has no copy of his reply, but it was to the effect, that as Mr. Wise had not furnished him with any extracts, or informed him as to what extent they had been handed about, and how he came to see them, he could not form any judgment on the subject; though at the same time, he felt sure that any such extracts could not by any just interpretation be considered injurious to Mr. Wise, yet, at the same time, their late difference in matters of business might therein be mentioned. Thus the matter passed; Mr. Wise never alluded to it again in any way whatever, although he was afterwards in daily personal communication with Sir James Brooke, during his four months' stay in England in 1847, when he received a substantial act of kindness from him, and although he continued his agent until November, 1848. Whatever annoyance, therefore, he felt at the time, Sir James Brooke naturally considered had passed away. There can, however, be no doubt that from this period dates his antipathy to Sir James Brooke; and when Sir James, in 1846, declined entering on any doubtful speculations, this antipathy began to find expression; for it can be proved by witnesses, that in 1847, whilst he was lauding Sir James AS A GREAT PHILANTHROPIST, he was *privately, and behind his back, maligning his character, and holding him up as* A TYRANT *and* A MURDERER. The following letters will show this fact clearly :—

Church Mission House, Sarawak,
December 16, 1850.

My dear Sir James,

In the communication I had with Mr. Wise, respecting you, before I left England, he, after speaking of all the good he had done you by his exertions, among other things said, that of course he had great influence with you, for your reputation was completely in his power, as there were passages in your Journal printed in Captain Keppel's book, which he had suppressed, but which, if given forth to the world, would make you appear a murderer, instead of the great philanthropist everybody thought you. This, even now, I remember distinctly was the purport of what he said, though not perhaps the exact words; and I was much surprised at his making such remarks to me—a perfect stranger, and the only object I could perceive in his doing so, was to make me apply to him rather than to you, in all matters concerning the Mission.

The bait, however, did not take, as I was never fond of go-betweens, and I certainly would never have fished in the dirty ditch at Austin Friars, when I had always ready access to the pure brook at Mivart's.

Very faithfully and affectionately yours,

F. T. M'Dougall.

18, North Bank, St. John's Wood,
June 23, 1851.

MY DEAR BROOKE,

WHEN I first became acquainted with Mr. Wise, he uniformly represented you to me, not only as a philanthropist, and the benefactor of the Indian Archipelago, but a truly great man. In this view of your character he persisted for a length of time, but afterwards changed suddenly, and began to say he had been deceived in you—that you were a very bad man—that all your proceedings in the East were carried on exclusively for your own aggrandisement—that he could supply me with proofs of these allegations—and that if he had not suppressed, or altered a portion of your "Journal," you would have appeared to the world in the light of a murderer, which it seemed to me evident he wished me to believe you. I replied, that if he would put into my hands the proofs he spoke of, I would attack and denounce you publicly. He promised to furnish me with the proofs (which, of course, he never did), but said the time was not come for bringing the matter before the world. This shook my faith in his trustworthiness, and I began to suspect he was playing some deep game of his own. Of this I became fully satisfied, when, on your return to England in 1847, he went down to meet you—invited you to dine at his house—and there, in the presence of numerous friends, pronounced the warmest eulogium on your character and on all you had done in the Archipelago. I was shocked and disgusted by this hypocrisy, and reproached him with it, as well as with causing your portrait, by Mr. Grant, to be copied, framed, and hung in his dining-room, to which his only answer was, that people are compelled sometimes to do such things by circumstances. The idea of my son's going out with you to Borneo had originated with him, but he now sought to dissuade me from allowing him to accept the appointment, saying you were the greatest tyrant in the world, as the poor youth would find as soon as he was fairly in your power. To this I replied that if I had fifty sons, I should be too happy to intrust them to you. Our intercourse now became unpleasant, and in a few weeks after you left England, ceased entirely. Allow me, for my own satisfaction, to add, that instead of repenting of having placed by son under your authority, I have every day more and more reason to rejoice at it, and to express my gratitude to you for the undeviating kindness and generosity with which you have treated him. Trusting you will excuse this expression of my feelings,

     I am, my dear Brooke,

      Most faithfully and gratefully yours,

        JAMES AUGUSTUS ST. JOHN.

It needs only to add, that Mr. Wise, in a letter addressed to the *Times* newspaper, stated that he was ready to meet any distinct charge brought against him. Here is a very distinct and grave charge, resting on the testimony of two gentlemen unknown to each other, and which could, in a lesser degree, be substantiated by Mr. Scott, the Lieutenant-Governor of Labuan, Mr. Low, and Mr. Spencer St. John.

APPENDIX No. 2.

REPORT of the PROCEEDINGS at a PUBLIC DINNER given to His Excellency SIR JAMES BROOKE, K.C.B., Governor of Labuan, and Rajah of Sarawak, at the London Tavern, Bishopsgate Street, on Friday, April 30, 1852.

ADVERTISEMENT INSERTED IN THE NEWSPAPERS.

IN order to mark the sense entertained by the Mercancantile and Shipping body—as well as by other members of the community—of the eminent services rendered by SIR JAMES BROOKE to the interests of commerce and humanity, in his endeavours to put down the evils of Piracy in the Eastern Archipelago, and in his labours to advance the interests of Civilization in that part of the world—a PUBLIC DINNER will be given to that Gentleman, at the London Tavern, Bishopsgate Street, on Friday, the 30th April. ROBERT WIGRAM CRAWFORD, Esq., in the Chair.

STEWARDS.

Nath. Alexander, Esq.	Charles Bayley, Esq.
John Armstrong, Esq.	W. Butterworth Bayley, Esq.
R. J. Ashton, Esq.	Peter Bell, Esq.
John Harvey Astell, Esq.	D. J. Bischoff, Esq.

H. D. Blyth, Esq.
James Blyth, Esq.
Robert Bradford, Esq.
James Brand, Esq.
Rev. C. D. Brereton.
Robert Brooks, Esq.
Alex. Stewart Brown, Esq.
C. D. Bruce, Esq.
W. Buchanan, Esq. Glasgow.
C. J. Bunyon, Esq.
J. C. Cameron, Esq.
Cha. Carnie, Esq.
Robert Carter, Esq.
John Cattley, Esq.
Philip Cazenove, Esq.
D. Barclay Chapman, Esq.
Right Hon. R. A. Christopher, Esq., M.P.
Matthew Clark, Esq.
Alex. Colvin, Esq.
James Cook, Esq.
R. W. Crawford, Esq.
J. J. Cummins, Esq.
Henry Drummond, Esq., M.P.
Edward Edwards, Esq.
The Right Hon. the Earl of Ellesmere.
John Lettsom Elliot, Esq.
William Fanning, Esq.
Alderman Finnis.
P. W. Flower, Esq.
J. G. Frith, Esq.
J. P. Gassiot, Esq.
Ellis James Gilman, Esq.
John Gilmore, Esq.
Baron de Goldsmid.
B. B. Greene, Esq.
Samuel Gregson, Esq.
Archd. Hamilton, Esq.
Wm. Hamilton, Esq., Glasgow.
Wm. Parker Hammond, Esq.
Thomson Hankey, Jun., Esq.

William Harrison, Esq.
John Harvey, Esq.
Thomas Haviside, Esq.
Captain Dalrymple Hay.
T. E. Headlam, Esq., M.P.
Robert Henderson, Esq.
George Herring, Esq.
Robert Hichens, Esq.
Henry Holroyd, Esq.
J. G. Hubbard, Esq.
John Hudson, Esq.
Robert Ibetson, Esq.
Frederick Janvrin, Esq.
Sir Richard Jenkins.
Horatio Kemble, Esq.
Stephen Kennard, Esq.
William King, Esq.
James Levick, Esq.
W. S. Lindsay, Esq.
Stillingfleet Locker, Esq.
Lt.-General Sir J. Law Lushington.
Robert M'Ewan, Esq.
K. R. Mackenzie, Esq.
Charles Marryat, Esq.
George Marshall, Esq.
George May, Esq.
George Meek, Esq.
Charles Mills, Esq.
T. A. Mitchell, Esq., M.P.
George Henry Money, Esq.
C. N. Newdegate, Esq., M.P.
J. D. Nicol, Esq.
Wm. Law Ogilby, Esq.
Thomas Olverson, Esq.
J. Horsley Palmer, Esq.
W. H. Plowden, Esq., M.P.
J. D. Powles, Esq.
H. T. Prinsep, Esq.
Henry Ranking, Esq.
Arthur Rasch, Esq.
C. R. Read, Esq.

G. C. Redman, Esq.
J. R. Reeves, Esq.
Stephen Reggio, Esq.
Edward Rigby, Esq., M.D.
T. C. Robertson, Esq.
W. G. Romaine, Esq.
Chas. Morris Roupel, Esq.
H. W. Schneider, Esq.
William Scott, Esq.
Thomas Sheppard, Esq.
Alexander Sim, Esq.
Joseph Somes, Esq.
Rev. T. F. Stooks.
E. P. Stringer, Esq.
Charles Stewart, Esq.
J. C. Templer, Esq.
H. H. Thomas, Esq.
James Thompson, Esq.

W. James Thompson, Jun., Esq.
Richard Thornton, Esq.
Thomas Thornton, Esq.
J. J. Travers, Esq.
Charles Trueman, Esq.
Richard Twining, Esq.
G. D. Tyser, Esq.
W. T. Wallace, Esq.
Andrew Walls, Esq.
Joshua Walker, Esq.
Wm. Thornton West, Esq.
James Weston, Esq.
John Wild, Esq.
Henry Wilson, Esq.
Henry W. Windsor, Esq.
John Young, Esq.
Edward J. P. Zohrab, Esq.

Tickets, £2. 2s. each, may be had by applying to the Committee for conducting the Dinner, at the London Tavern.

LIST OF THE COMPANY PRESENT.

Robert Wigram, Crawford, Esq., Chairman.

Admiral Sir Charles Adam, K.C.B.

The Hon. Baron Alderson.

Vice-Admiral Sir Thomas Cochrane, K.C.B.

Henry Drummond, Esq., M.P.

Vice-Admiral Sir James Gordon, K.C.B.

Thomas Emerson Headlam, Esq., M.P.

Lieut.-General Sir James Law Lushington, G.C.B., Director of the East India Company.

William H. C. Plowden, Esq., M.P., Director of the East India Company.

Rear-Admiral Renton Sharpe, C.B.

John Harvey Astell, Esq., Director of the East India Company.

William Butterworth Bayley, Esq., Director of the East India Company.

John Cattley, Esq., Chairman of the London Dock Company.

Thomson Hankey, Jun., Esq., Governor of the Bank of England.

J. G. Hubbard, Esq., Deputy-Governor of the Bank of England.

Sir Richd. Jenkins, G.C.B., Director of the East India Company.

Charles Mills, Esq., Director of the East India Company.

Henry Thoby Prinsep, Esq., Director of the E. I. Company.

James Weston, Esq., Prime Warden of the Fishmongers' Company.

William Adam, Esq.

Packenham Alderson, Esq.

Nathaniel Alexander, Esq.

Nath. C. Alexander, Esq.

Robert Alexander, Esq.

William Anderson, Esq.

Rev. Dr. Archer.

John Armstrong, Esq.

J. Arnould, Esq.

R. J. Ashton, Esq.

H. Astell, Esq.

R. N. Bacon, Esq.

E. Barber, Esq.

Peter Bell, Esq.

Alexander Bellamy, Esq.

D. J. Bischoff, Esq.

James Blyth, Esq.

H. D. Blyth, Esq.

W. H. Bowen, Esq.

Robert Bradford, Esq.

James Brand, Esq.

Rev. C. Brereton, M.A.

Rev. C. D. Brereton, M.A.

Robert Brooks, Esq.

Rev. J. Browell, M.A.

W. H. Brown, Esq.

Charles Dashwood Bruce, Esq.

Joseph Buchanan, Esq.

Thomas Buchanan, Esq.

C. J. Bunyon, Esq.

John Campbell Cameron, Esq.

James Campbell, Esq.

Charles Carnie, Esq.

William Carr, Esq.

Robert Carter, Esq.

Philip Cazenove, Esq.

Montague Chambers, Esq., Q.C.

D. Barclay Chapman, Esq.

C. Churchill, Esq.

Matthew Clark, Esq.

Gordon W. Clark, Esq.

Thomas Collyer, Esq.

Alex. Colvin, Esq.

James Cook, Esq.

W. H. Covington, Esq.

J. H. Crawford, Esq.

J. J. Cummins, Esq.

S. D. Darbishire, Esq.

N. de St. Croix, Esq.

J. Earl, Esq.

Edward Edwards, Esq.

Captain B. Elder.

J. L. Elliot, Esq.

S. H. Ellis, Esq.

William Fanning, Esq.

Captain Farquhar, R.N.

Alderman Finnis.

J. Fitzpatrick, Esq.

P. W. Flower, Esq.

Charles Freeman, Esq.

J. G. Frith, Esq.

A. W. Gadesden, Esq.

C. Gassiot, Esq.

J. P. Gassiot, Esq.

Ellis James Gilman, Esq.

J. Gilman, Esq.

John Gilmore, Esq., R.N.

Thomas Gladstone, Esq.

H. Goschen, Esq.

B. B. Greene, Esq.

Samuel Gregson, Esq.

Archibald Hamilton, Esq.

Wm. Parker Hammond, Esq.

Lieut. H. B. Hankey, R.N.

William Harrison, Esq.

Thomas Haviside, Esq.

Captain Dalrymple Hay, R.N.

Robert Henderson, Esq.

George Herring, Esq.

Hugh Hill, Esq.

Robert Hichens, Esq.

H. Holroyd, Esq.

Commander Wilmot Horton.

John Hudson, Esq.

Seymour Huffam, Esq.

G. W. Hunt, Esq.

W. Hunt, Esq.

Robert Ibetson, Esq.

Frederick Janvrin, Esq.

Rev. F. C. Johnson, M.A.

Charles Johnson, Esq.

William Just, Esq.

Captain Justice, R.N.

Horatio Kemble, Esq.

Adam Kennard, Esq.

Stephen Kennard, Esq.

The Hon. Captain Keppel, R.N.

William King, Esq.

A. A. Knox, Esq.

Robert Knox, Esq.

W. Lacaita, Esq.

J. Lethbridge, Esq.

James Levick, Esq.

H. H. Lindsay, Esq.

W. S. Lindsay, Esq.

Stillingfleet Locker, Esq.

H. Low, Esq.

George Malcolm, Esq.

Charles Marryat, Esq.

George Marshall, Esq.

George May, Esq.

Lobert McEwan, Esq.

George Meek, Esq.

Geo. Henry Money, Esq.

A. Nesbitt, Esq.

William Law Ogilby, Esq.

Thomas Oliverson, Esq.

R. S. S. Padday, Esq.

Edward Howley Palmer, Esq.

J. Parkinson, Esq.

H. Phillips, Esq.

Charles Pietroni, Esq.

Rev. Charles J. Plumher.

John Diston Powles, Esq.

Rev. R. Cowley Powles.

Thomas W. Powles, Esq.

W. S. Price, Esq.

J. V. Prior, Esq.

G. T. Ranking, Esq.

Henry Ranking, Esq.

Arthur Rasch, Esq.

C. R. Read, Esq.

G. Clavering Redman, Esq.

J. R. Reeves, Esq.

Stephen Reggio, Esq.

Edward Rigby, Esq., M.D.

T. C. Robertson, Esq.

W. G. Romaine, Esq.

Dr. Roots.

C. M. Roupell, Esq.

B. R. Saunders, Esq.

Robert Saunders, Esq

Henry William Schneider, Esq.

William Scott, Esq.

Captain Selby.

C. J. Selwyn, Esq.

Charles Sheppard, Esq.

Captain Shugrha.

G. A. Shuttleworth, Esq.

Alexander Sim, Esq.

Joseph Somes, Esq.

John Stanley, Esq.

Horace St. John, Esq.

J. A. St. John, Esq.

Rev. T. F. Stooks, M.A.

E. P. Stringer, Esq.

Charles Stuart, Esq.

G. D. O. K. Templer, Esq.

J. C. Templer, Esq.

H. H. Thomas, Esq.

James Thompson, Esq.

W. J. Thompson, Jun., Esq.

James Thorne, Esq.

Richard Thornton, Esq.

Thomas Thornton, Esq.

Rev. Joseph Tombs, M.A.

J. J. Travers, Esq.

W. Trixford, Esq.

Charles Trueman, Esq.

Richard Twining, Esq.

G. D. Tyser, Esq.

Joshua Walker, Esq.

W. T. Wallace, Esq.

Andrew Walls, Esq.

William Thornton West, Esq.

John Wild, Esq.

Hiram Williams, Esq.

Henry Wilson, Esq.

H. W. Windsor, Esq.

John Young, Esq.

E. J. Zohrab, Esq.

Viscount Palmerston, and many other Members of Parliament, were prevented attending in consequence of important business occurring in the House of Commons on the same evening.

Dinner to Sir James Brooke, K.C.B.

The *Chairman.*—Gentlemen, the toast I have first to propose is one which, on such occasions as the present, always takes precedence over every other toast, and it is one that needs no comment from me; it is—The health of Her most Gracious Majesty the Queen. with all the honours.

The *Chairman.*—The next toast, gentlemen, is the proper compliment to the one that has preceded it, and needs, like the other, no special commendation to recommend it to your notice. I give you—The health of His Royal Highness Prince Albert and the rest of the Royal Family.

The *Chairman.*—Our next toast. gentlemen, is one that is always well received in any company of Englishmen— The health of that distinguished body of our fellow-countrymen connected with the United Services. I think, gentlemen, you will drink this toast with more than ordinary enthusiasm on the present occasion, when you remember that it was in the army that Sir James Brooke first became distinguished in the public service, and that it has been his lot still further to distinguish himself in conjunction with the navy. (Hear, hear.)   Gentlemen, I think that the toast I now propose to you is one that cannot fail to obtain your most hearty applause ; and if any particular credit is to be given to those with whom Sir James Brooke was associated in these services, it will be better to reserve that acknowledgment for a special toast.   Gentlemen, I will now give you—The Army and Navy, coupled with the names of two distinguished officers, which will be handed down with honour to posterity,— Admiral Sir Charles Adam, and Lieutenant-General Sir James Law Lushington.   (Loud cheers.)

Admiral Sir Charles Adam.—It must always be a high gratification to any man called upon as I am upon the present occasion, to return thanks for the service to which I have the honour to belong ; I feel it particularly on this occasion, for the manner in which your Chairman has given the toast, and I feel that that satisfaction is enhanced very much because the toast is given in the City of London. No officer who has served in war can fail to remember that when any high service was performed by the navy, those who suffered in the fight were always solaced by the cordial feeling of the City of London, who relieved the wounded and comforted the widow and the orphan.   (Loud cheers.) I trust that if it should ever happen again that this country is called upon to engage in such a war, you would find the navy equal to the same exploits as those which had brought such honour to it hitherto, and that its services would be received in a similar manner by the generous City of London. But, gentlemen, there is another reason why I feel the satisfaction very much enhanced,—that we are met to do honour to a gallant and noble-minded person who is our guest this night. (Loud cheers.) I have served in India long enough to know that piracy is a deep stain on that country, and that it can only be obliterated by the means that have been pursued by our excellent guest. It gives me the highest satisfaction to reflect, that whenever Sir James Brooke came into communication with the officers of the British navy, he acted most cordially with them. That there had been some bloodshed, I am convinced no one more sincerely deplores than my gallant friend. (Loud cheers.) From my experience, I am convinced that there are no means of putting an end to piracy in the Eastern Archipelago, than those which our friend has adopted. Gentlemen, in the name of my brother officers, I return you our best thanks for the honour you have conferred upon us, in drinking our healths on this interesting and important occasion.

Lieutenant-General Sir James Law Lushington.—I beg, gentlemen, to return you my most sincere thanks for the honour you have conferred upon the service to which I belong. I am quite sure that toast has arisen from a conviction that the Army has hitherto done what was needed from them. I rejoice that at the present moment we are at peace with

all the world, and I most heartily desire that that peace
may long continue. I beg again to thank you, gentlemen,
for the kind manner in which you have received the toast
so well proposed by the Chairman.

The *Chairman.*—Gentlemen, we have now arrived at
that period in the course of the evening when I think I
may appropriately allude to the object for which we are
assembled in this place. We are met for the purpose of
manifesting, after the manner which the convivial customs
of our age sanction, to our countrymen and to the world at
large, the high esteem and grateful admiration with which
we regard the services rendered by Sir James Brooke, in
the promotion of the moral influence of his country in
those parts of the world with which he has been connected,
—in the extension of our commerce,—and in imparting
the blessings of civilization to the people of those inhospitable regions wherein his lot has been cast. We are met
here also for the purpose of conveying to him an expression
of our sympathy in that most unmerited and calumnious
requital —(loud and long-continued cheering)—in that
most ungenerous requital which he has met with at the
hands of certain parties in this country, to whom I feel it
is doing an honour to say of them that they are his countrymen. And we are met, further, to assure him of our
unshaken and unabated confidence in his ability and will-
ingness to maintain on his return to that part of the world
the honour and glory of his country, and the high reputation
he has already earned for himself. And, gentlemen, when
I look around this table,—when I look through the list of

...to do honour to our guest by
...ling,—when I see at this table
...ouse of Commons, (and know
...en present had they not been
...of public business, and by the
...g before the House,)—when I
...pany is graced by a member
...ly and ornament of our age,
...I see around this table not
...Services, to whom I have
...,—when I see here many
...ection of the affairs of that
...paramount of the East,—I
...(cheers),—to render their
...nd integrity of Sir James
...ighest executive officers of
...er, the Bank of England.
...every creed and caste in
...vey to Sir James Brooke
...ling confidence,—I may
...belief that we shall hear
...ations upon his character
...attacks upon his character
...n disappointed expectation
...red by that morbid avidity
...mongering on the part of
...discredit upon those from
...him to whom they wish to
...) If I deplore this exhibition

of feeling on the part of some, it is not on account of any
stain it can attach to Sir James Brooke; for the more he
is attacked, the more brightly will his character shine
after the investigation. But if there is one reason why I
should deplore this conduct more than another, it is, that I
feel it to be in the highest degree impolitic that the
motives of officers, intrusted with the performance of
arduous duties in foreign parts of the globe, should be
brought under the critical examination of the House of
Commons as Sir James Brooke's have been. I do not,
of course, complain that the House of Commons should
have the power of exercising a right discretion in investi-
gating such matters when they are properly brought under
its notice; but I do complain that such opportunities
should thus be given to men who have private interests to
serve, and whose object is not the public good. I say, it
is lamentable that such men should have an opportunity
given to them of thus enlisting others in their private cause,
and that they should command that attention on the part
of others who have nothing to do but to hunt up imaginary
cases of grievance and wrong. Now I believe that it
would be quite within my province, on this occasion, but I
do not think there is any necessity for it, to carry you
through a long personal account of Sir James Brooke since
he left this country in 1838 down to the present time.
The pages of Keppel, of Mundy, and other officers who
have served with him in his trials and his dangers, and who
now share with him, I am proud to say, the honours which
his countrymen, and his countrywomen too (as testified by

their presence here to-night), desire to render to him—those pages are open to all; and there are few, probably, whom I have now the honour to address who have not thus made themselves acquainted with the main features of Sir James Brooke's extraordinary career. It is not to the facts connected with Sir James Brooke's career that I wish now particularly to allude;—I would rather advert to the consequences which I think will spring from his great exertions on the inhospitable shores of Borneo to the commerce of this country, and to the extension of that moral influence which England is entitled to exercise even in that distant part of the world. When you contrast the present state of Borneo with what it was some time ago, I think it will be difficult to deny to Sir James Brooke the credit of most unfailing sagacity, of a wonderful self-denial, of an equally wonderful facility of adapting himself to the exigencies of the station in which he has been placed; and I think I can cite no better instance of the extraordinary fame which his name has acquired, than by reading an extract from a note put into my hands since I came into the room :—

" Sir,

" Just hearing that you are to preside at the dinner to be given to him whom all honest men delight to honour, I venture to relate to you a circumstance which occurred to myself about two years since, whilst surveying the coast of Palawan (from which I have but a few days returned), which I conceive a strong evidence of the moral influence the proceedings of the rajah (Sir James Brooke) have obtained in that quarter, even beyond where he has been seen:—Landing on the eastern shore of Palawan, in a boat, with six men, in the execution of surveying duties, I was met by a corresponding number of Malays, armed, who, assuming a threatening attitude, warned me off. I told them we were English, and inquired what they were afraid of? This appeared to inspire something like confidence; when one of the party asked, 'Did I know Tuan Brooke?' Replying in the affirmative, he exclaimed, 'Bargoose! Tuan Brooke,' or, 'Very good Mr. Brooke;' placing his arm on my shoulder at the same time, his confidence being fully confirmed.

"It was my good fortune, a few months later, to meet a man on the same coast, named Sheriff Hassen, a native of Malludu, which was so notorious in 1845 as being a den of piracy. This man produced a paper, given him by the rajah, certifying to his honest character, and recommending him to any Europeans with whom he might meet. The certificate was dated on board H.M.S. "Mæander," at Malludu, in 1848.

"That His Excellency may long be spared as an instrument of Divine Providence for the good work he has so successfully commenced in the Eastern Archipelago, whose children already join in singing songs of gratitude to their benefactor, is the humble, but hearty prayer of

"Your obedient Servant,

"C. Pasco,

"Lieut., R.N.

"10 Wharton Street, Pentonville, April 30th, 1852."

Now, gentlemen, this may seem a very trivial matter, but it will show you to what extent Sir James Brooke's moral influence has penetrated, when these Malays threw down their arms and accepted as friends those whom they were previously disposed to massacre. (Cheers.) You may receive this as one out of numerous testimonials accessible at the present time,—testimonials of the influence which the English nation possesses through the rightful exercise of the power with which Sir James Brooke has been invested. And I will ask you, whether it is not monstrous that such a career of humanity and righteous dealing should be cut short through the machinations of a disappointed few. I am disposed to attribute to those gentlemen, by whom the motion adverse to Sir James Brooke was proposed in the House of Commons last year, a conscientious motive in the discharge of their duties, but I cannot go futher than that; for I believe the whole of the opposition he has met with to have been originated by personal considerations. And, gentlemen, if further evidence were wanting of the change which has taken place in that part of the world under the administration of Sir James Brooke, it might be found in that excellent letter from the Bishop of Calcutta, which was read in the House of Commons by the honourable member for Newcastle (Mr. Headlam). It is impossible for any man to read that letter and not give full credit to the sentiments there set forth; and I ask you whether the measures Sir James Brooke has taken to pacify that country, whether the great and wonderful change from the barbarism existing in that country when he first visited it, is to be stopped by such proceedings as I have mentioned. We require nothing more, at the present time, than a strong manifestation of the feeling of this country, with a fair and reasonable judgment,—not one dictated by personal feeling. Nothing more than this is needed to enable Sir James Brooke to return to that country, and to carry out the great objects in which he has been interested; and I believe that in whatever position he may be placed there, whether as an independent ruler, or as her Majesty's representative and governor of the island of Labuan, I say it requires nothing more than a strong expression of feeling on the part of the British public, to ensure all that we can expect of him in our most sanguine moments. (Cheers.) Now, gentlemen, I do not wish to occupy your time, at the present moment, with long charges against those whom we have considered inimical to Sir James Brooke. We may think that they have taken misguided views. I allude more particularly to those who voted for an inquiry into Sir James Brooke's proceedings; but I think it is very much to be lamented that such a state of things should be again allowed to occur. Of the individual who took the lead on that occasion, I would always wish to say nothing that is harsh or unpleasant; but I must say (for at the time referred to I held a seat in the House of Commons), that it will be to me a very great satisfaction to reflect upon the vote that I had then the opportunity of giving; and it seems to me that if that gentleman has not proved that the object of his attack was a Verres in his Pro-consulship, he has certainly not acquired for himself the character of a Cicero in the prosecution of his case. (Laughter and cheers.) We have met to-night for the purpose of exhibiting to Sir James Brooke our undiminished confidence in the integrity of his views, and in his ability to carry out the great undertaking he has before him ; and you will render him no stronger assistance in carrying out his purposes than by cordially accepting the toast I will now propose,--that of the health of Sir James Brooke, and long life and prosperity to him. (Loud and long-continued cheering.)

Sir James Brooke, in acknowledging the toast, spoke as follows :—Mr. Chairman and Gentlemen,—I am deeply sensible of the honour which has been conferred upon me at this present moment, and, if anything would have enhanced the pleasure I already experience, it would have been the manifestation of your feeling in responding to the toast proposed by the Chairman. I will not pretend, gentlemen, to that species of pride which apes humility; I will not humble myself that you may exalt me. I will not say that I am utterly unworthy of your regard; but I will venture to tell you something of my own feelings and something of the position I hold in the East. I am deeply sensible, gentlemen, that such an expression of opinion from an assembly like this, is important and valuable to me, not only as a token—a public testimony—of approval of my conduct, and my sincere desire to advance the interests of this country in a distant quarter of the globe, but it justifies the conviction—the unchangeable conviction —that I have ever entertained, that truth and justice will

314

country when he first vi
proceedings as I have
more, at the present ti
the feeling of this count
ment,—not one dictat
more than this is nee
return to that country.
in which he has been
whatever position he
independent ruler, or
governor of the island
more than a strong e
British public, to en
our most sanguine m
I do not wish to occ
with long charges a
inimical to Sir Jar
have taken misgui
to those who vote
proceedings; but
that such a state
Of the individu
would always w
at I

and when he has trampled upon private
...ill always find one who will tell you that it
...member of parliament to act as a scavenger
...other men, or,—to borrow a simile from my
...,—to become a cesspool for every foul slander
...he Antipodes or manufactured in London.
...nciples of justice supposed to be implanted in
...eart, and which are certainly acknowledged by
...of all nations. It is a principle of justice, that
...on of crime shall not be disposed of by one
...tribunal, and again and again preferred year
... It is a principle of justice that suspicion is no
...truth,—that ignorance is no ground of inquiry,—
...a principle of justice that trivial offences shall not
...ed up in the category of deadly crimes. It is a
...le of justice, that deadly crimes shall not be charged
...it and frivolous pretences. It is a principle of jus-
...that trials shall precede condemnation, and it is a
...nandment of God, as well as a principle of justice,
..." Thou shalt not bear false witness against thy neigh-
...r." (Loud cheers.) These, gentlemen, are the
...rnal principles upon which the foundations of society
...st, and to violate them is to injure society ; and yet, if
...ou will weigh what has passed with those principles, and
...ry them by their balance, you will find that there is one
...member of the House of Commons who has not only
...abused his privilege as a member of Parliament, but who
...has made unto himself a new law. There are principles
...more important than the welfare of nations, and there are

triumph, in the present state of society, over any outcry
fomented in the popular mind against the character of an
honest man. (Loud cheers.) Gentlemen, your approval
of my conduct is no light condemnation of the conduct of
those who have sought by every means, fair and unfair, to
blast my reputation, even at the risk of injuring their own;
who, under the pretence of humanity have screened their
injustice, and on the plea of inquiry, have been unscrupulous
enough to charge murder. It is now but little more than
four years since I was the idol of a spurious popularity; it
is more than three years that I have been the object, but
happily not the victim, of an unprecedented persecution;
and it will afford me no light satisfaction, gentlemen, if
this night a fair and moderate estimate can be formed of
my motives, and of my conduct. Praise and blame have
been lavished upon me with no sparing hand. I have been
accused of every crime, from murder to merchandize.
(Laughter.) I have been held up as a prodigy of perfec-
tion,—and I have been cast down as a monster of iniquity.
These, gentlemen, are the extremes which human folly
delights in; these are the distortions which the tribunes of
the people represent as Bible truths to the multitude:
these the delusions which a hackneyed politician uses
lightly, to wound feelings he has long outlived, and to cast
a slur upon Her Majesty's servants. The evil, gentlemen,
I fear is inevitable; but it is no less an evil, that public
morals in such hands should sink, like water, to its lowest
and its dirtiest level; and, Mr. Chairman, you will always
find some sapient senator, when he has infringed upon

public principle, and when he has trampled upon private feeling,—you will always find one who will tell you that it is his duty as a member of parliament to act as a scavenger to the vices of other men, or,—to borrow a simile from my friend near me,—to become a cesspool for every foul slander invented at the Antipodes or manufactured in London. There are principles of justice supposed to be implanted in the human heart, and which are certainly acknowledged by the virtuous of all nations. It is a principle of justice, that an accusation of crime shall not be disposed of by one competent tribunal, and again and again preferred year after year. It is a principle of justice that suspicion is no proof of truth,—that ignorance is no ground of inquiry,— and it is a principle of justice that trivial offences shall not be mixed up in the category of deadly crimes. It is a principle of justice, that deadly crimes shall not be charged on light and frivolous pretences. It is a principle of justice, that trials shall precede condemnation, and it is a commandment of God, as well as a principle of justice, that "Thou shalt not bear false witness against thy neighbour." (Loud cheers.) These, gentlemen, are the eternal principles upon which the foundations of society rest, and to violate them is to injure society ; and yet, if you will weigh what has passed with those principles, and try them by their balance, you will find that there is one member of the House of Commons who has not only abused his privilege as a member of Parliament, but who has made unto himself a new law. There are principles more important than the welfare of nations, and there are

plain rules for the guidance of mankind; but we all know
that men's passions and men's moral obliquity cause a
departure from these grand truths. There is a duty which
teaches one man to filch his neighbour's purse—there is a
duty which teaches another man to steal his neighbour's
good name; but until this new code of morals be established,
I shall continue to call things by their right names,—I
shall call persecution, persecution; and the persecution
which has pursued me has been as dogged and as fierce as
though it had been caused by religious hatred; it has over-
leaped the barriers of testimony, defied the voice of reason,
till honest men loathe the injustice done, and you, gentlemen, have marked your sense of principles violated, and of
feelings outraged. Had I said less, gentlemen, I should
not have conveyed what I wish to express. I feel that
those principles cannot be lightly violated; but for those
personally who have honoured me by their suspicions, I
wish to dismiss them from my thoughts with the charitable
contempt I feel. There can be nothing common between
us. A tardy conviction is due to their own character, but
I have never mingled in the " filthy fray,"

" Where the soul sours, and gradual rancour grows
    Embitter'd more from peevish day to day."

But I know that there are men who love notoriety better
than justice, and who live upon the breath of popular
applause. I do not wish to comprehend their motives—I
do not respect their calling, neither do I envy their fame
or success. (Cheers.) Our tastes and our feelings assi-
milate upon no single point, and for my part, gentlemen,

" I would rather be a kitten, and cry Mew,
  Than one of these same metre ballad-mongers."

It has been said, gentlemen, that when I set sail for the
shores of Borneo, now fourteen years ago, I carried a deep
design in my bosom to suppress piracy, and to carry
civilization to the Malayan race.   This is most flattering to
my wisdom and foresight, but unfortunately, it is not true.
I had but one definite object when I left England, and
that was, to see something of the world and to come back
again.   The extraordinary events that occurred after my
arrival in Sarawak I need not detail.   I found a country
ruined by its native princes, and which they could no
longer govern.   I had everything to do.   I was a reformer
in the most extended sense of the word; but I recognised
the principle, that to effect any adequate measures of reform
you must respect vested interests,   (Hear, hear.)   This, I
need hardly say, is the same in England as in Borneo.   I
had a government to support; small, it is true, but a
government far beyond the means of the country to pay for.
I had prohibited the native princes from plundering the
unfortunate people, and the consequence was, that I had to
pay these princes myself.   Many evils existed, and for the
first two years I had to support a starving people, and I
had to revive the first glimmerings of trade.   A system of
usury had become common in the country, 24 per cent.
a-month being charged for small loans.   This abuse was
corrected by my paying off the original sums lent.   I
mention this to illustrate what I had to do, for all these
expenses had to be defrayed out of my own private fortune.

alleged I have heaped up, I regret to say that Sarawak
boasts a national debt, not so large as that which the
Chancellor of the Exchequer is explaining just now in the
House of Commons, but still quite large enough to be
burdensome and inconvenient. But I will say, with great
boldness, that I have refrained from imposing taxes upon a
rude people. (Cheers.) I have resisted those who wished
to impose taxes. I knew always that a long confidence
must precede taxation; and I hope still that the benefits of
good government will in time induce the people to impose
taxes upon themselves. I could not, from my very nature,
be covetous enough to wring the earnings from the peasant's "hard hand," though that peasant's skin was of a
different colour from my own. (Cheers.) It was during
the time that I was struggling against pecuniary difficulties,
and difficulties of every other sort, that I first became
acquainted with the character of the Serebas, and Sakarran
pirates, that is, of the Malays and the Dyaks of those rivers;
and, after twelve years of minute experience, I may be
supposed to be able to distinguish between piratical attacks
and intertribal feuds—and these intertribal feuds are such
as the wolf wages on the lamb. Gentlemen, there has
been much vain declamation upon this subject; but I
should much like to ask the most peaceable man in England,—the man who is peaceful in words as well as in
deeds,—the man who is peaceful by habit and peaceful by
religious persuasion,—such a man I respect, although I
differ from him,—but I should like to ask such a man
what he would do if a horde of bandits frequently burst

forth from Brest or Cherbourg, ravaging the shores of the
Channel, and carrying women and children into captivity,
with the heads of their decapitated husbands and fathers?
Would he not resist? Would he not defend his own
hearth? Would he not, to save his family, seek those
marauders on the high seas, or crush them in their own
dens? Would he preach,—and suppose those deaf adders
would not listen—would he preach when he saw his
daughter dishonoured, and his son murdered? and then
would he proclaim his shame and cowardice amongst men?
I do not myself believe that such a man breathes in England, from length to length. (Cheers.) But how, gentlemen, does this differ from what has already occurred?
Have not the natives of Borneo suffered, and have they not,
when the proper time arose, in obedience to the impulse of
self-preservation, acted in accordance with the common
laws of nature? The rest is leather and prunella,—soap-
bubbles blown by our popular legislators to obtain temporary applause. The pirates were punished because they
are the enemies of mankind. The natives of Borneo
attacked these marauders, and they obeyed the law of
nature. Her Majesty's forces acted in obedience to the
law of nations; for it is a law of nations that the powerful
should protect the innocent from the guilty; and the law
was applied, on these occasions, as it is applied at home.
If a smuggler evades capture, and resists the law, he is
fired into, and shot and shell do their work. If a felon is
collared by a policeman, and resists, he receives a tap on
the head to make him quiet: and so it has been in Borneo.

—the pirates would not be quiet, and measures were taken to compel them to be so. When the police of this country can reason your criminals into virtue, the same may be done with the pirates, but not till then.

Gentlemen, I had desired to seize this opportunity of expressing to the Noble Lord (Palmerston) who was expected here this evening, my sincere sense of the constant and generous support which I have received from him and from her Majesty's late Ministers. I should be ungrateful, indeed, if I did not thank my honourable friend the member for West Surrey (Mr. H. Drummond). I thank him not in an idle form of words, but from my heart—I thank him for his defence of an absent man, and a stranger. (Cheers.) To the honourable gentleman the member for Newcastle (Mr. Headlam), and to many friends who are now present, I owe a debt of gratitude which I can never forget, though I can never repay. I am, indeed, a beggar in this respect, gentlemen; for I have to remind the gallant admiral now present, of the time he commanded on the coast of Borneo, when I served as a volunteer under his command, whilst he was carrying out a course of measures which may well serve as an example to other nations, as well as to our own. An English squadron then made a circuit of those seas, and the natives knew the power of this country. To the gallant captains (Captain Keppel and Captain Farquhar) with whom I have acted so cordially, I will only say that, should we ever hear again of attacks, I trust to find them near me. (Cheers.) I am a bankrupt, but a bankrupt proud of his obligations; and if I have suffered,—and I do not deny that I have suffered from the machinations of my enemies,—my sufferings have been more than balanced by the devotion of my friends, by your kindness, and by the justice rendered me by my countrymen at large, and I think I may say, by my countrywomen also. (Cheers.)

Gentlemen, I am proud to avow that the position I hold in the East has enabled me to introduce social and political improvements amongst the natives, and this will lead in the fulness of time to great commercial development. I am proud to say that I possess some power; that power, however, has been conferred upon me by the fountain-head of all power, and it may be resumed whenever it is misused. I will respond to what the Chairman has said, by declaring that I do possess an influence over the native mind, and this influence, joined to power and knowledge, is the chief element of future success. But, gentlemen, this influence would never have arisen, had I been actuated by base motives of any kind; nor could it, indeed, survive a day that child-like confidence which is the fruit of a long experience. Whatever may be the course of our future policy, it should be worthy of a great nation, and it should not be dictated by the meddling parsimony which begrudges a small outlay to obtain great future advantages. (Cheers.) The countries of the Archipelago are the fairest and richest of the world. There are resources to employ British enterprise—there are outlets for English commerce; and it would be lamentable indeed if they were lost. We have something to do and some difficulties to overcome before we clutch these advantages. There is an imbecility, which hopes to attain everything by doing nothing, and which weakens every executive power in every distant part of the empire. Borneo has not escaped this evil, but for this country she may yet preserve that commerce, and may develop it a hundred-fold; but unless England is awake to its importance, it will be closed against her enterprise. Others will awake, though England may sleep. Short of this firm and consistent course of action, better would it be to withdraw from the enterprise than to continue it, and to attempt what you will never carry out successfully. It is an injury to the natives to excite false hopes that are never to be realized. There is one page in history, and the history of this country, which tells us of a native people in the Archipelago betrayed by our carelessness, and British interests sacrificed to ignorance. One single record is sufficient on our annals, for I am convinced that the time has now arrived that England must maintain her position in these seas. She must suppress piracy,—she must secure stepping-stones for her infant steam communication, which is to join her possessions in Australia to her possessions in China,—she must develope her commerce. She must do this, or she must abandon a glorious enterprise to another: and, when that happens, I shall say, to a greater nation. The alternative is before us. I look forward myself with warm hope that the nobler alternative will be chosen; but I do not conceal that I am not unprepared to meet the meaner one.

Gentlemen. I will now say that your confidence, which

the Chairman has so well expressed, will cheer me in the path of public duty, or will solace me in the retirement of private life, in the deep solitude of a Borneon existence. I have only now, gentlemen, to implore you, not only in my own name alone, but in the name of those who, like myself, have suffered from the licence of men's tongues,— I implore you not to believe what is said of an absent man unless it be proved. Pause long, consider well before you give ear to a slander affecting a man of integrity. Do not disgrace your public servants by inquiries generated in the fogs of base suspicious ; for remember, a wrong done is like a wound received,—the scar is ineffaceable. It may be covered by glittering decorations, but there it remains to the end. The wound may be healed, and the injury may be repaired. Gentlemen, I have now to thank you for your kindness in listening to me, for the high honour you have done me, for the feeling of confidence you have expressed, and for that remedy which you have applied to a wrong which shall be obliterated henceforth from my mind. (Sir James Brooke resumed his seat amidst demonstrations of applause which lasted several minutes.)

Sir James Brooke again rose, and said,—I fear I have been acting the part of a Pharisee, and have been as selfish as most men who are placed in my position ; but I have a pleasing duty to perform, and one that gratifies me as it will gratify all present. I beg leave to propose the health of our worthy Chairman, and if I may add my small tribute of praise to the praises of his daily life and conversation, I am sure you will heartily join me in it. I am proud on this occasion of making his acquaintance, and I hope the acquaintance thus commenced will ripen into a warmer and better feeling of friendship. (Cheers.)

The toast having been warmly responded to,

The *Chairman* said,—I feel I should do but poor justice to my own feelings if I were not to thank you for the compliment you have passed upon me. I beg to thank you in terms of the most unaffected gratitude for that great compliment. For myself, I can only say, as the best excuse for occupying this seat, that I possess an interest in this great matter second to none in this country. As a merchant of the City of London, and connected with the commerce of the East, I feel a peculiar interest in the success of Sir James Brooke's proceedings, and if my conduct on this occasion has met with your approbation, it is the best reward I could ask.

The *Chairman*.—Gentlemen, we have been honoured on this occasion by the company of gentlemen whose presence is always acceptable. I allude to those members of the Bar who have favoured us by coming amongst us this evening. And when I say that we have here this evening a member of that distinguished body, the Bench of England, I am sure you will drink with cordiality—The Bench and the Bar, and the health of Baron Alderson. (Loud cheers.)

Mr. Baron Alderson.—I do not mean to return thanks for the Bar, nor for anything but the Bench. The Bar has its representatives here, and they must speak for themselves. I am obliged to listen to them very often, and I

intend to do so to-night.   We on the bench do the best we
can in equally administering justice, and I think we do no
more than equal justice when we acquit Sir James Brooke.
It gives me very great pleasure to be here this evening.   I
ask myself this question,——What are we here for this evening?   Why do I stand between Sir James Brooke and the
gallant officers who have so often stood by him on other
occasions?   Why are there present so many persons of
different professions, opinions, and ages,——from the old,
whose fears exceed their hopes, to the young, whose hopes
exceed their fears?   Simply to do honour to an English
gentleman of indomitable will, great philanthropy, great
humanity, who has endeavoured to spread amongst a benighted people the blessings of knowledge, the advantages
of civilization, and the blessings of religion.   It is for this
reason that we are here to-night, and I am sorry to say that
in one respect I differ from Sir James Brooke and the
Chairman, in that they expressed something of regret that
our distinguished guest had not the approbation of all mankind.   I do not think Sir James Brooke would deserve it
if he had it; for I have always observed,——and I believe
history will confirm me,——that the greatest benefactors of
the human race have been most abused in their own time,
and I therefore think that Sir James Brooke ought to be
congratulated *because* he is abused.   I look to the future and
not to the present, because I look to the time when he will
come out as the sun from behind the clouds.   When this
takes place, his calumniators and detractors will be obscured
in the oblivion of their own insignificance.   Then will

come the time when full justice will be done him. I cannot hold out any hope to him that this will occur in his lifetime or mine. I cannot promise to him universal approbation, because that does not generally accompany desert; but I think I can promise him the approbation of his own conscience, the approbation of all good and reasonable men, and of Almighty God who does justice and who will reward. (Loud cheers).

Mr. Montague Chambers, Q.C., in returning thanks for the Bar, said,—We ought to be greatly obliged to the learned judge who has just sat down, for so admirable a speech. I had little thought of being called upon to return thanks for the Bar of England. It is known that the occupation of the profession to which I belong is, if possible, to discover truth, to obtain justice, and to vindicate the oppressed. We have it in our power on many occasions to do justice to the present as well as the absent, and I am delighted to think that we have heard this parting injunction—"When I am a stranger in a foreign land, don't forget that you are my friends." I for one will not forget that injunction (cheers), and I am sure that my friends who are engaged in a noble profession will never allow it to escape their memory, and will never forget those great principles so well stated by Sir James Brooke,—ever to do justice to the absent, and never to condemn unheard. The Bar of England, in the associations in which they are permitted to mix in public festivals, always esteem the high favour which they receive in one of the standing toasts of England. They are vain and proud enough to suppose that they will do their duty, and be esteemed just and honourable men. I desire to express, on the part of the Bar of England, their thanks for the opportunity we have had afforded to us of giving our feeble, but feeling testimony, towards the estimation in which Sir James Brooke is held by the common profession. We know his merits—we have felt his wrongs as though they were our own. We have watched his proceedings with deep anxiety. Speaking for myself, I may say that I was not invited here. I solicited to be invited. A friend of my own accidentally mentioned to me that this dinner was to take place, and I immediately expressed my deep anxiety to be present. It is well known to Sir James Brooke that I am related to one of those noble captains who assisted him in repressing those piratical proceedings he has mentioned, and I felt as though a wound was inflicted upon myself when slanders were uttered against Sir James Brooke. Independently, therefore, of the Bar of England, I am deeply anxious about the meeting of to-day. It has struck me as one of the most important things in this matter, that there should be an assembly of men of all classes united in one common feeling to do justice to an honourable man, not to pay him an empty compliment, but to carry to his heart the conviction of his fellow-countrymen that he deserved their regard. (Cheers.)

The Chairman. — The best arrangements are always liable to unforeseen interruptions, and it is to the Chancellor of the Exchequer having fixed this evening for his budget

> " I would rather be a kitten, and cry Mew,
>   Than one of these same metre ballad-mongers."

It has been said, gentlemen, that when I set sail for the
shores of Borneo, now fourteen years ago, I carried a deep
design in my bosom to suppress piracy, and to carry
civilization to the Malayan race.   This is most flattering to
my wisdom and foresight, but unfortunately, it is not true.
I had but one definite object when I left England, and
that was, to see something of the world and to come back
again.   The extraordinary events that occurred after my
arrival in Sarawak I need not detail.   I found a country
ruined by its native princes, and which they could no
longer govern.   I had everything to do.   I was a reformer
in the most extended sense of the word; but I recognised
the principle, that to effect any adequate measures of reform
you must respect vested interests,   (Hear, hear.)   This, I
need hardly say, is the same in England as in Borneo.   I
had a government to support; small, it is true, but a
government far beyond the means of the country to pay for.
I had prohibited the native princes from plundering the
unfortunate people, and the consequence was, that I had to
pay these princes myself.   Many evils existed, and for the
first two years I had to support a starving people, and I
had to revive the first glimmerings of trade.   A system of
usury had become common in the country, 24 per cent.
a-month being charged for small loans.   This abuse was
corrected by my paying off the original sums lent.   I
mention this to illustrate what I had to do, for all these
expenses had to be defrayed out of my own private fortune.

think it worth while to propose its health at all. (Laughter.)   As you have called upon me to return thanks, I do so, because I adhere to the first teaching of my school-boy days,—" Obedience from a sense of duty."   It is perfectly true that I do not stand here as an old friend of Sir James Brooke.   It happened, that being much abroad at the time to which he has alluded, I had scarcely heard his name, until a gentleman in the House of Commons—a worthy, good sort of man, in his narrow way—I have no objection to mention his name, it was Mr. Cobden—said to me one day, when the piracy question was coming on,—" Did you ever look into this question?   I wish you would look into these papers," at the same time giving me a host of books on the subject.   Well, I read all these wondrous blue books and white books ; and I came from the perusal with a conviction exactly the opposite to that at which Mr. Cobden had arrived—with the strongest possible conviction that Sir James Brooke had taken the right course;—the only proper course that, under the circumstances, he possibly could have taken. (Cheers.)   Now, I don't believe that this contest is yet at an end.   I look to this meeting, here assembled, as of very great importance ; not as a thing that is to pass away like a glass of effervescing champagne, but as evincing a determination on your part to screw your courage to the sticking-point.   I tell you that this persecution will not cease—will not abate.   On the votes of the House to-night a motion on this subject has been renewed, and it will be your duty to unite and stand by us to see that right is done to a noble and slandered man.   I thank you on behalf of the House of Commons, such as it is. (Laughter.)

Mr. Headlam, M.P.—The duty of proposing the next toast has been intrusted to me. It will not want a word of recommendation; but I propose, if you will allow me to say one word for myself. The only part I had to take in the House of Commons in reference to this matter was to state a plain unvarnished tale,—to tell that tale to an assembly who, however it may be influenced by circumstances which have a temporary effect, is still an assembly of English gentlemen, upon whose verdict any man may rely for justice. The toast I have to propose is—The progress of Civilization in Borneo. It expresses a deeper feeling, and a higher tone of sentiment, than is usually given from the dinner-table. But I look upon this meeting as one of no ordinary character. We do not come here for mere enjoyment, or for idle ceremony, but in pursuance of a solemn act of duty and justice. With that view I have come away from scenes of some interest in the House of Commons, to express my sympathy with a man who, amidst difficulties almost unparalleled, difficulties in a foreign land, has struggled for the noblest object it is given to man to accomplish,—to beat back the barriers of darkness and barbarism, and to spread the light of civilization and true religion amongst a benighted people. (Cheers.) I have to propose—Progress to that civilization. It is not for us to say how that shall advance in future ages; but the seed has been sown, the light has been kindled, and no man can say what fruit it shall bring forth in after ages. The House of Commons has vindicated the character of Sir James Brooke, and has thrown back the calumnies cast upon him, upon their authors; but his vindication would not have been complete had not the citizens of London met on this occasion to express their sympathies with Sir James Brooke, and their hopes that the blessing of Providence may rest upon his labours. (Cheers.)

Toast—The progress of Civilization in Borneo.

Mr. J. D. Powles.—Sir, I have very great satisfaction in bringing to the notice of this meeting the next toast upon the Chairman's list, conveying a tribute of respect to Vice-Admiral Sir Thomas Cochrane and the other gallant officers who have so zealously served in the measures taken against the pirates of Borneo. (Cheers.) Often has it happened in this City of London, that its merchants have had to express their grateful sense of the exertions of the national marine in the protection of its commerce. Some of us here can remember, during the long war this country was engaged in, when our convoys of merchant marine stretched from shore to shore, how vigilantly they were guarded by our naval officers; and, although it not unfrequently happened that three or four hundred vessels were left to the care of a single vessel of war, how rarely it occurred that the wolf was able to snatch one from that large fold intrusted to their care. And in the long peace which has since ensued, we find the national marine ever on the watch to protect our commercial interests on distant coasts, whenever cases of collision arising between other states call for their interference. But there can be no service in which the national marine can be engaged more useful to commerce or more interesting to humanity than when it is repressing the dreadful evil of piracy—the greatest crime of any that can be found in the catalogue of human offences. Strange, indeed, it is, that when engaged in putting down an offence so direfully destructive in its character, suspicion or mistrust should have been cast upon men occupied in so holy a cause. Stranger still is it, that men are to be found in this metropolis who affect to be ignorant of the existence of piracy in those seas. Why, we have in this room a merchant who has had as large dealings in that part of the world as any other man, whose own brother was taken captive by these pirates, his life inhumanly sacrificed, with a ship and cargo worth 30,000*l.*; and yet in this very house a meeting was held—I was almost going to say, of idiots, pretending to rebuke the manner in which the great crimes prevailing there had been put down. I have attended many meetings of a public character in this city, but I have never one so substantially attended as that in which we are now taking part, and I trust it will go forth to the world not only as a vindication of Sir James Brooke, but as a determination expressed by the citizens of London, that they will not allow such scandals to go unanswered. (Loud cheers.) It is a great evil that is to be put down, and we offer our earnest hope that the attempts already made will be steadfastly followed up, until the evil shall be utterly annihilated. I beg to propose the health of Vice-Admiral Sir Thomas Cochrane

... The House ...
... Sir James ...
...
...
... of London ...
... with Sir J...
... the ...
...

... progress ...
H... J. P...
... in the ...
... the ... Sir ...
... Sir Thomas C
... have ...
... the pirates of Bor...
... in the City of Lo...
... to express their grateful ...
... marine in the ...
Some of us here can remem...
... country was engaged in, wh...
... marine stretched from shore
... were guarded by our naval
... infrequently happened that ...
... were left to the care of a sing...
... the wolf was ...
... to their co...
... we find...
... our com...
... of coll...

Penang, and I think, therefore, I am qualified to bear testimony to his character. (Hear, hear.)   Various circumstances induced me to proceed to the coast of Borneo, in consequence of representations made to me, and Sir James Brooke placed himself at my disposal.   Upon that occasion I went to Borneo and destroyed a piratical place called Malludu, and on another occasion captured the town of Bruné.   On these and other occasions I found in Sir James Brooke a person most devoted, and most kind and liberal to the people, and on every occasion we went there, he stated his strong impression as to the necessity of forbearance, and his anxiety for the welfare of the people. I visited parts of Borneo where no European had ever been before, and even in those parts the people came out and mentioned with delight the name of Brooke; in fact, wherever I went, I found his name was a sort of talisman. These are strong illustrations of the feeling entertained towards him by the natives, and of the strong anxiety he evinced to secure good feeling amongst the people over whom he was placed, and to protect them.   When I went to the city of Bruné, and captured it, the sultan ran away, and, in fact, had abdicated.   Now, I had very strong impressions at that time, and I may mention them, to show you what my feelings were with regard to your honoured guest.   I am not sure whether I have ever conveyed those impressions to Sir James Brooke or not.   I was strongly impressed; if I could at that moment, I would have conferred upon him the Sultanship. (Loud cheers.) I had the power to do it, and I felt it would have been

received with acclamation by the whole population, and
that it would have been a most important thing for that
country, both as regards the civilization and the happiness
of the people.   I cannot bear stronger testimony to Sir
James Brooke's character than by telling you what were
my impressions of him at that moment, and I deeply regret
that I did not feel empowered to carry out my views.   But
since that time Sir James Brooke has been attacked and
calumniated by certain members of the House of Commons.   They never attacked the naval officers who commanded there, but they fixed all their charges upon Sir
James Brooke, who was not responsible, and had nothing
whatever to do with the matters to which they referred.   I
wish also to state to you that those persons who have so
improperly attacked Sir James Brooke were told that if
they liked to come to me, I would give them every information fully and honestly, having been out at Borneo a
long time; but not one of them ever came to me.   (Cheers.)
I have felt, gentlemen, that what I have said was not only
due to you, but due to your honoured guest.   I cannot
pity Sir James Brooke, on account of the attacks which
have been made upon him, for his calumniators have
brought out his character in a manner which probably
would not have been the case if the attacks had not been
made.   I thank you, gentlemen, once more, for the honour
you have done me in drinking my health.

The *Chairman.*—Gentlemen, I have had occasion already
to allude to the gentlemen connected with the East India
Company who are present this evening, and I am sure the

toast I am about to propose will be acceptable to you. I think there is no public body whose members are more capable, on account of the scenes they have themselves witnessed, of delivering a free and impartial opinion on such matters as we have had under our consideration this evening. I propose the health of the Directors of the East India Company, who have been so good as to honour us with their company this evening. (Cheers.)

Sir J. Law Lushington.—In returning thanks for the toast you have just drunk, I may be allowed to say, that in his endeavours to diminish piracy in the Archipelago, not only has Sir James Brooke done a great service to England, but he has done a great service to all that part of the world. We are anxious that that country should be preserved. I can only say, that the East India Company is deeply grateful to Sir James Brooke for his endeavours to put down piracy, and to promote the general improvement of the country with which he has now been, for some years past, so honourably connected.

The *Chairman.*—Gentlemen, there is another great body most efficiently represented here this evening — I mean, the Bank of England. In proposing that institution, I think I may say, as there are several of my brother proprietors present, that it may be well for them to ascertain how they manage, in Borneo, to get 24 per cent. a-month on small loans; for it is not a usual or customary per-centage in this country. As a proprietor, I would suggest to the Directors the expediency of sending over a commissioner, according to the fashion of the day, to ascertain how this is done. It might prove a satisfactory way of investing the spare capital that is now coming over to this country. (Laughter.) I propose to you—The Directors of the Bank of England.

Mr. Thomson Hankey, Jun.—I may say, on the part of the Directors of the Bank of England, that they feel it to be a great compliment to be allowed to be present on such an interesting occasion as this. It gives us great and sincere gratification to bear our testimony, as members of one of the oldest corporations of the City of London, to your distinguished guest on this occasion. It has very often been my lot to dine in this room, and to take part in many public assemblies; but I never witnessed so mixed an assembly as this in support of a common object. (Cheers.) The Directors of the Bank of England owe a deep debt of gratitude to Sir James Brooke, and they are anxious fully to express that feeling on this interesting occasion. They felt it but due to him to express their opinion of his proceedings on every available opportunity, and witnessed with great satisfaction the entertainment now given to him. I have not attended this festival to vindicate the character of Sir James Brooke, for I never thought it wanted any vindication (loud cheers); for the facts have been patent to all the world, and must carry conviction to the mind of every person who is not warped by prejudice. On behalf of the Directors of the Bank of England, I beg to acknowledge the toast you have drunk, and thank you for the opportunity you have afforded us in expressing our opinion of Sir James Brooke and the course he has pursued.

The *Chairman.*—Gentleman, the last but not the least of the toasts I beg to submit to you is—The Corporation of the City of London. I have great satisfaction in giving this toast, because Sir James Brooke is a member of that Corporation—a Fishmonger and Goldsmith. The satisfaction I have in proposing the toast is considerably enhanced by being enabled to couple with it the name of Mr. Alderman Finnis. (Cheers.)

Alderman Finnis.—At this late hour of the evening, I will not detain you. I had the honour of being present, some few years ago, when Sir James Brooke publicly stated the course of proceeding he should adopt; and I have the satisfaction of saying that he has most nobly fulfilled his engagements. I hope he will live long to uphold the British character in the land of his adoption. (Loud cheers.)

The company then separated.

THE END.

.

LONDON:

PRINTED BY W. CLOWES AND SONS, STAMFORD STREET
AND CHARING CROSS.

think it worth while to propose its health at all. (Laughter.) As you have called upon me to return thanks, I do so, because I adhere to the first teaching of my school-boy days,—"Obedience from a sense of duty." It is perfectly true that I do not stand here as an old friend of Sir James Brooke. It happened, that being much abroad at the time to which he has alluded, I had scarcely heard his name, until a gentleman in the House of Commons—a worthy, good sort of man, in his narrow way—I have no objection to mention his name, it was Mr. Cobden—said to me one day, when the piracy question was coming on,—"Did you ever look into this question? I wish you would look into these papers," at the same time giving me a host of books on the subject. Well, I read all these wondrous blue books and white books; and I came from the perusal with a conviction exactly the opposite to that at which Mr. Cobden had arrived—with the strongest possible conviction that Sir James Brooke had taken the right course;—the only proper course that, under the circumstances, he possibly could have taken. (Cheers.) Now, I don't believe that this contest is yet at an end. I look to this meeting, here assembled, as of very great importance; not as a thing that is to pass away like a glass of effervescing champagne, but as evincing a determination on your part to screw your courage to the sticking-point. I tell you that this persecution will not cease—will not abate. On the votes of the House to-night a motion on this subject has been renewed, and it will be your duty to unite and stand by us to see that right is done to a noble and slandered man. I thank you on behalf of the House of Commons, such as it is. (Laughter.)

Mr. Headlam, M.P.—The duty of proposing the next toast has been intrusted to me. It will not want a word of recommendation; but I propose, if you will allow me to say one word for myself. The only part I had to take in the House of Commons in reference to this matter was to state a plain unvarnished tale,—to tell that tale to an assembly who, however it may be influenced by circumstances which have a temporary effect, is still an assembly of English gentlemen, upon whose verdict any man may rely for justice. The toast I have to propose is—The progress of Civilization in Borneo. It expresses a deeper feeling, and a higher tone of sentiment, than is usually given from the dinner-table. But I look upon this meeting as one of no ordinary character. We do not come here for mere enjoyment, or for idle ceremony, but in pursuance of a solemn act of duty and justice. With that view I have come away from scenes of some interest in the House of Commons, to express my sympathy with a man who, amidst difficulties almost unparalleled, difficulties in a foreign land, has struggled for the noblest object it is given to man to accomplish,—to beat back the barriers of darkness and barbarism, and to spread the light of civilization and true religion amongst a benighted people. (Cheers.) I have to propose—Progress to that civilization. It is not for us to say how that shall advance in future ages; but the seed has been sown, the light has been kindled, and no man can say what fruit it shall bring forth in

Lightning Source UK Ltd.
Milton Keynes UK
UKOW07f2028090715

254907UK00009B/217/P